AF604811

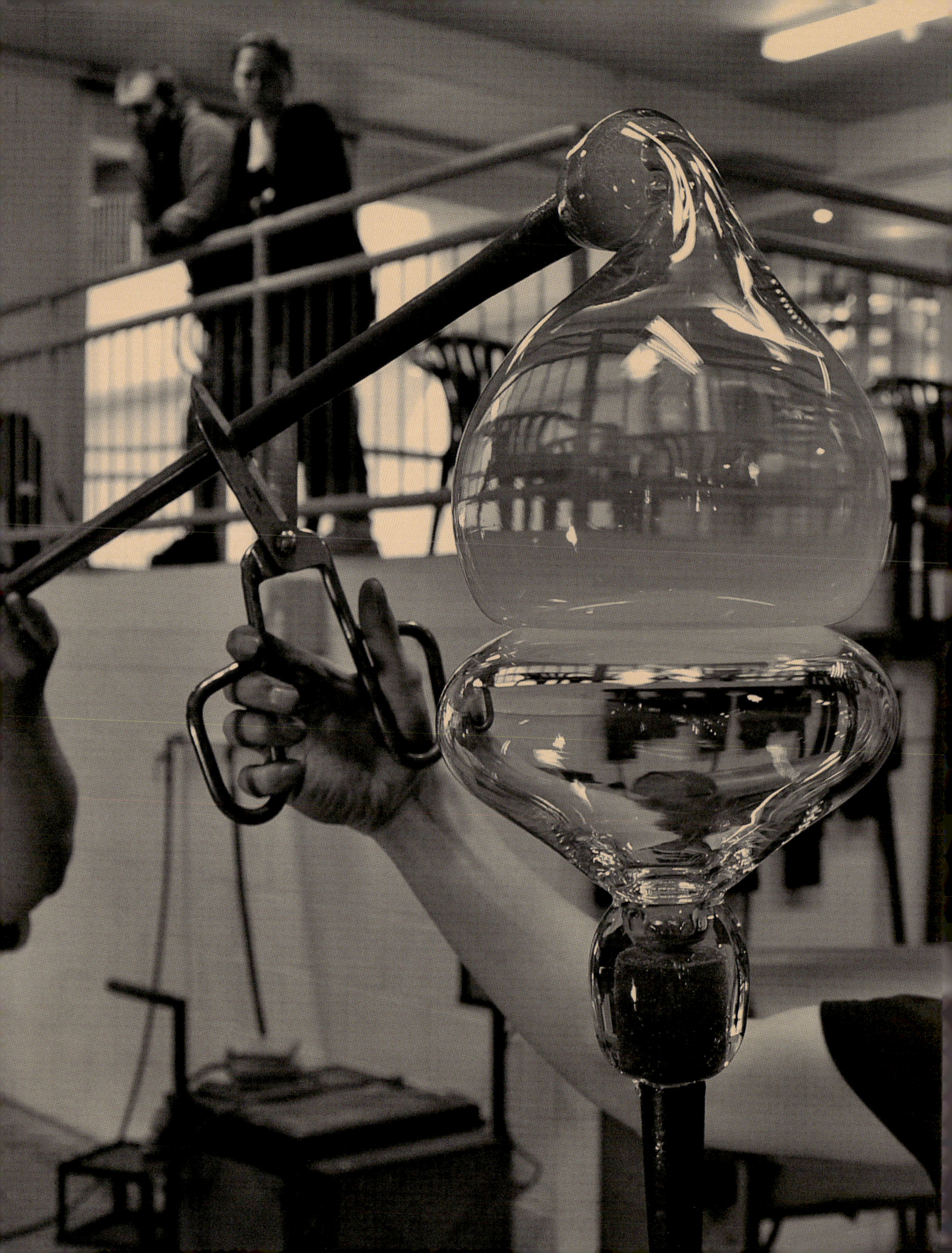

DESIGNING CRAFT/ CRAFTING DESIGN: 40 YEARS OF JAMFACTORY

Editors
Margaret Hancock Davis,
Margot Osborne and
Brian Parkes

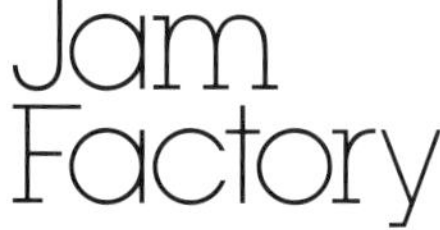

First Published in Adelaide, Australia in 2013

Published to coincide with the exhibition *Designing Craft/Crafting Design: 40 Years of JamFactory* shown in Adelaide from 19 April - 9 June 2013

Published by JamFactory
19 Morphett Street Adelaide SA 5000
www.jamfactory.com.au

ISBN 978-0-9807910-3-7

Co-curators: Margaret Hancock Davis, Margot Osborne and Brian Parkes
Copy Editor: Theresa Willsteed
Design: Sophie Guiney
Printed in China for Imago

All quotes by exhibiting artists have been drawn from interviews conducted by the curators.

All measurements have been given height x width x depth

All photographs have been credited throughout except the following:
Grant Hancock pages 10, 12, 15, 24, 27 and all exhibition work
Mick Bradley pages 2, 5, 22, 40, 45, 59
Tom Roschi pages 42, 54, 56
Michal Kluvanek page 10
Portrait photography courtesy the artist

Cover:
Peta Kruger
Geranium, 2012
brass, paint
60 x 80 x 110mm

Principal Sponsor

ANZ is proud to be the official 40th anniversary partner for JamFactory's program of exhibitions and events throughout 2013, and is the Principal Sponsor of *Designing Craft/Crafting Design: 40 Years of JamFactory.*

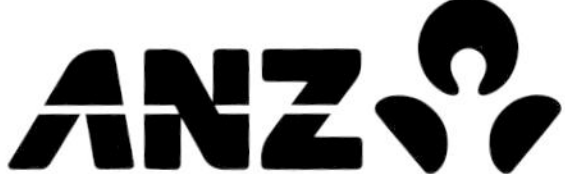

Government Support

The exhibition has been supported by the Government of South Australia through Arts SA's New Exhibitions Fund.

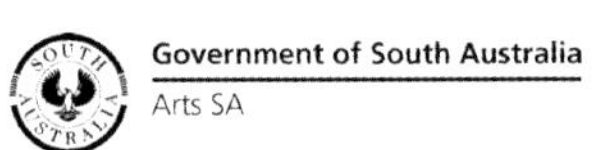

The exhibition has also been supported by the Contemporary Touring Initiative through Visions of Australia, an Australian Government program; and the Visual Arts and Crafts Strategy, an initiative of the Australian, State and Territory Governments.

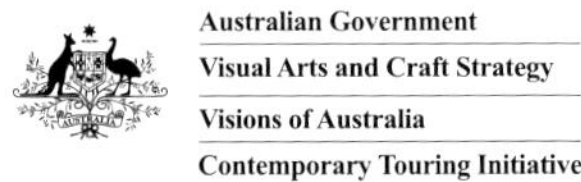

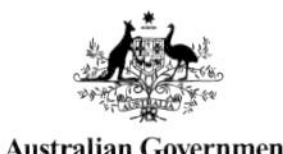

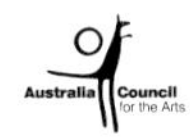

JamFactory acknowledges the support of the South Australian Government through Arts SA and the assistance of the Visual Arts and Crafts Strategy, an initiative of the Australian, State and Territory Governments. JamFactory's Exhibitions Program is assisted by the Australian Government through the Australia Council, its arts funding and advisory body.

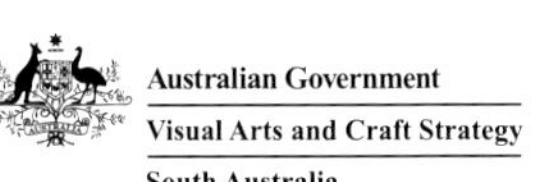

Touring Partner

The exhibition will be toured nationally by Country Arts SA.

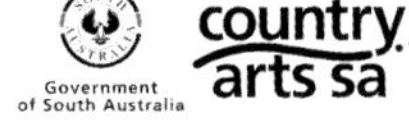

JamFactory has changed its name several times over the years from its original establishment as the South Australian Craft Authority by an Act of the South Australian Parliament in 1973. It was incorporated as the Jam Factory Workshop Inc. in 1977, then changing to the Jam Factory Craft and Design Centre Inc for the move to the Lion Arts Centre in 1992. In 1997 'the' was finally dropped and the two words were merged to JamFactory Contemporary Craft and Design Inc. Finally, in 2010 the name became simply JamFactory. For the sake of clarity 'the Jam Factory' has been used for the St Peters years and 'JamFactory' after the move to the Lion Arts Centre.

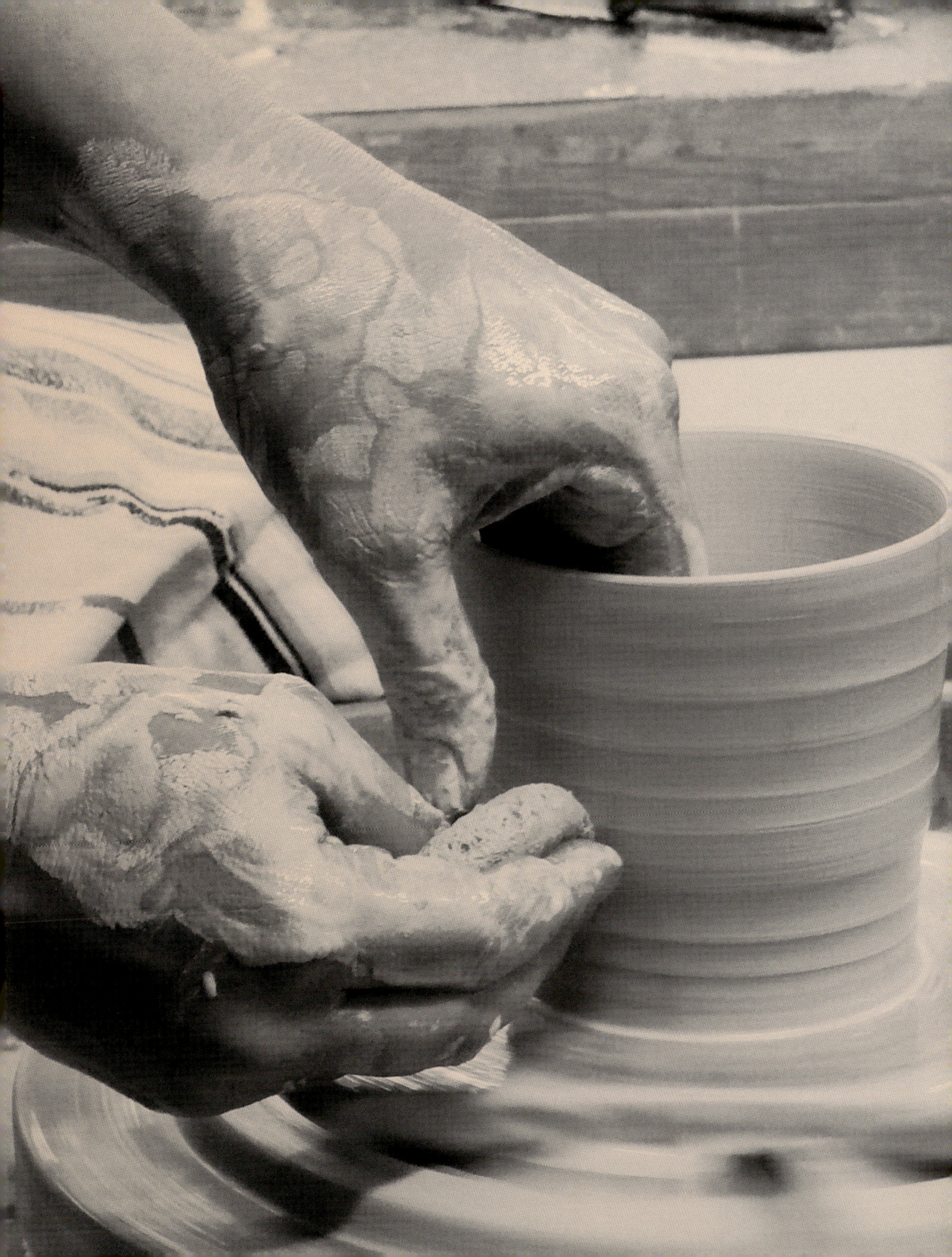

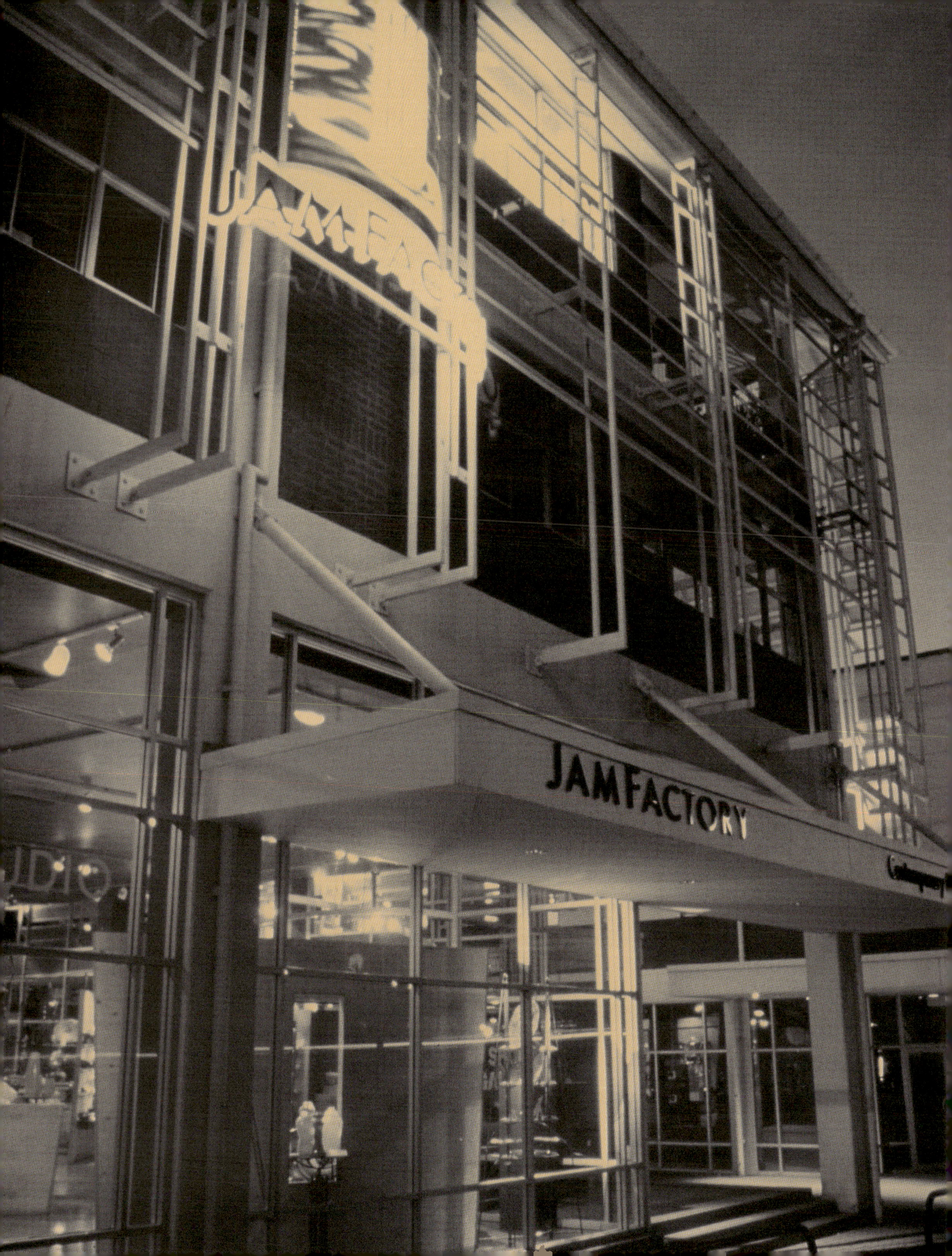
JAMFACTORY

CONTENTS

FOREWORDS

The establishment of the South Australian Craft Authority in 1973, which soon after became the Jam Factory, was a visionary initiative of the South Australian government. Even now, 40 years later, there is still no other organisation in Australia that can rival the breadth and scope of its activities in the support and promotion of contemporary craft and design. Through its training programs, studios, galleries and shops it has nurtured and supported the careers of hundreds of artists, craftspeople and designers – many of whom are now recognised as national and international leaders in their fields.

As well as developing local talent, JamFactory has, since its inception, attracted outstanding artists and designers from around Australia and across the globe. Some have come to work as staff, some to rent studio space or use facilities and many others to undertake JamFactory's intensive training program. A significant proportion of these creative entrepreneurs have subsequently chosen to stay in South Australia.

JamFactory has also provided an important public interface between professional art, craft and design practitioners and the wider public. South Australians and visitors to our state have had the opportunity to learn about and be inspired by outstanding work in the regularly changing exhibitions in JamFactory's galleries. Importantly, they have also had the opportunity to purchase something of lasting value and quality through JamFactory's retail shops. Each purchase made has directly supported incomes for artists and has helped to fund JamFactory's training and exhibitions programs.

The South Australian Government is proud to provide JamFactory with its core funding and the purpose-built building which has been its home since 1992. This investment has been returned to the people of South Australia many times over through the vibrant culture it has created and I am personally pleased that this government has been able to support JamFactory's 40th anniversary through Arts SA's New Exhibitions Fund.

I am confident that JamFactory will continue to be an important part of the cultural life of South Australia in another 40 years time.

Jay Weatherill

The Honourable Jay Weatherill MP
Premier of South Australia
Minister for the Arts

Designing Craft/Crafting Design: 40 years of JamFactory is the centrepiece in a year-long celebration of JamFactory's 40th anniversary. First and foremost, I would like to thank the 40 exhibitors whose works are included in the exhibition. Each has a significant relationship with JamFactory and together their works and stories provide insight into the history and influence of this unique organisation over the past four decades. These exhibitors were selected – from literally hundreds of artists, craftspeople and designers who have been associated with JamFactory – by the curators, Margot Osborne, Margaret Hancock Davis and JamFactory's current CEO, Brian Parkes. I thank them for the care and attention they have applied to this important project.

JamFactory's 40th Anniversary celebrations will include the launch of a new annual magazine called *Marmalade*, a city-wide program of exhibitions and events across Adelaide from April to June 2013, the development of three nationally touring exhibitions and the opening of an ambitious regional facility incorporating studios, a gallery and a shop at the iconic Seppeltsfield Village in the Barossa Valley.

Designing Craft/Crafting Design: 40 Years of JamFactory has been made possible through funding from Arts SA and I thank the South Australian Government and in particular the Premier and Minister for the Arts, Jay Weatherill MP.

We are delighted to be working closely with Country Arts SA who will manage a 15-venue national tour of the exhibition funded by the Commonwealth Government through Visions of Australia. I thank the Minister for the Arts, Simon Crean MP for this valuable support.

The principal sponsor for this exhibition – and JamFactory's 40th anniversary celebrations – is the ANZ. This is an exciting new relationship we hope will continue into the future and I would particularly like to thank the South Australian Chair of the ANZ, Jane Yuile.

This beautiful catalogue will stand as a lasting record of the exhibition and of JamFactory's first 40 years. Special thanks to catalogue designer Sophie Guiney and photographer Grant Hancock.

JamFactory is now a confident and mature organisation with a clear vision, a committed Board and a dedicated staff. We are thankful for the efforts of past and present Board Members, staff, customers and supporters who have weathered many storms over 40 years to create the strong foundations evident today.

Your legacy will live on in the bright future to be enjoyed by JamFactory as it undertakes the next chapter of its history.

Peter Vaughan
JamFactory Chair

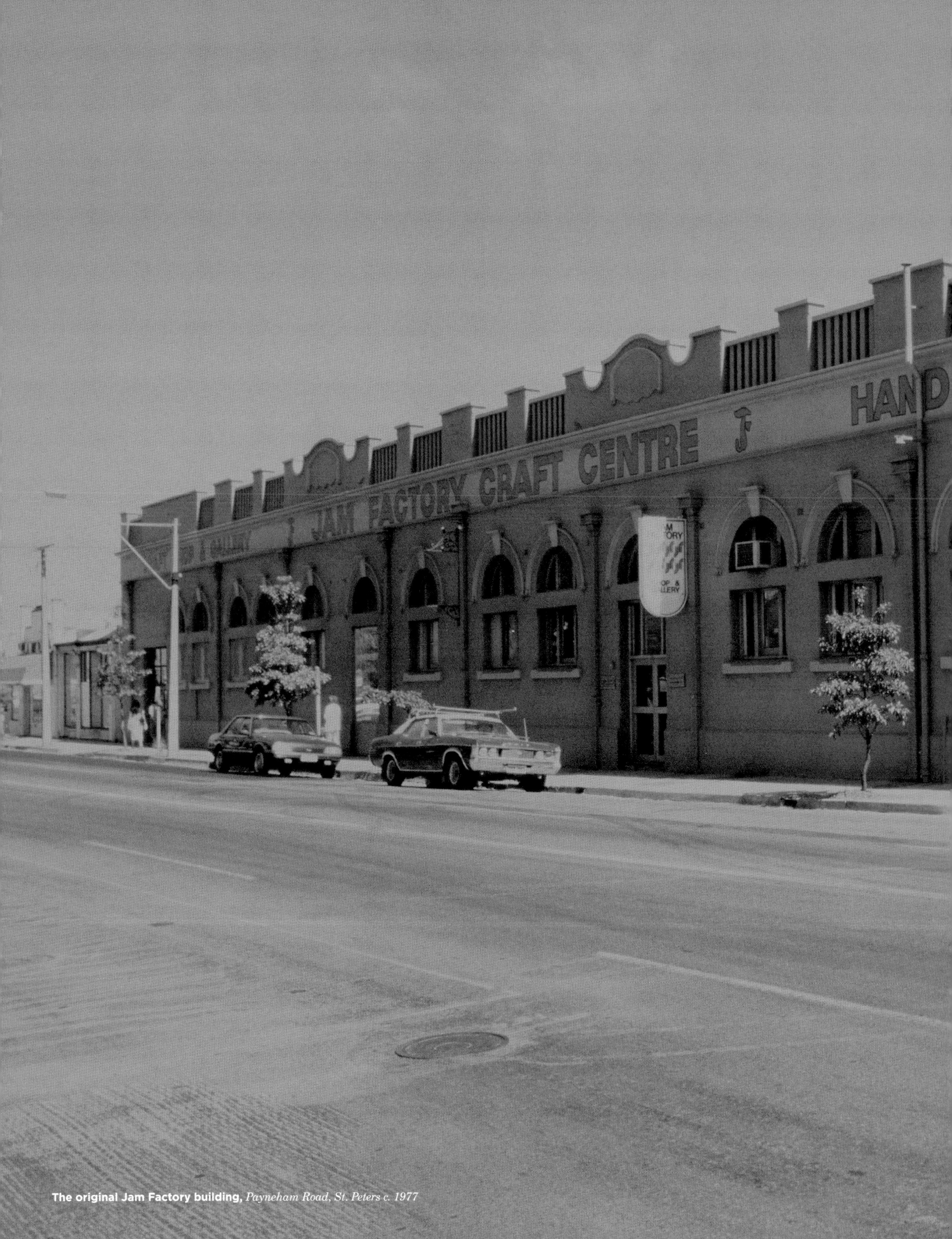

The original Jam Factory building, *Payneham Road, St. Peters c. 1977*

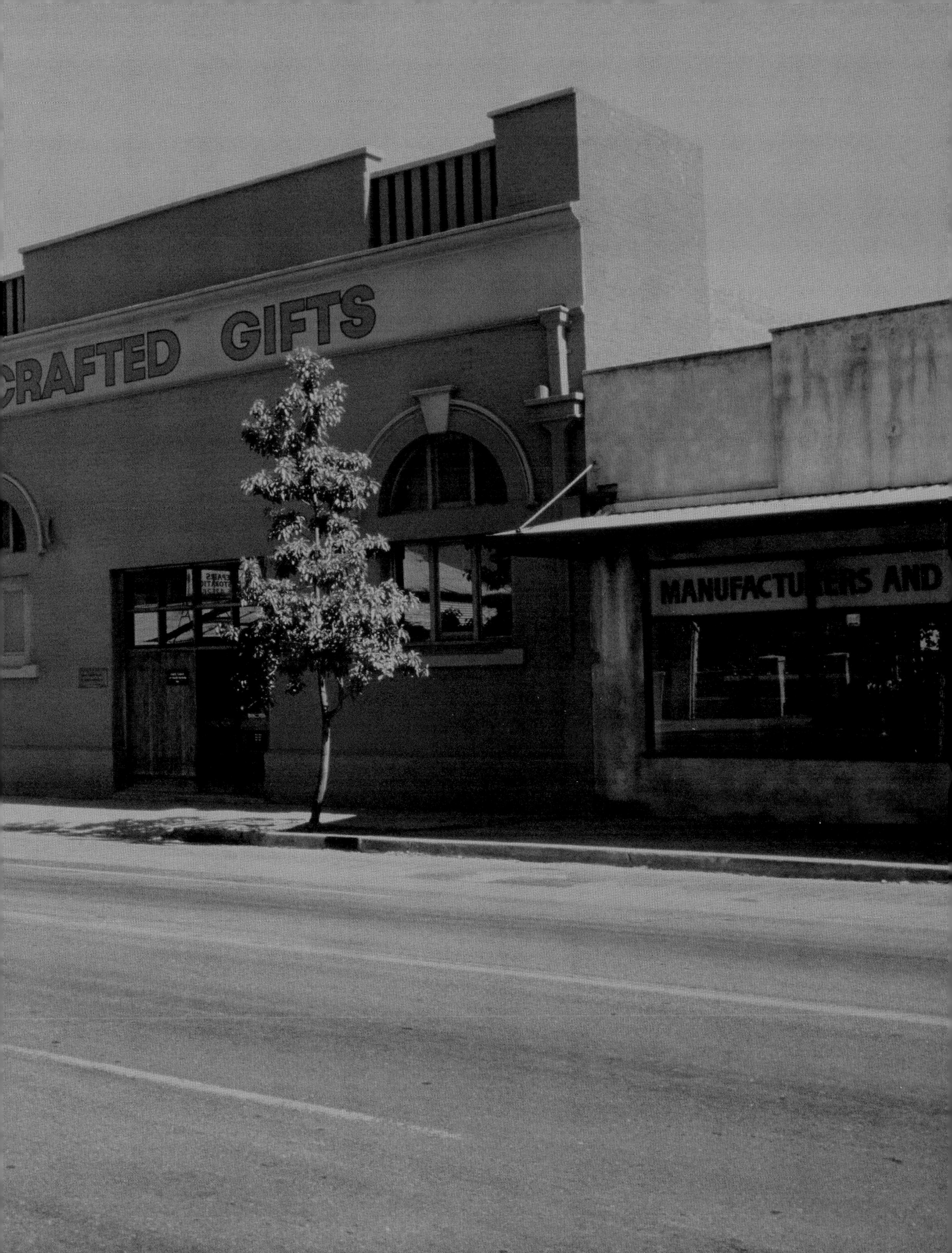
CRAFTED GIFTS
MANUFACTU ERS AND

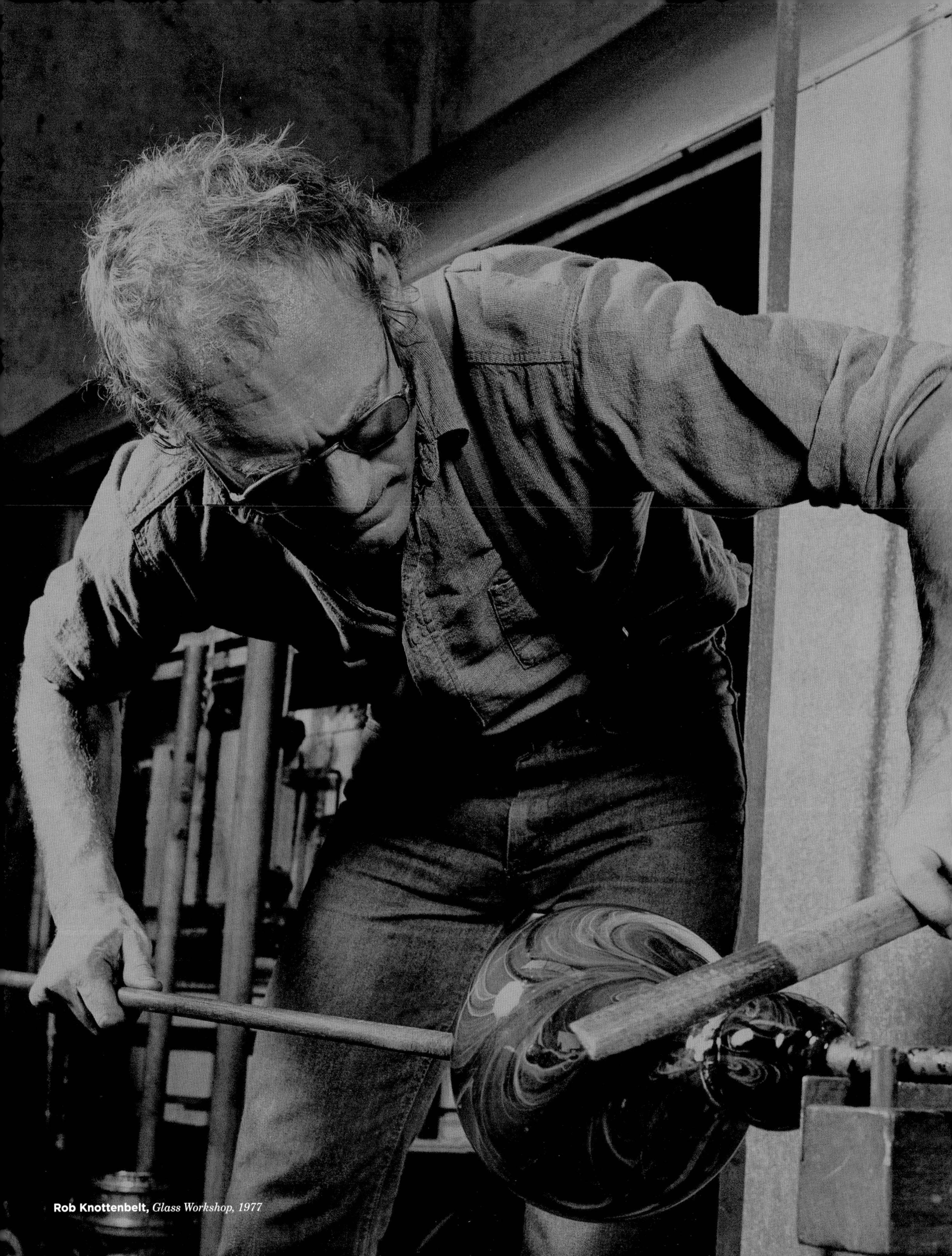

Rob Knottenbelt, *Glass Workshop, 1977*

BEGINNINGS

“*September 1976.... The potters were lined up along the western wall of the Jam Factory. I put a plastic roof on mine to keep dust and pigeon droppings off. I would have been working on the* This woman is not a car series *at this stage. It received a big write up in the Australian by Peter Ward, then a journalist working in Adelaide. The article was actually a critique of* The Womens Art Show *I helped organise at the Jam Factory, which took up the centre of the huge workspace behind the Jam Factory shop on Payneham Road.* This woman is not a car series *was featured in the 1977* Link *the exhibition at the Art Gallery of South Australia, organised by curator Dick Richards.*”

Margaret Dodd
Ceramics Studio Tenant
1976

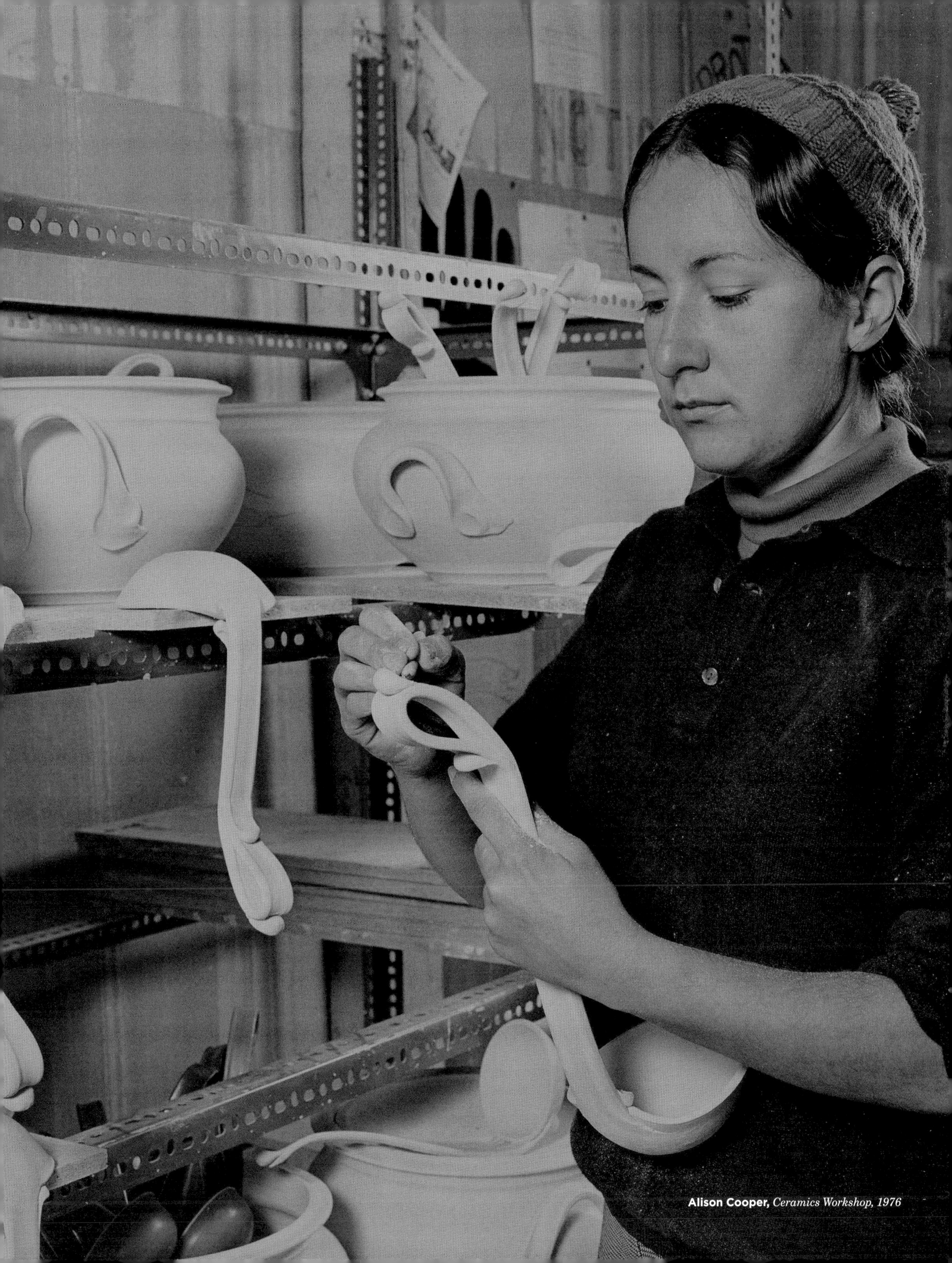

Alison Cooper, *Ceramics Workshop, 1976*

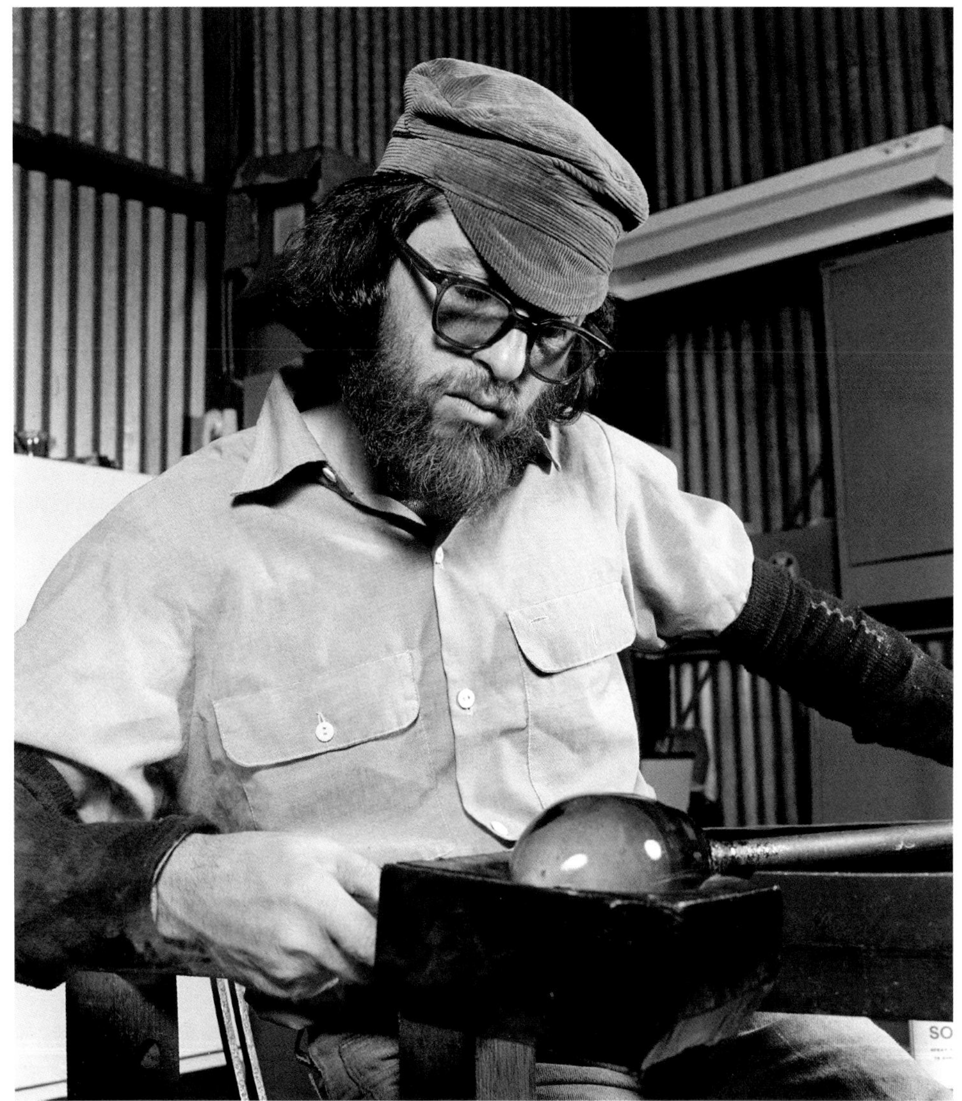

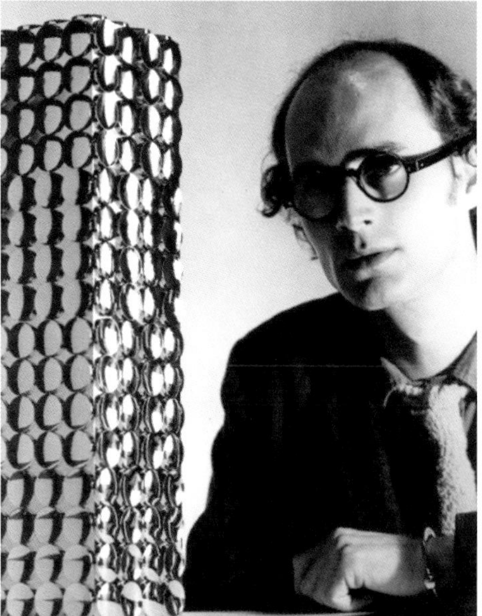

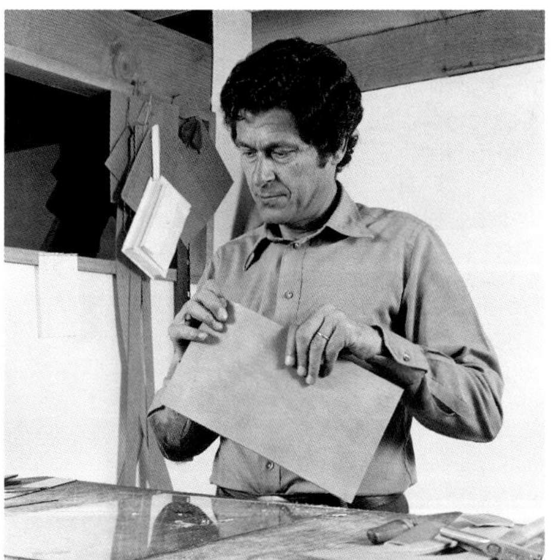

JAMFACTORY — THE BEGINNING, A PERSONAL VIEW

Dick Richards

The 1960s was an exciting time to be in Australia: Germaine Greer set dinner parties on fire, the Vietnam War polarised Australia, politics suddenly engaged the population and there was a sense of entitlement among young people. Sleepy but awakening observers, we felt empowered to bring about change. It is true that it was my idea to start something like the Jam Factory, but ideas like that were in the air, and it was Don Dunstan and his close staff, Peter Ward and Len Amadio, together with other specialists, including Marcia Del Thomas, President of both the Adelaide and national Crafts Councils, who made it happen.

From the late 1950s the Australian craft movement began to be influenced by international developments in design, through publications like the American *Craft Horizons*, the Italian *Domus*, the British *Design* magazine, and *Craft Australia* and the British *Crafts,* which came later.

The 1960s saw the advent of shops and galleries in Adelaide that specialised in well-designed imported wares and local craft. Quality Scandinavian glass, ceramics, tableware, clothing and jewellery became available in department and specialty stores like White Studio, Habitat and The Design Centre. Aldgate Crafts, in the Adelaide Hills and later the city, became an important venue for exhibitions and sale for local craft workers.

In 1964 the New South Wales branch of the Crafts Association of Australia, which was modelled on the American Crafts Council (established 1943), began to raise standards, and foster education and marketing. An Adelaide chapter followed soon after.

In 1971 a national Committee of Enquiry into the Crafts, driven by Dr Jean Battersby and chaired by Kym Bonython, was set up by the Coalition Government under Prime Minister William McMahon and continued under the Labor Prime Minister, Gough Whitlam. The findings of the committee were published in 1975, with far-reaching affects. In 1973 the Australia Council was created and quickly brought about major changes. The various boards of the new council developed national policies to give aspiring and established artists, writers, musicians and craftspeople new opportunities. Craftspeople benefited from access to education facilities, travel, exhibitions and individual workshop development grants. There was also an emphasis on Aboriginal arts and crafts. It was an exciting time for men and women who were frustrated by a lack of learning and marketing opportunities. Also, there was a shift from male-dominated practice with the entry of more women into both craft and design as artists, and as curators and teachers.

By the mid to late 1960s, it also became apparent in Adelaide that the import of manufactured goods from overseas was a threat to local industry, which had been so carefully nurtured after World War II by long-serving conservative Premier Tom Playford. New enterprises had to be developed to provide places for displaced workers and the growing number of young adults born after the war. Some observers feared a future *Grapes of wrath* environment, with unemployed young people forced to move from state to state to find work.

clockwise from left
Sam Herman, *Glass Workshop, 1976*
Photo: Grant Hancock

Frank Bauer, *1973*
Photo: Max Dupain

Pietro Salemme, *Leather Workshop, 1976*
Photo: Grant Hancock

Don Dunstan became Premier briefly in 1969 and was re-elected in 1970. His political philosophies were underpinned by theoretical Fabian socialist ideas, the confluence of Bauhaus and Fabianist craftwork, and 'En-nobled' Labour Romanticism. Dunstan had a passionate concern for the arts and an interest in craft and design heritage going back to William Morris, the legendary 19th-century British craftsman, designer, writer and typographer.

South Australia has an enviable connection with William Morris through Robert and Joanna Barr Smith and their family who, from 1884 to 1929, furnished several of their large mansions almost exclusively with Morris & Company carpets and textiles, furniture, wallpaper, ceramics and glass. One or two families followed suit and several Adelaide churches, even the Stock exchange, have Morris & Company stained glass. Given Dunstan's background and education he would have been aware of both Morris's Fabian philosophies and his connection with South Australia. There was also a strong tradition in the early days of South Australia, the 'Paradise of dissent', for the support of social justice issues.

Fertile ground existed in the late 1960s, as a result of the development from the mid 1950s of Australian furniture and textile design, the early Australian studio craft movement, and the growing number of galleries that exhibited fine craft and design. South Australian students and artists were influenced by such people as the studio potter and sculptor Alex Leckie and other South Australian School of Art lecturers, including Margaret Douglas and Helen Macintosh; the seminal teacher and potter, Milton Moon, who arrived in the state in 1969; the potter and weaver Pru Medlin (now La Motte), who returned to Australia in 1967; the architect Newell Platten and his colleagues; and also by the often forgotten, yet important Scandinavian Design exhibitions mounted in Adelaide by Karin Lemercier. The students and associates of these teachers and practitioners were encouraged to exhibit their work locally and to see themselves as part of a growing international movement in craft and design. The improving Australian economy and the arrival of the Australia Council Crafts Board also provided opportunities for graduates to travel and study abroad. The internationally recognised hot glass maker Nick Mount was an early recipient of a Council travel grant.

My interest in develoing design and craft education and related craft-or design-based industries for South Australia grew from three years (1956–59) I spent studying

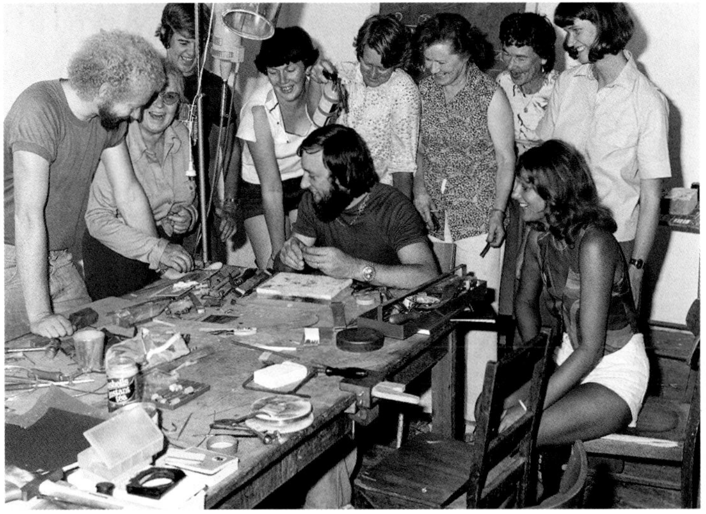

above
Norman Crichton running a summer school class,
Jewellery Workshop, 1978
Photo: Grant Hancock

opposite top
Sewing Leather,
Leather Studio, c. 1978
Photo courtesy JamFactory

South Australian Craft Authority Exhibition,
Jam Factory Gallery, 1976
Photo: Grant Hancock

and working at Chrysler Australia as a trainee. On my first day in the plant I bent down to pick up some discarded bolts on the floor, and the whole production line ground to a halt and a stop-work meeting began—I was staff! From then on I wore overalls in the factory and merged with the workers on day and night shifts. The months spent studying in the plant were intensely interesting, but there were also downsides to such a large and complex operation: mass sackings during downturns in the economy, industrial safety issues (I saw a young Hungarian refugee lose an arm in a press), and there were some disturbing problems with human relations in the plant. For example, Chrysler had an enlightened policy of providing jobs for intellectually challenged workers, but these individuals were subjected to inhuman bastardisation by some of their fellow workers, unbeknown to management.

Appointments to the National Craft Enquiry Committee and the Crafts Board brought me in contact with a large number of specialists involved with craft and design. The artist Tony Tuckson and his wife Margaret introduced me to leading east coast artists and designers, including the jewellers Helga Larsen and Darani Lewers, Frank Bauer and the potter-sculptor Marea Gazzard, who had all travelled widely and were deeply committed to fostering design and craft practice and education. My own studies at the South Australian School of Art and work at the Art Gallery of South Australia under the enlightened Director John Baily also brought me into contact with many local and international artists and designers.

As Premier, Dunstan made a strong speech at the opening of an exhibition at the Rundle Street Design Council Gallery in 1970, which affirmed his desire to support design-based industries in South Australia. Inspired by his stand, I called an informal meeting of a small group of artists, lecturers and craftspeople at my house to discuss Dunstan's ideas and how we might be involved in developing craft-based industry and education in South Australia. It was a lively meeting, probably fuelled by Darry Osborn's flagon claret served in ceramic mugs because I had vowed not to drink from glass until it was made in Adelaide.

To our amazement our report from the evening's discussion drew the attention of the Premier's executive assistant Peter Ward, who arranged for me to have lunch with Dunstan to explain our ideas. Subsequently the Premier sent me on a fact-finding tour of Europe. Coincidently I was already a recipient of a Calouste Gulbenkian Foundation grant to study art gallery and museum design in Europe and America and had been granted several months leave from the Art Gallery of South Australia. Following visits to Sweden, Denmark, Holland and Germany, I was staying in London, which coincided with one of Dunstan's regular visits there. I was able to meet with the Premier and Peter Ward to discuss my first report.

My key recommendations were:

• adopt the marketing strategies employed in Scandinavia and Europe, where handmade, and also well designed and manufactured goods utilising local materials are freely available in large supermarkets and 'home ware' emporiums

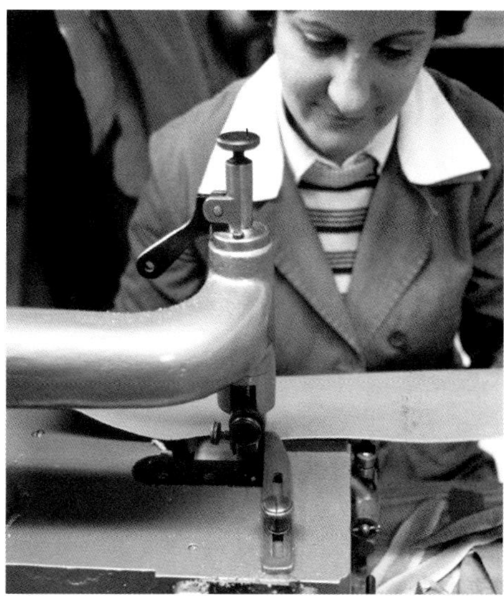

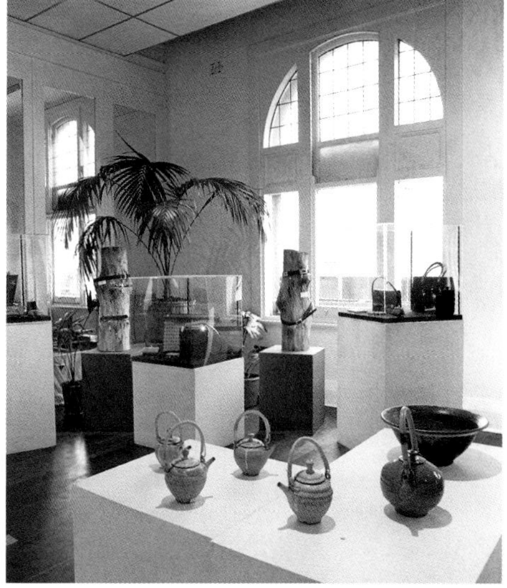

• develop state support for national and international travelling exhibitions of South Australian handmade and production craft and design

• encourage government support for tertiary design and craft education

• investigate the forces that led to the success of the Kilkenny Design Workshops in Cork, Ireland (1963–88), one of the first state-owned design consultancies in the world, and determine how the ideas that worked so well in Ireland and the United Kingdom might be adapted for South Australia

• examine the methods of the successful British Design Council and the Council for Small Industries in Rural Areas, which have been key instruments for positive change in the United Kingdom—the holistic support of these innovative institutions for small, medium and large enterprises proved to be highly successful during the 1960s and 1970s

• evaluate Sam Herman's program at London's Royal College of Art, which provided glass workshop facilities, separate from the college, for senior students to work independently while developing their craft and marketing skills. By the time the students graduated, they had established a client base and had gained experience in running a small business. (Herman was the first artist–craftsperson with an international reputation to agree to come to South Australia to set up a teaching studio. His support for the project was crucial to the creation of the Jam Factory.)

In 1972, under the umbrella of the Premier's Department, Don Dunstan formally decided to commission a far-reaching study of 'design and craft industries in South Australia'. Cabinet agreed to support the project and a committee was formed to carry out a detailed investigation. Their report was completed in May 1973 and it strongly recommended, among other initiatives, that a 'Craft Authority' be created to establish a craft and design training and production workshop in Adelaide. In response to the changing economic environment, it was mooted that the state's abundant resources of clay, sand, wool, leather, gemstones, jade and opal could be productively managed while providing creative employment opportunities, particularly for the young.

Don Dunstan then invited James Noel White (formerly of the British Council of Industrial Design and President, World Crafts Council of Great Britain) to Adelaide to review the report and offer advice. Noel White had been extremely supportive to me while I was in London, but needed to look at South Australia objectively. Again, he was extremely positive and the Premier responded accordingly.

The Craft Authority opened the Jam Factory retail shop and gallery in 1974 in the old Mumzone Factory, obtained from the Commonwealth for a peppercorn rent. The first workshop/studios, which trained apprentices and produced work for sale, were run by leading national and international craftspeople: glass blowing (Sam Herman, USA, UK); leather working (Pietro Salemme, Italy); weaving (Prue Medlin, Australia); and jewellery (Vagn Hemmingsen, Denmark).

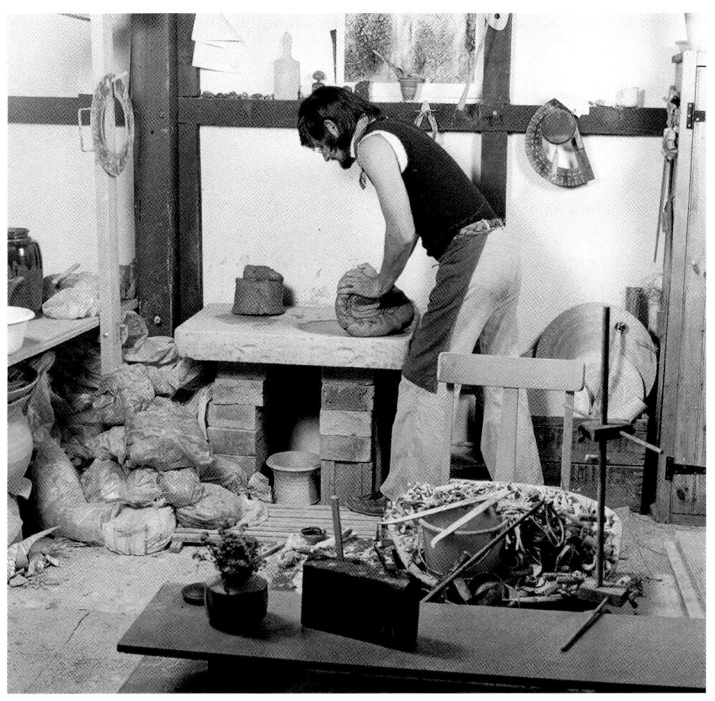

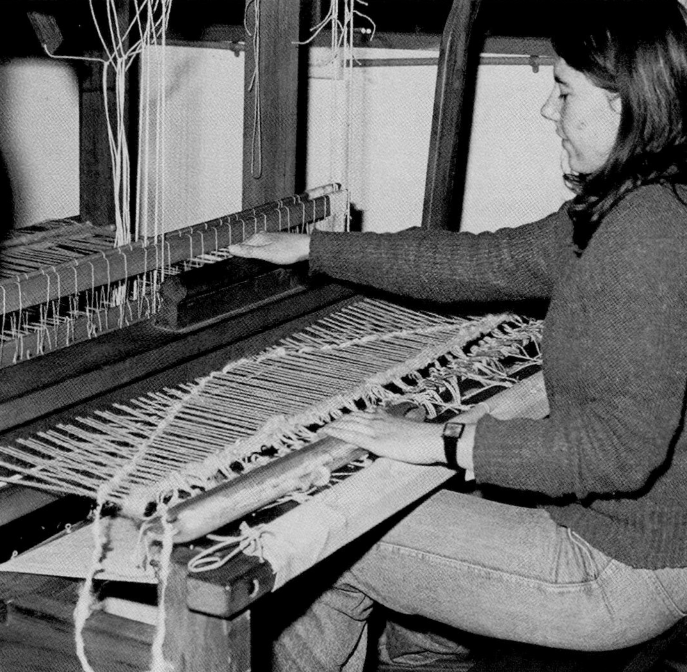

The Jam Factory's goal was to create an environment where small craft-and design-based enterprises could grow and contribute to the South Australian economy by producing high quality, value-added goods made from local raw materials for the local and Asian markets, particularly Japan.

Don Dunstan summed up his reasons for supporting the Jam Factory project in a speech at an exhibition opening there in November 1974:

The South Australian Craft Authority was established by the government for a number of reasons. Firstly, we had craftspeople in the state whose achievements were so distinctive that we believed they needed support. Secondly, the government wanted a situation in which such achievements affected the design criteria of the State's mass production industries. Thirdly, we wanted to encourage the development or the continuation of rare or interesting skills, gratuitously, not because any one person or group of people would necessarily make a profit from such a program, but because it was a nice thing to do, a civilised thing to do.

top
Jeff Mincham,
Ceramics Studio, 1976
Photo: Grant Hancock

Helen Bennett,
Woven Textiles Workshop, 1977
Photo: Grant Hancock

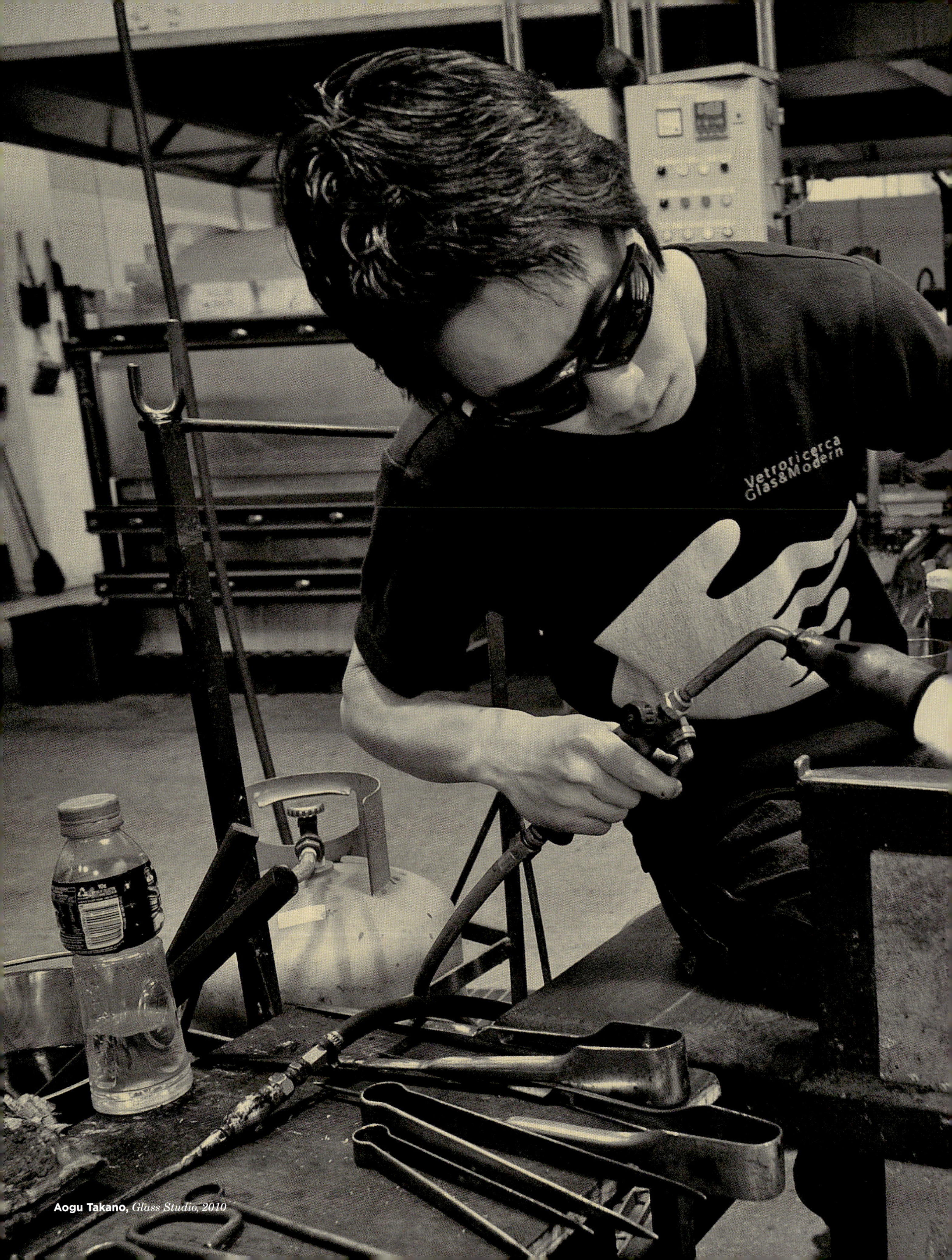

Aogu Takano, *Glass Studio, 2010*

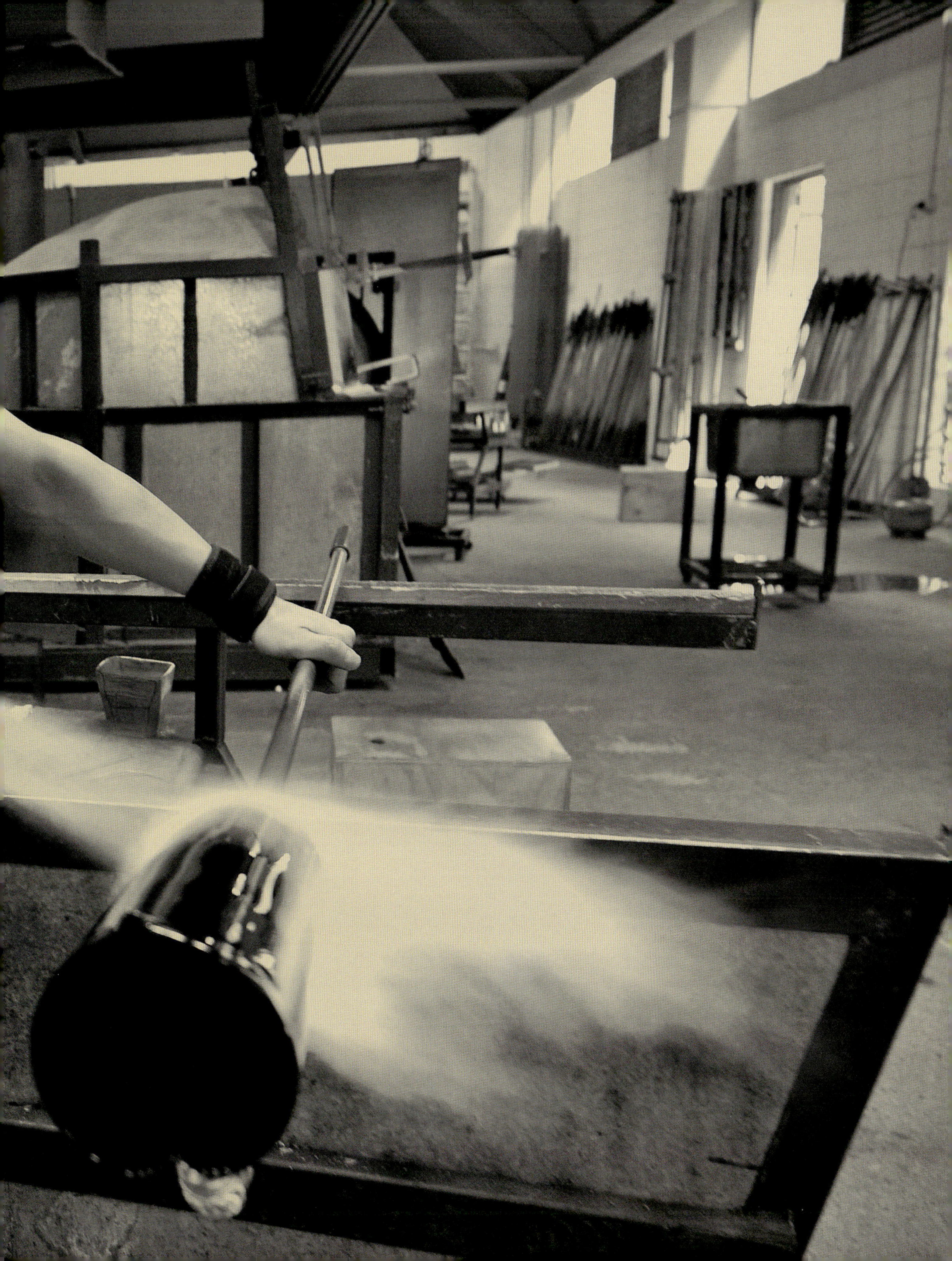

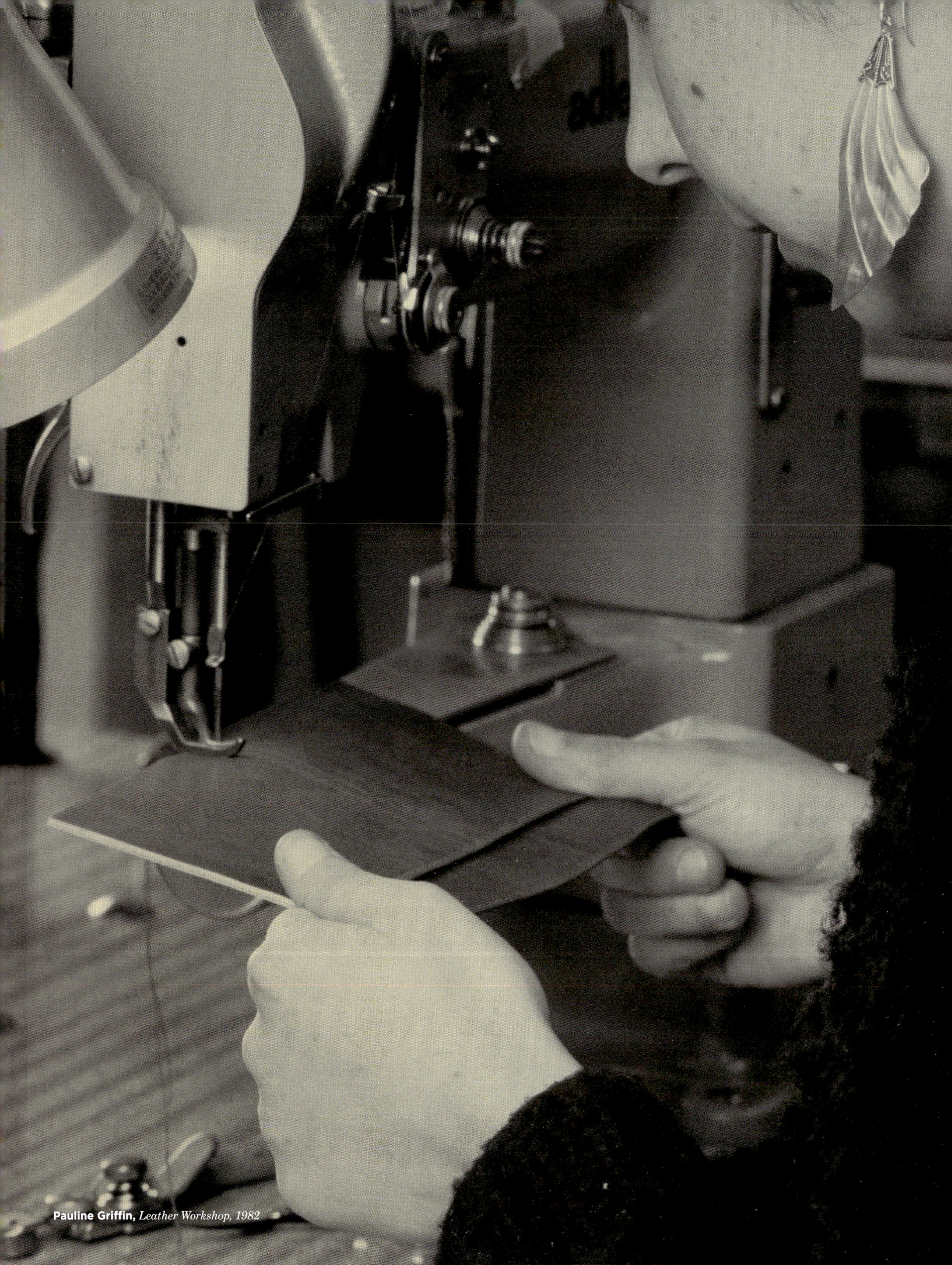

Pauline Griffin, *Leather Workshop, 1982*

DEVELOPMENT

“There were so many amazing projects happening all the time at the JamFactory during the 1980s – people working on product ranges in the training workshops, curated exhibitions involving trainees, workshop heads and others, visiting artists using the spaces, in particular the bullring space, visiting resident artists, etc. There was a lot of engagement across the studios involving collaborative work practices and commissions, but also lots of social activities – usually involving food and drink!

One of the most memorable things for me about my time at the Jam was the generosity of spirit - the willingness to share ideas, to be truly collaborative - displayed by all who worked there. There was a lot of cross fertilisation of ideas.”

Jennifer Layther
Head of Workshop Knitted
Textile Design 1982 - 1990

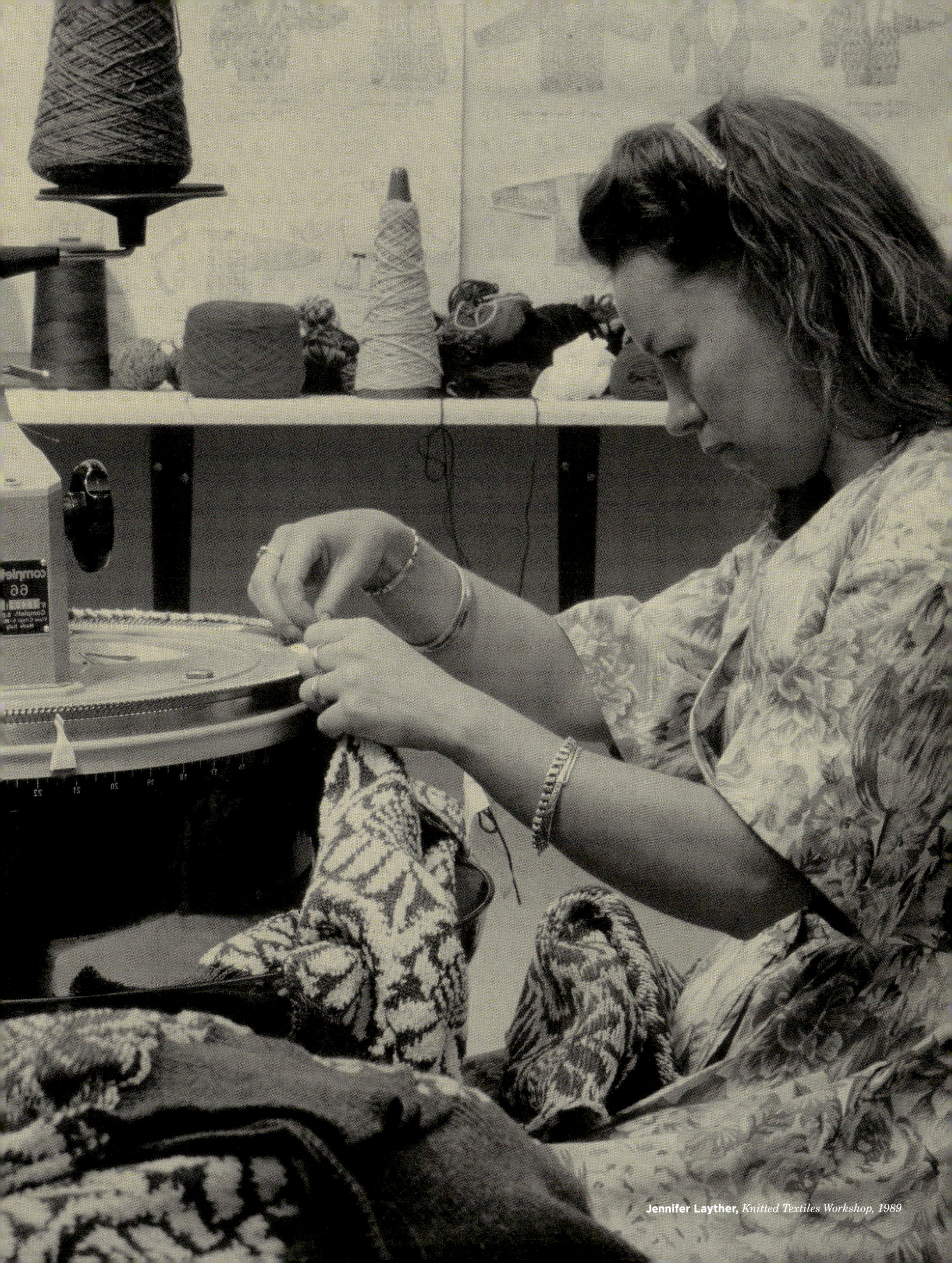

Jennifer Layther, *Knitted Textiles Workshop, 1989*

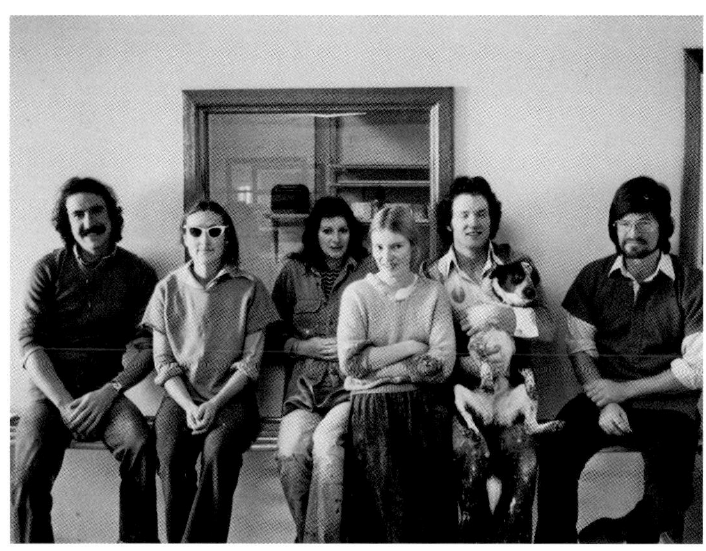

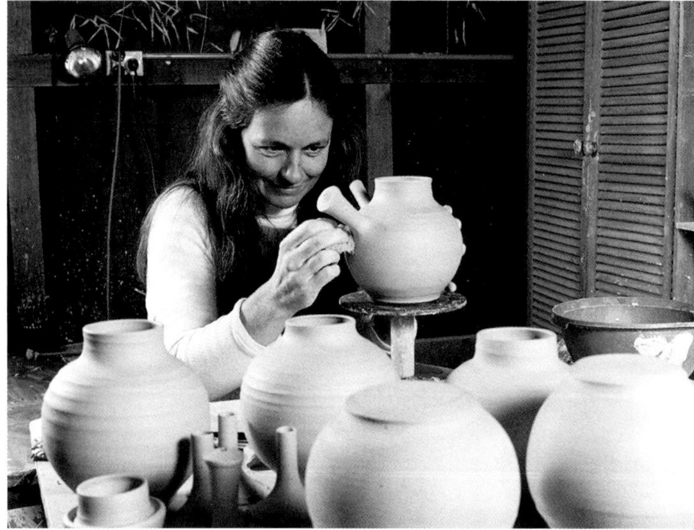

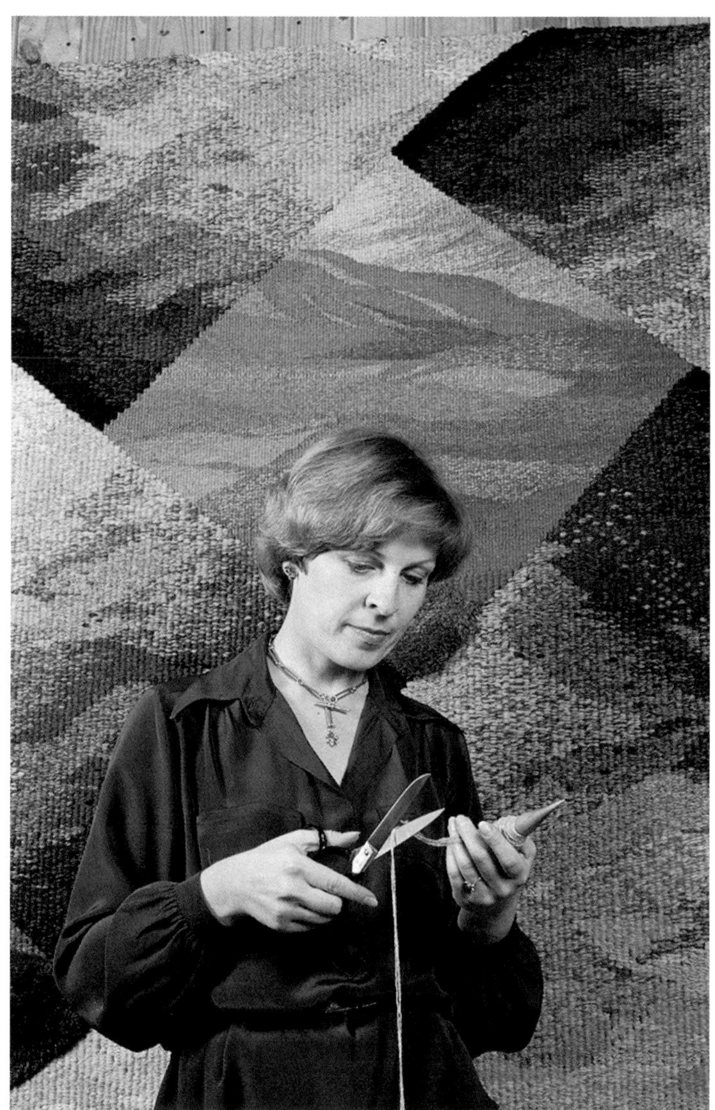

A PLACE AND AN IDEA—JAMFACTORY 1973 TO 2013

Margot Osborne

JamFactory[1] today is a wonderful, truly unique creative centre, generating innovative people, products and programs, which both respond to local needs and have global reach. It is a much-loved Adelaide institution, which attracts a broad public and fulfils a vital role for South Australia's professional craft and design practitioners. That it has survived for 40 years is a small miracle. It is also vindication for all those who, over the years, have contributed in incremental ways to its development and survival, often with very real sweat and occasional tears.

Looking back over those 40 years it is possible to discern many changes, but there is even more that remains the same. Now, as then, JamFactory is a place where a lot is happening.
It is an incubator, where emerging craft and design practitioners learn from leaders in their field and get to try out their ideas, with access to some of the best facilities available.
It is a creative production hub, where work is constantly being conceived and produced for commissions, and for distribution to galleries and shops throughout Australia and the world.
It is an exhibition venue, where the public can see exhibitions of some of the most innovative Australian craft and design. It is a shop and tourist attraction, where both locals and visitors from interstate and overseas can buy the finest handcrafted Australian products.

Much, though by no means all, of this present-day scenario was part of the original vision of those key movers in the early 1970s—Premier Don Dunstan, his advisor Peter Ward, and Art Gallery of South Australia curator Dick Richards.[2] The South Australian Parliament legislated to create the South Australian Craft Authority in October 1973. The following year a home was found for it in a run-down former jam factory at St Peters. After some relatively superficial refurbishment and the painting of the facade in fashionable chocolate brown, the Craft Authority was officially opened by Dunstan on 1 November 1974, with an exhibition of jade, nephrite and silver jewellery by the first Jewellery Workshop Head, Danish master-craftsman Vagn Hemmingsen. At the opening, Dunstan stated his reasons for establishing the Authority. These were to support craftspeople, to affect 'the design criteria of the State's mass production industries' and to encourage the development of 'rare or interesting skills'.[3]

Almost certainly, neither he nor anyone else could envisage how this fledgling venture would look 40 years on, when it had matured and evolved with the changing times. In many, but not all respects, Dunstan's vision has been fulfilled. Stephen Bowers once said that JamFactory was both a place and an idea. As a man of many parts—not least, as JamFactory's former Managing Director and Head of its Ceramics Studio, and also as a one-time arts bureaucrat and a professional ceramicist—Bowers can speak with some authority on JamFactory. His comment points to how it has become a mirror—or perhaps a sponge is a better analogy—for changing notions of what crafting and designing objects might be all about. It has survived partly because of its flexibility in adapting to these changes. But this comment pinpoints, as well, the tensions that have always existed

clockwise from top left
Christopher Headley, Bronwyn Kemp, Lorraine Lee, Nicola Purcell, Peter Andersson, Smithie (dog), Jeff Mincham, *Ceramics Workshop, 1978*
Photo courtesy Bronwyn Kemp

Winnie Pelz, *1979*
Photo: Grant Hancock

Liz Williams, *1976*
Photo: Grant Hancock

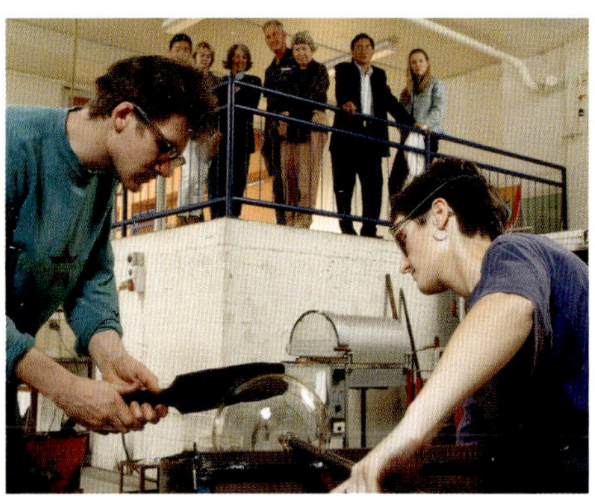

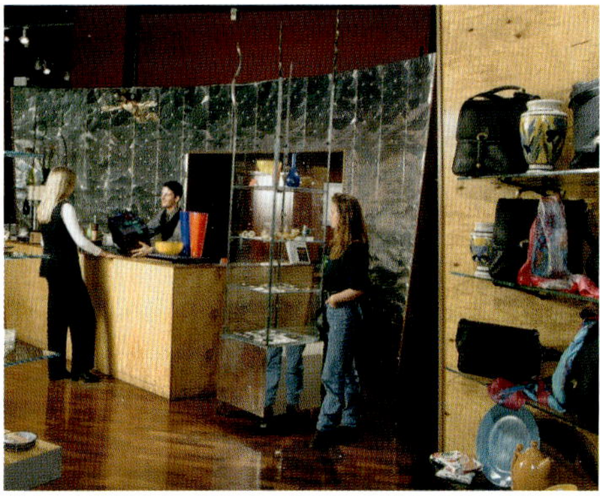

top
Tom Moore and Clare Belfrage, *Glass Studio, c. 1997*
Photo courtesy JamFactory

Retail Shop, *Morphett Street, c. 1997*
Photo courtesy JamFactory

between what JamFactory is, and what it has been expected, or aspired, to be. It has been tethered to a founding vision encoded in its formative DNA, even as it has mutated through a succession of 'mission statements' developed over time by its Boards, CEOs and focus groups. The miracle is how it has transcended all this to become a deeply embedded and highly valued part of the South Australian craft and design scene. For to view JamFactory's evolution only through official mission statements of what it aspired to be would be to miss the point entirely of what has been the life and heart, the key driver of the organisation—its people.

Over the years there has been a constantly changing cast of Associates, Creative Directors, CEOs and Board Members, with almost every year a slightly different blend of people. This perpetual renewal has created an organisation living in the present, oriented to future goals, with little corporate memory—hence the importance of markers like this 40th anniversary. However, some have had a more ongoing relationship and left an enduring legacy. Former Creative Director Nick Mount has continued his connection with the Glass Studio over many years, as a user of its facilities and as a mentor. Sue Lorraine played a significant role as longstanding Creative Director of the Metal Studio. Stephen Bowers had a long connection in differing roles as trainee, Creative Director of the Ceramics Studio and eventually Managing Director. Pauline Griffin presided over JamFactory's retail and wholesale operations at the height of their success during the late 1990s and into the 2000s. Phil Hart, who was a trainee under Bronwyn Kemp in the 1980s, contributed greatly to the Ceramics Studio over the years as Studio Technician and then Creative Director. Tribute should be paid here to the longest-serving staff member of JamFactory, Tom Persson, who retired in 2011 after working as Technician - in the Glass Studio mostly, since 1975!

Most visitors experience the JamFactory through its public zones—the galleries and retail areas. Between 60,000 and 75,000 visit the exhibitions annually, including many school groups and cultural tourists. But there is much more that most visitors do not see (unless they are part of an organised tour). If you could take a hypothetical video-tour tracking through JamFactory's three-level building in the Lion Arts Centre, on any day you would find dozens of creative practitioners at work from the early hours until late. They would include not only the 20 or so Associates and Creative Directors in each of the four main studios—Ceramics, Glass, Furniture and Metal Design—but also other professional practitioners hiring equipment, furnaces and kilns on an access basis, and more working independently in shared studio tenancies. There may even be a master class in progress, run by one of the regular artists-in-residence visiting from interstate and overseas.

There is a palpable energy generated by this hum of activity, and a cross-fertilisation between individual practitioners, between each of the studios, and between the studios and the galleries and shops. In a very real sense there has always been creative room for individual decision-making at every level, and this in turn leads to a sense of ownership. Successive CEOs

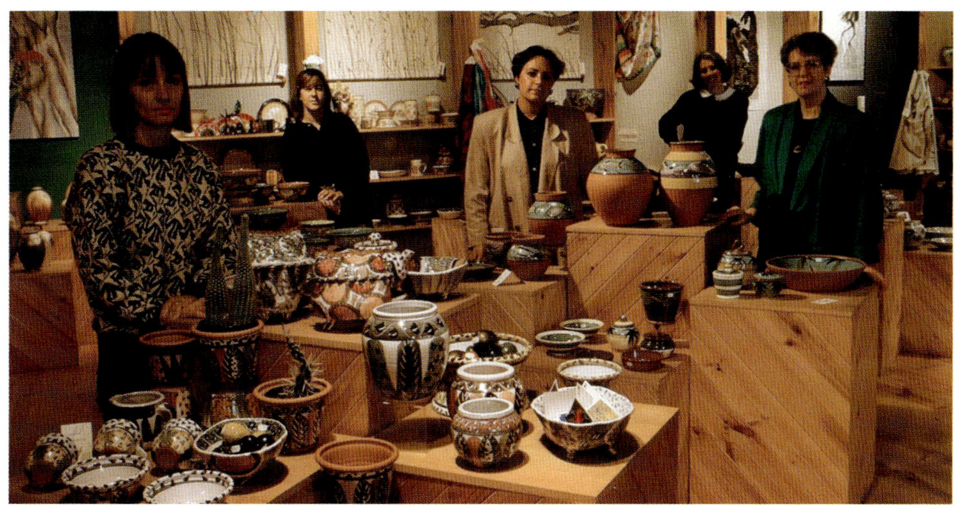

Retail Shop, *Payneham Road, c. 1985 Photo courtesy JamFactory*

have had the unenviable task of marshalling all this creative energy and moving the organisation forward in line with the Board's corporate vision at any given moment—not always with much success.

JamFactory is a truly synergetic, complex organisation where the whole is greater than the sum of its parts. This complex, interdependent relationship of parts has been the source of its creative strength, although it has also contributed to recurring financial crises when a weakness in one part threatened the sustainability of the organisation. It has always survived, and usually thrived, but this has been a hard-won survival. In the process it has matured into a unique arts organisation, and one of which South Australians and the government can be proud.

Arguably, the first few years were some of the toughest, as the organisation struggled to get established and live up to the political rhetoric. By the end of 1976 all four workshops - Glass, Leather, Textiles, Jewellery - were running with master-craftsmen supervising groups of trainees.[4] From the outset the gallery and shop were the successful public face of the former St Peters Jam Factory. Not only were there solo exhibitions by leading and emerging crafts practitioners from South Australia and interstate, but there were also landmark national surveys such as the first Ausglass exhibition in April 1979. Touring exhibitions of Indigenous craft was part of the program mix from the early days, with *Bags and Baskets from Australia and the South Pacific* in March 1976, and *Tiwi Carvers and Desert Weavers* in February 1978. Ceramicist Mark Thompson was appointed Gallery Manager in 1978.

Even as these programs were getting established there were underlying ideological differences emerging, both among the Board Members and in the wider South Australian craft community, concerning the South Australian Craft Authority's mission, management model and operating budget. At issue was how to live up to the government's claim that the Authority would be self-supporting, and how to respond to opposition from some craft practitioners who saw this government enterprise as competing unfairly in the market place. These problems came to a much-publicised head in November 1977, when the Opposition arts spokesman Murray Hill raised questions in State Parliament about the South Australian Craft Authority's financial losses and the expensive overseas study trip of its Chairman Earle Hackett and Board Member Karin Lemercier. In an unlikely alliance, potter Jeff Mincham and Donald Brook of the Experimental Art Foundation each wrote letters to *The Advertiser* arguing against commercialising the Jam Factory's operations (14 November 1977).

Meanwhile in *The Australian* (1 December 1977), Peter Ward argued that there needed to be a distinction between 'the artist craftsman producing one-off gallery pieces and the industrial designer producing craft-based industrial design suitable for mass production and the mass market'. Thus the foundations were laid for the running debate on what the JamFactory should be doing, which has continued virtually unabated to the present day, with successive CEOs and Boards addressing this in differing ways. Ward, who remained a 'true believer' in Dunstan's (and his) founding vision, has criticised JamFactory over the years for diverging from it. Writing in *The Australian* (14–15 March 1992) at the time of the move to the Lion Arts Centre, he commented that the JamFactory had 'negligible success' in influencing design standards, but on the positive side had 'helped markedly increase the diversity and quality of artist-craft work'. Again, in his review of the *2001 JamFactory Biennial* he expressed his disillusionment that instead of prototypes he found 'the precious world of artist-craftsperson one-offs', whereas 'the Jam Factory was meant to be so much more than that'.[5]

In August 1977 the South Australian Craft Authority was put in permanent mothballs and the Jam Factory Workshops were incorporated.[6] For the next two years it was run by bureaucrat Tony Richardson (formerly of the scrapped Monarto Project). As Chairman and General Manger he introduced financial controls and could boast in the annual report for 1977–78 that sales, rental income and commissions had generated $211,902, with 32,000 visitors to the shop and gallery.

The next potential crisis came with the change of state government in late 1979, prompting fears that the Jam Factory would be abolished or commercialised. In the event, the incoming Liberal Government appointed Winnie Pelz as Executive Chairman in April 1980. Her first official function was to open an exhibition of ceramics by Bruce Nuske and glass by Nick Mount. The appointment of Pelz proved to be an inspired move, as it was under her adept and energetic management that the Jam Factory finally achieved a new stability and credibility as a flagship for craft development in South Australia.

She was under no illusions about her brief from the Government, commenting recently that:

There was enormous pressure on us to become financially stable. Whilst it was never openly stated, I was appointed with an unwritten but clearly understood message of 'make the place less reliant on subsidy, or we might be forced to close it down'. From memory, the government subsidy in 1980 was around 70%. By 1986 it was down to approx 35–40%, with the retail shop and wholesaling contributing significantly.[7]

Pelz introduced quarterly *Bulletins* promoting exhibitions and events. The first Bulletin (January - March 1983) publicised the forthcoming joint exhibition by ceramicists Robin Best and Stephen Bowers—both of whom would go on to have a long involvement with the organisation. By October 1983 the Jam Factory

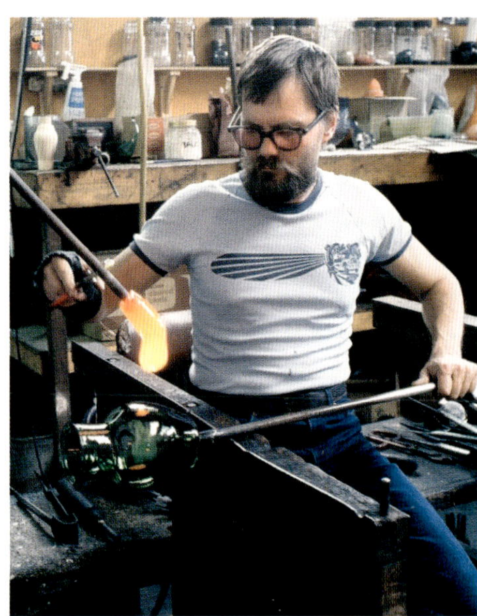

above
Tom Persson, *Glass Workshop, 1989*
Photo courtesy JamFactory

opposite top
Stephen Bowers, *1982*
Photo: Grant Hancock

Robin Best, *1982*
Photo: Grant Hancock

had survived its first decade. In Bulletin No 3 (October - December 1983), Pelz wrote:

The path has had its ups and downs (and a few hairpin bends too!) but all in all we've come a long way ... Part of the success of the organisation lies in its flexibility to adapt to changing conditions.

In his review of the 10th anniversary exhibition, Neville Weston commented that 'the Jam Factory has gained strength and status each year'.[8] In 1985-86, attendances peaked at 76,000.

Working conditions at the Payneham Road premises had always been fairly basic at best, and would never pass Health and Safety standards today. Jeff Mincham, who was Head of the Ceramics Workshop from 1979 to 1982, once joked that you could paddle a kayak down the main concourse after it rained. By 1984 Pelz was starting to lobby for new premises. The success of the 1984 Adelaide Fringe, held on the site of the old Fowler's Flour factory on North Terrace (now the Lion Arts Centre), prompted the formation by Arts SA of a committee to investigate the feasibility of housing a range of arts organisations, including the Jam Factory, in a Living Arts Centre on the site. In 1986 Pelz resigned to become Development Manager of the Living Arts Centre. It was not until 1990 that the first soil was turned on the site. Providentially this was just before the collapse of the State Bank, which would bring down the Labor Government and might have caused the project to be abandoned. The new purpose-built JamFactory, designed by architect Steve Grieve, was officially opened by HM Queen Elizabeth II on 25 February 1992. By then Pelz had moved on to become Chief Executive of Arts SA, while still continuing to keep a protective eye on JamFactory.

Lynn Collins, who took over running the Jam Factory in 1986, straddled the art/craft divide as both a recognised contemporary artist and former executive officer of the Crafts Council of South Australia (now Craftsouth). His relatively brief tenure with the Jam Factory was notable for a series of innovative exhibitions that expanded notions of the handmade. *Selected Affinities* (October 1986) featured artists Alison Clouston, Clinton Garofano, David Hawkes, Narelle Jubelin, each of whom used handcrafting in their art practices. *Makers' Choice II* (June 1987) was a critically successful exhibition, with each artist selecting three who had influenced him or her. It was reviewed by John Neylon in *The Advertiser* (20 June 1987) as 'an innovative and exciting exhibition at the experimental edge of contemporary craft'.

When Frank McBride, a former senior staffer of the Australia Council's Visual Arts/Crafts Board, took over from Collins as CEO in June 1989 there was a noticeable shift in aims and objectives. McBride was far more oriented than his predecessors to fulfilling JamFactory's original mission of establishing a connection between designer-makers and industry. When Don Dunstan was appointed Chair in 1990, these views made the pair a natural fit. Together they presided over the move to the Lion Arts Centre. In conjunction with the relocation there was a new name, Jam Factory Contemporary Craft and Design Centre, and there was a change in the training workshops. McBride closed the Leather and the

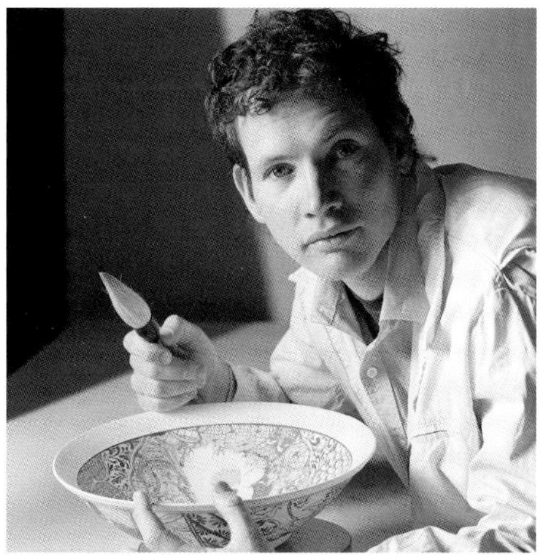

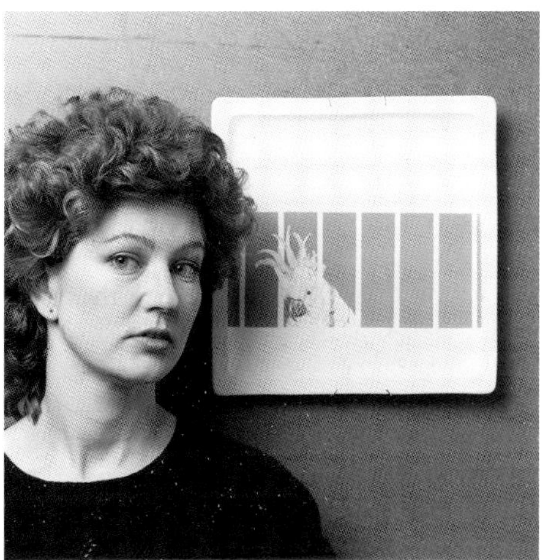

Knitted Textiles Workshops, and in turn established two new workshops of Metal+Design and Furniture.

Shortly after the move, in a June 1992 interview with John Emery, McBride talked of returning to the founding vision of widening South Australia's industrial base, with craftspeople to have a role in industry. He proposed a redefinition of the kind of craft object that was relevant to the 1990s and advocated a direct link between craft and commerce, stating:

Commercial furniture design is politically interesting to us because it means, rather than designing things that only have a life as far as very wealthy people are concerned, we will be designing things that are actually in people's everyday lives.[9]

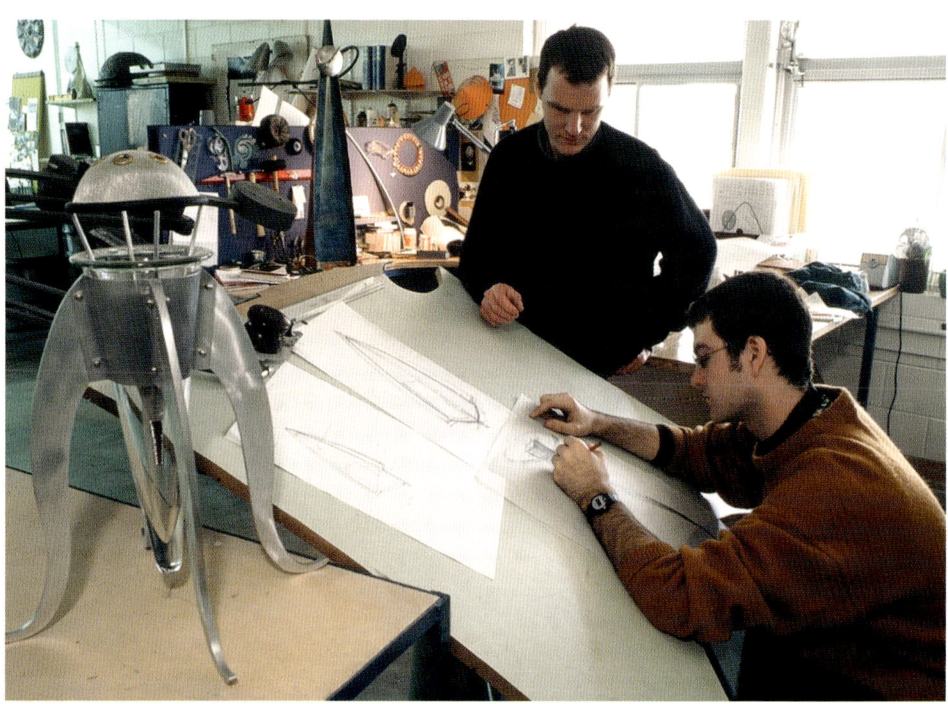

One of the triumphant features of the new JamFactory was the large exhibition space with two galleries, one able to accommodate major exhibitions, and an intimate glass-enclosed space, ideal for jewellery and small objects. The gallery was then, and continues to be today, the most impressive public gallery in Australia dedicated to the display of craft and design. Janene Pellarin was appointed as Gallery Curator and launched the exhibitions program with *Real and Forged Contemporary Australian Metal* in Gallery 1 and *Wearable Glass* in Gallery 2. Pellarin, who continued as Gallery Curator until 1996, presented several significant exhibitions, including the *Second Contemporary Jewellery Biennial* (1993), *Italian Gold* (1995), *Homocraft* (1995), and a major survey of architect Alvar Aalto for the 1996 Adelaide Festival. Over the years since then, under its subsequent curators and

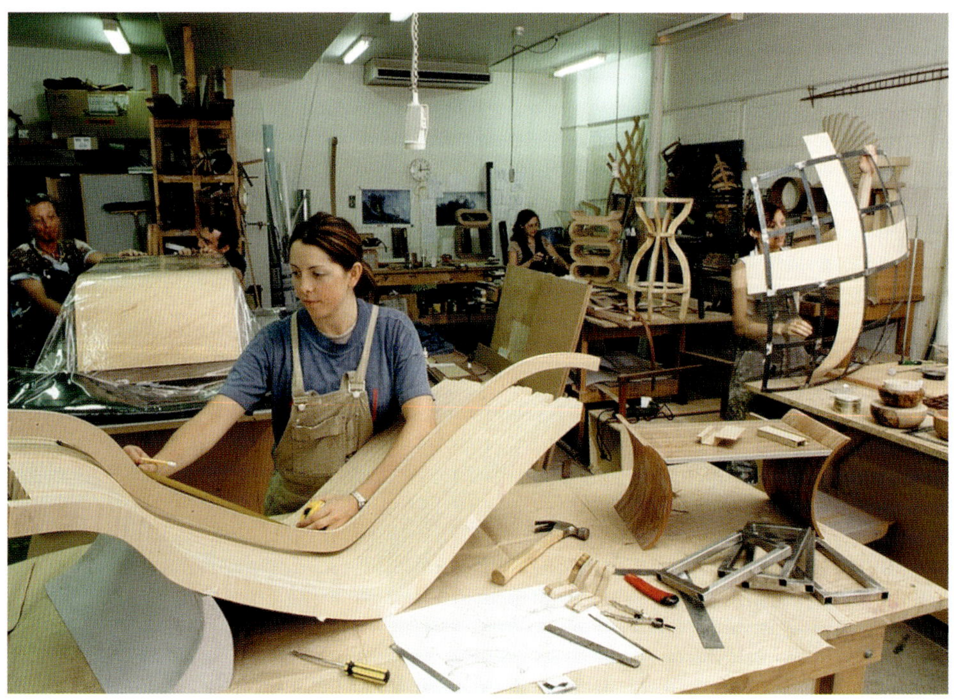

managers, JamFactory's exhibitions program has consistently been a vanguard showcase for the latest developments in craft and design both in South Australia and nationally.

The Board and McBride saw the relocation as an opportunity to leave behind the 'folksy' image of crafts and launch JamFactory into the 1990s with new premises and a new identity. They were to discover that enticing visitors loyal to the old St Peters location, let alone building new audiences, was not going to be achieved overnight. The shop changed from 'folksy' to sharp, shiny and slick—an exemplar of late 1980s purple and metallic décor. This was too much for the more traditional craft-lovers, still holding on to memories of 1970s-style 'back to the earth' wares. Or maybe they could not find a car park, or did not wish to venture into the city's slightly sleazy West End. Taxi drivers were slow to catch on and still wanted to take their fares to St Peters. Whatever the reason, it took a few nail-biting years for shop revenue to recover and for audiences to build—but build they did.

For the first three years, though, there were cost over-runs and revenue downturns, leading to a spate of questioning in the media. The Advertiser's craft writer Noris Ioannou was persistent in his attacks on JamFactory's 'design-led recovery', even suggesting at one stage that JamFactory was a failure and that its funding should be directed instead to Craftsouth. This criticism was largely directed at the financial performance rather than at creative achievements. It prompted a riposte from Dunstan in *The Adelaide Review* (January 1993), deflecting accusations of bad management and asserting that 'the Board strongly suggests that the changes we have made over the past two years present a new and challenging view of the crafts for the 1990s'.

Loene Furler (1994-1996) was appointed Chair replacing Dunstan in 1994, and shortly afterwards took on the double role of Executive Chair after the resignation of McBride, who left to take up a position in Brisbane. She realised that JamFactory needed to sell itself more effectively in order to build audiences and revenue, and used the 21st anniversary celebrations in October 1994 as an opportunity to raise the profile of the Lion Arts Centre site. She focused also on overseas projects, including taking work to *SOFA* (Sculpture, Objects, Functional Art + Design) Chicago for the first time in 1994.

Furler was fortunate to have supporting her a particularly strong team of Studio Heads, with Nick Mount running the Glass Studio, Donald Fortescue in charge of Furniture, Stephen Bowers as Head of Ceramics and Greg Healey in the Metal+Design Studio. All the studios contributed to developing a range of JamFactory product lines, including a folding table by Fortescue, a fruit bowl and a tray from the Metal Design Studio, the Jam 95 *Grrrange* jug, bowl and vase from the Glass Studio and the *Andamooka* range of marbled ceramics. The latter, which was designed by Bowers and produced by a professional team within the Ceramics Studio (and not by the Associates), would prove a long-running success, being produced continuously for over a decade.[10]

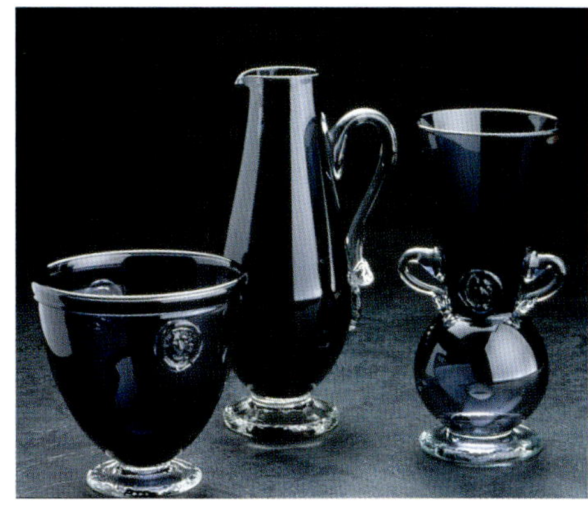

above
Grrrange, *1995*
blown glass
dimensions variable
Photo courtesy JamFactory

opposite top
Greg Healey and Jason Moss
Metal Design Studio, 1992
Photo: Michal Kluvanek

Michael Hill, Toby Thomas, Kelly-Anne Capuano, Amanda Twyford, Anne-Claire Petre
Furniture Studio, 1992
Photo courtesy JamFactory

The *Grrrange* glass products were awarded Australian Gift of the Year 1995 and the JamFactory shop won the SA Tourism Retailing Award for 1995. It would be in cultural tourism retailing and wholesale distribution of South Australian craft that JamFactory would play a significant and often overlooked role in supporting the livelihoods of South Australian craft practitioners. Sale of their work through JamFactory has provided crucial income for a wide range of craft and design practitioners, including those directly connected to JamFactory and others with independent practices.

The foundations laid in the first part of the 1990s in establishing the new location and identity were built upon in the latter part of the decade. During the next few years under the next CEO Mark Ferguson (1997–2004) and Chair Richard Krantz (1996–2001), JamFactory fully realised some of its potentials, not only in retail and tourism, but also in other areas of its operations including the exhibitions program, studio commissions and awards, residencies and international exchanges. Re-badging for the fourth time, the Board adopted the name, JamFactory Contemporary Craft and Design in 1997, and in 2010 shortened this to simply JamFactory. A lot happened during the late 1990s and early years of the new century, far too much to even skate over here, so I will cover just some of the key events, moments and achievements.

Retail, wholesale, gallery and studio operations grew to a peak combined turnover of $2.26 million in 1999–2000, with the major portion being returned to craft practitioners. JamFactory could claim in 2000 that it was the leading Australian wholesaler of contemporary craft and design. Retail again won an award for Tourism Retailing in 1998 and in 2000, and was recognised with an Award of Distinction. There were awards also to Associates and Studio Heads. Furniture Associate Mark O'Ryan won Best New Furniture Design Award at Interior Designex 2000; ceramicist Robin Best (who would later become Creative Director) received a Design Institute of Australia award for her *Concertina* bowl; and Metal Design Studio Associate Alisa Dewhurst won an emerging artist award at *Talente*, Munich, in 1998. The following year *Talente* was won by Furniture Studio Associate Ian Hope and in 2000 by Aaron Robinson from the Glass Studio. The Furniture Studio under Peter Walker had its most successful year in 2000 when it undertook a major commission for Adelaide's Pedare Christian College.

There was a program of regular residencies and master classes by visiting interstate and international artists. These raised the bar for local practitioners, not only enhancing

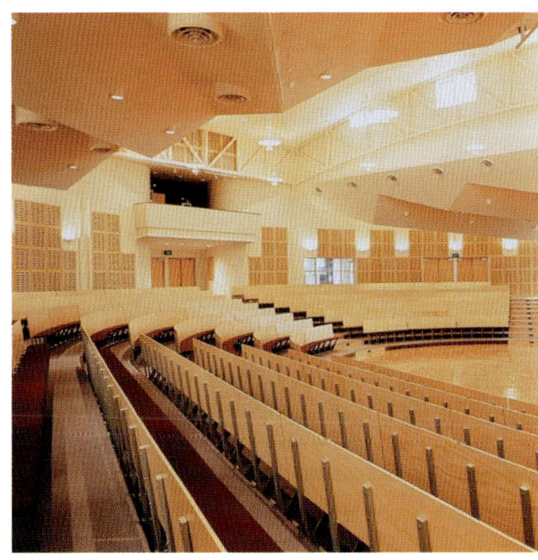

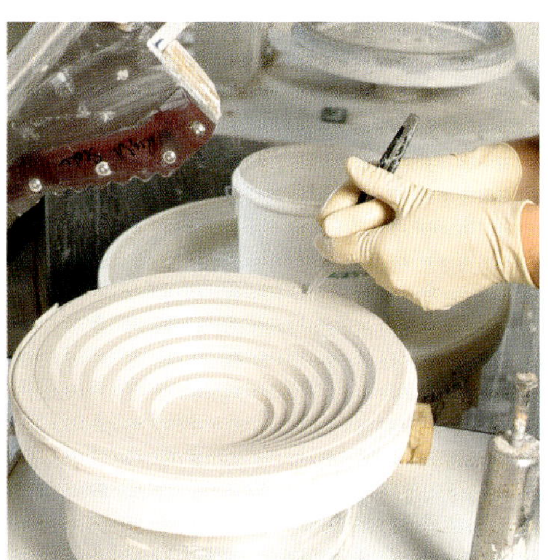

above left
Pedare Christian College Chapel Pews *Furniture Studio Commission, 2000 Photo courtesy JamFactory*

Concertina Bowl in production
Ceramics Studio, 1999 Photo: Michal Kluvanek

opposite top
Chihuly Masterworks in Glass
JamFactory Gallery One, 2000 Photo: Grant Hancock

Wild Nature
JamFactory Gallery One, 2002. Photo courtesy JamFactory

their skills but also enabling them to measure their work against the best in their field. One project that has left a continuing legacy was the first residency in the Ceramics Studio in 1997 by Indigenous artists from Ernabella in central Australia. This led to a partnership between JamFactory and Ernabella Arts that involved ceramic blanks being produced in the Ceramics Studio before being sent to Ernabella for hand-painting by women artists there. The first fruits of this exchange were exhibited to great acclaim at JamFactory in November 1998. This was the beginning of a continuing connection between the two organisations and led to regular exhibitions at JamFactory since that time.

The gallery under this author as Exhibitions Curator (1998–2001) and then Janice Lally (2001–04) developed an ambitious exhibitions program. The *JamFactory Biennial* of work by final year Associates and Studio Heads was launched in 1999 and became a recurring and very successful showcase of what was happening in the four studios. Exhibitions generated by JamFactory, which toured Australia and overseas, were *The Return of Beauty* (Adelaide Festival and Object, Sydney, 2000); *Designing Minds* (tour to Object, Sydney, 2000); a Frank Bauer retrospective (presented jointly with the Powerhouse Museum, 2000); *GlassState 2001* (interstate tour); *Wild Nature* (national tour 2002–04); *Permutations* (Seattle, 2003); *Ritual of Tea* (tour to Object, Sydney, 2002); and *Light Black* (Asialink tour to Japan, 2003–04). Easily the most ambitious exhibition ever presented by JamFactory was *Chihuly Masterworks in Glass*. This wildly successful exhibition attracted

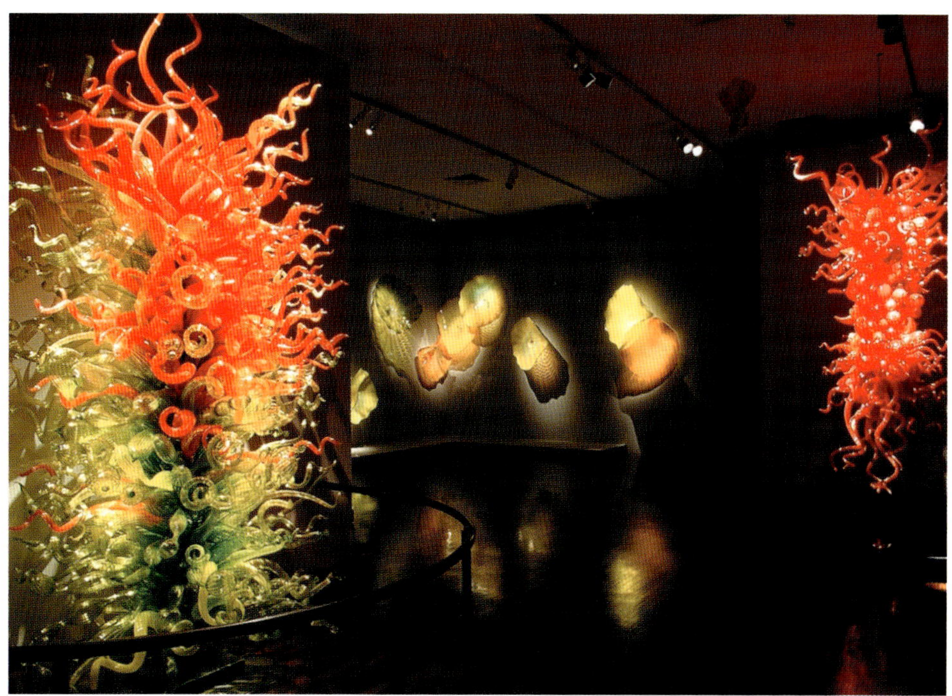

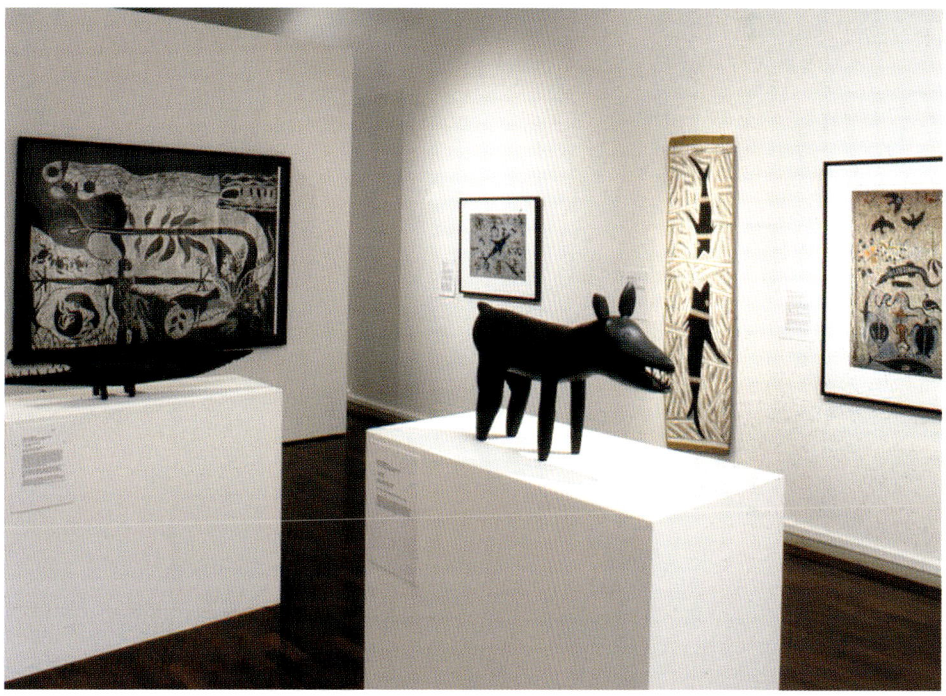

20,000 visitors, even with an admission charge, and was made possible by a large guarantee against loss from the State Government. This helped lift attendances in 2000 to a record 74,600.

More than simply providing exposure for South Australian practitioners, the curatorial concepts behind these exhibitions positioned work in a wider cultural context and presented differing aesthetic rationales for viewing handcrafted objects. In this sense the exhibitions program has been an invaluable counterpoint to retail operations, in providing entry points for understanding handcrafted and designed objects and how they can be distinguished from mass-produced consumer merchandise.

Other achievements during Ferguson's term included securing delegated funding from the Australia Council to coordinate the Australian presence at international events *Talente*, Munich, *SOFA Chicago* and *Collect*, London; the commitment of substantial additional funding towards the exhibitions program from the Myer Inquiry; securing the international GAS (Glass Art Society) Conference for Adelaide; and forming a partnership with UniSA to present a Masters program for Studio Associates. It would be his successor Stephen Bowers who actually implemented these programs.

JamFactory's revenue sources in retail and corporate commissions have always been susceptible to economic and tourism downturns. By the time Bowers took over from Ferguson in mid 2004, there were pressures once again from the Board, chaired by accountant Jane Yuile, to improve economic performance and find a 'sustainable business model'. He chose a stringent cost-cutting regime, leaving positions unfilled, reducing Associate numbers, and continued to run the Furniture Studio as an access studio without a Creative Director until it reopened in 2006 under Creative Director Tom Mirams.[11]

Bowers re-invigorated the organisation, placing particular emphasis on making a shift from 'product to people' as a guiding principle.[12] He saw JamFactory as a 'creative laboratory' and during his term there was an increase in residencies by local, interstate and overseas artists. Among these, sound composer Michael Yuen's four-month residency to experiment with 'wearable technology' pushed the boundaries of craft and design conventions. Former Furniture Studio Head Peter Walker brought students from Rhode Island School of Design to create designs in response to the natural environment of Kangaroo Island. There was a two-month residency by three Taiwanese artists in 2006. In the galleries, significant exhibitions included the *Here and there* (HAT) exchange between jewellers from Australia and England (2005); *Surface Tension*, ceramics by visiting artists Paul Scott, Stephen Dixon and Sergei Isupov (2006); *Salon South*, furniture design selected by guest curator Joanne Cys, Program Director of Interior Architecture at UniSA (2006); *Porcelain* (2008); *From the Earth*, the first national exhibition of Indigenous ceramics (2008); and *A Secret History of Blue and White* (Asialink tour, 2009).

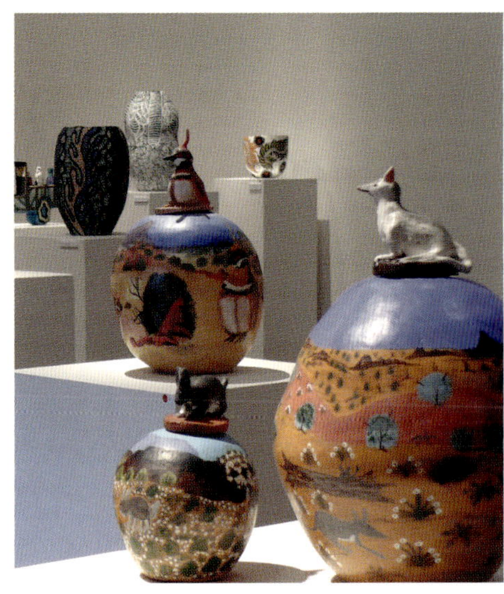

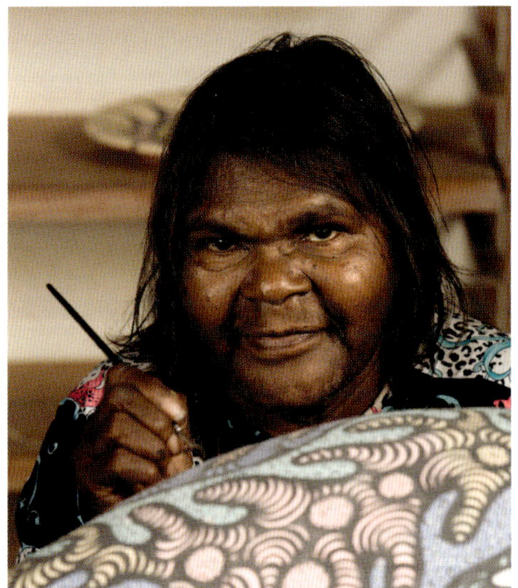

top
From the Earth,
Gallery One, 2008
Photo courtsey JamFactory

Nyukana (Daisy) Baker,
Central Craft, Alice Springs, 2008
Photo: Peter Eve

Bowers bowed out with the February 2010 launch of a major refit of the retail space, designed by Khai Liew. Incoming CEO Brian Parkes inherited an organisation in good shape in every respect. He has spent the past three years subtly shifting it in a new direction that increasingly integrates craft and design, as suggested by the very title of this 40th anniversary exhibition. He outlines his vision and approach elsewhere in this publication.

In conclusion, in its 40 years of ceaseless creative production, JamFactory has helped shape many of the individuals who lead Australian contemporary craft and design practice, and it has challenged and extended our understanding of what contemporary craft and design might be. It has become a vital part of South Australia's creative culture and a resource for all South Australian professional craft and design practitioners. It has survived and thrives. Long may it do so.

---

1. JamFactory has changed its name several times over the years from its original establishment as the South Australian Craft Authority by an Act of the South Australian Parliament in 1973. It was incorporated as the Jam Factory Workshop Inc in 1977, then changing to the Jam Factory Craft and Design Centre Inc. for the move to the Lion Art Centre in 1992. In 1997 'the' was finally dropped and the two words were merged to JamFactory Contemporary Craft and Design Inc. Finally, in 2010 the name became simply JamFactory. However, for the sake of clarity I have used 'the Jam Factory' for the St Peters years and 'JamFactory' after the move to the Lion Arts Centre.

2. Dick Richards gives an insider account of those formative years in his essay (see p 17). In 1987 Peter Ward recalled the same period in his catalogue essay for the Workshop Heads' and Trainees' exhibition 1987 (chronological clippings files, Art Gallery of South Australia Library). See also Christopher Menz's historical essay for Jam Factory Craft & Design Centre: 21 years, Jam Factory Craft & Design Centre, Adelaide, 1994, pp 2–9.

3. Ward, op cit, 1987.

4. In addition to Hemmingsen's Jewellery Workshop, there was the Textile Workshop run by South Australian weaver, Pru Medlin, the Glass Workshop run by British glass blower Sam Herman and the Leather Workshop by Italian Pietro Salemme. In 1975 German metal-smith Frank Bauer was enticed to South Australia by Dick Richards and established a practice within the Jewellery Studio. Czechoslovakian-trained Stanislav Melis joined Herman in the Glass Studio and Japanese weaver Jun Tomita worked for two years with Medlin, instructing in Kasuri dying and weaving. Graduate potters from the South Australian School of Art, including Jeff Mincham, Bruce Nuske and Liz Williams, had access facilities, but a Ceramics Workshop would not be established until 1979 under Mincham as its first workshop head.

5. 'Jammed in the works', The Australian, 26 October 2001, p 23.

6. As the South Australian Craft Authority could only be abolished by an Act of Parliament, it presumably still exists in a dormant state.

7. Winnie Pelz, email to the author, 12 September 2012.

8. 'Jam packed with talent', The Advertiser, 3 November 1983.

9. 'Clever craft', The Advertiser, 6 June 1992.

10. The *Andamooka* range was re-branded as *Terra Australis* in 2005

11. Bowers did not re-appoint a Gallery Curator when Janice Lally left in August 2004, instead creating a more junior Gallery Manager position. Until 2006 he continued to run the Ceramics Studio under manager Philip Hart (who was subsequently appointed Creative Director).

12. It may be argued that 'people not product' was always the unofficial modus operandi on the 'factory floor', but it was made explicit in the Board's 2002–05 Strategic Plan, and was subsequently given particular emphasis by Bowers.

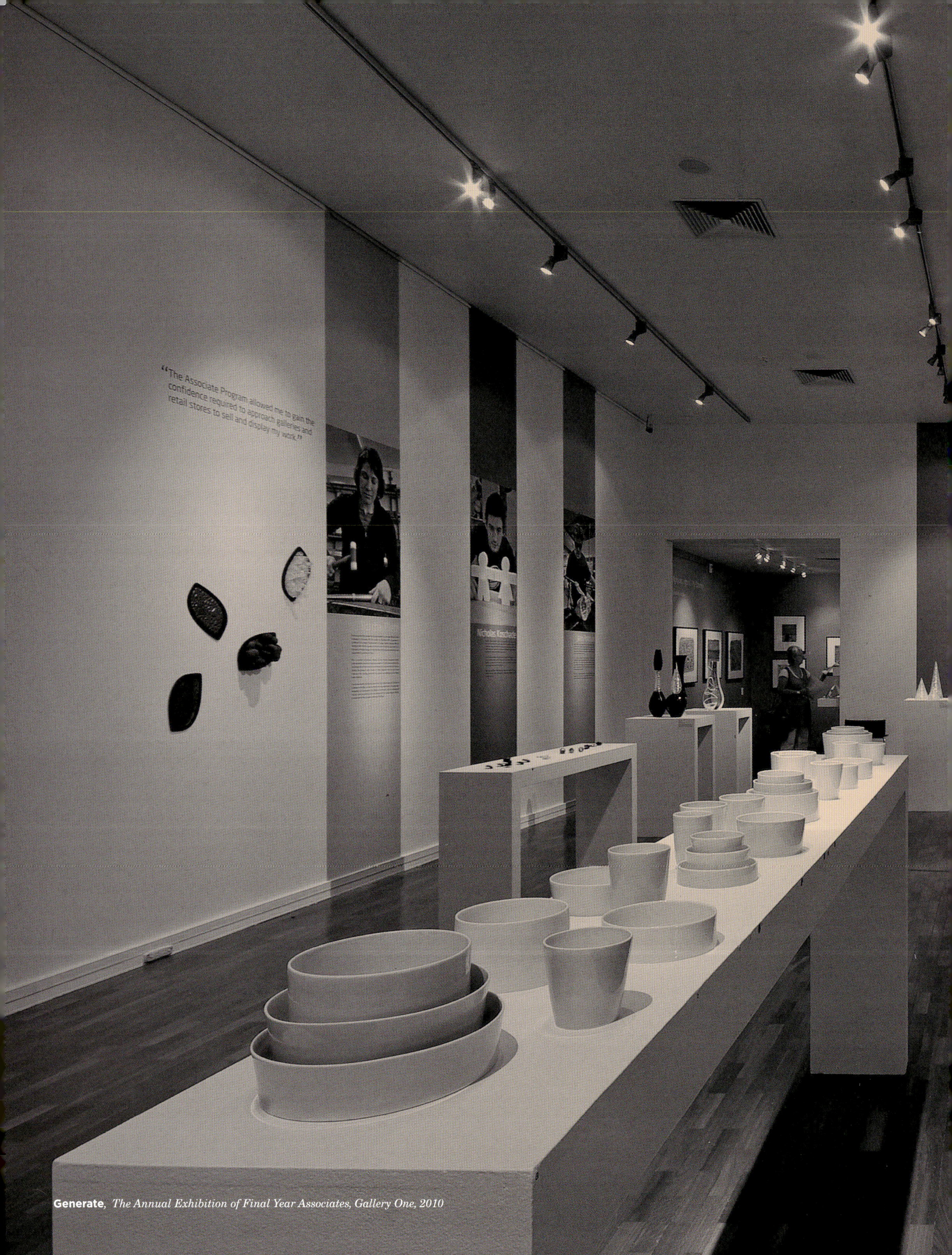

Generate, *The Annual Exhibition of Final Year Associates, Gallery One, 2010*

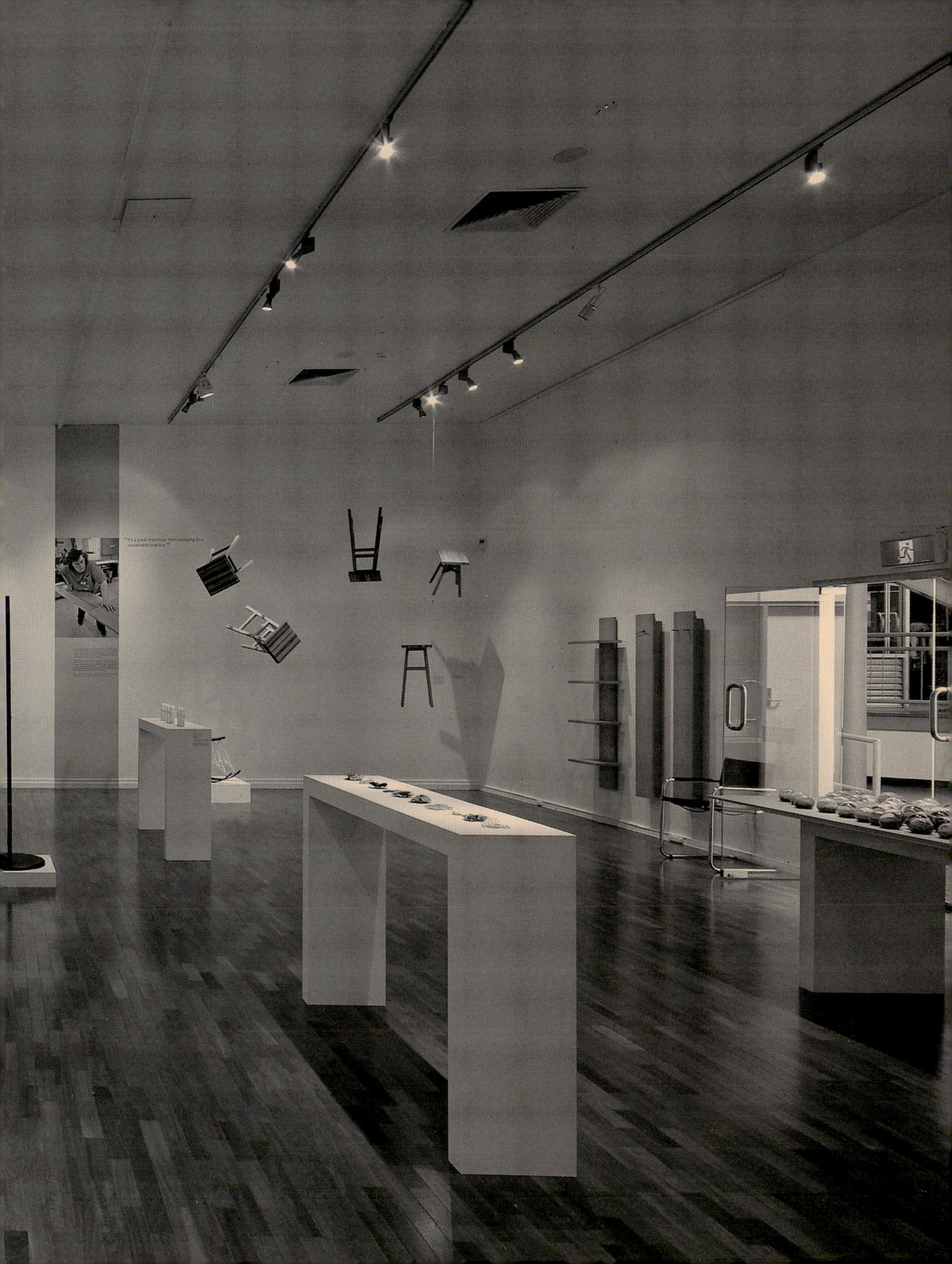

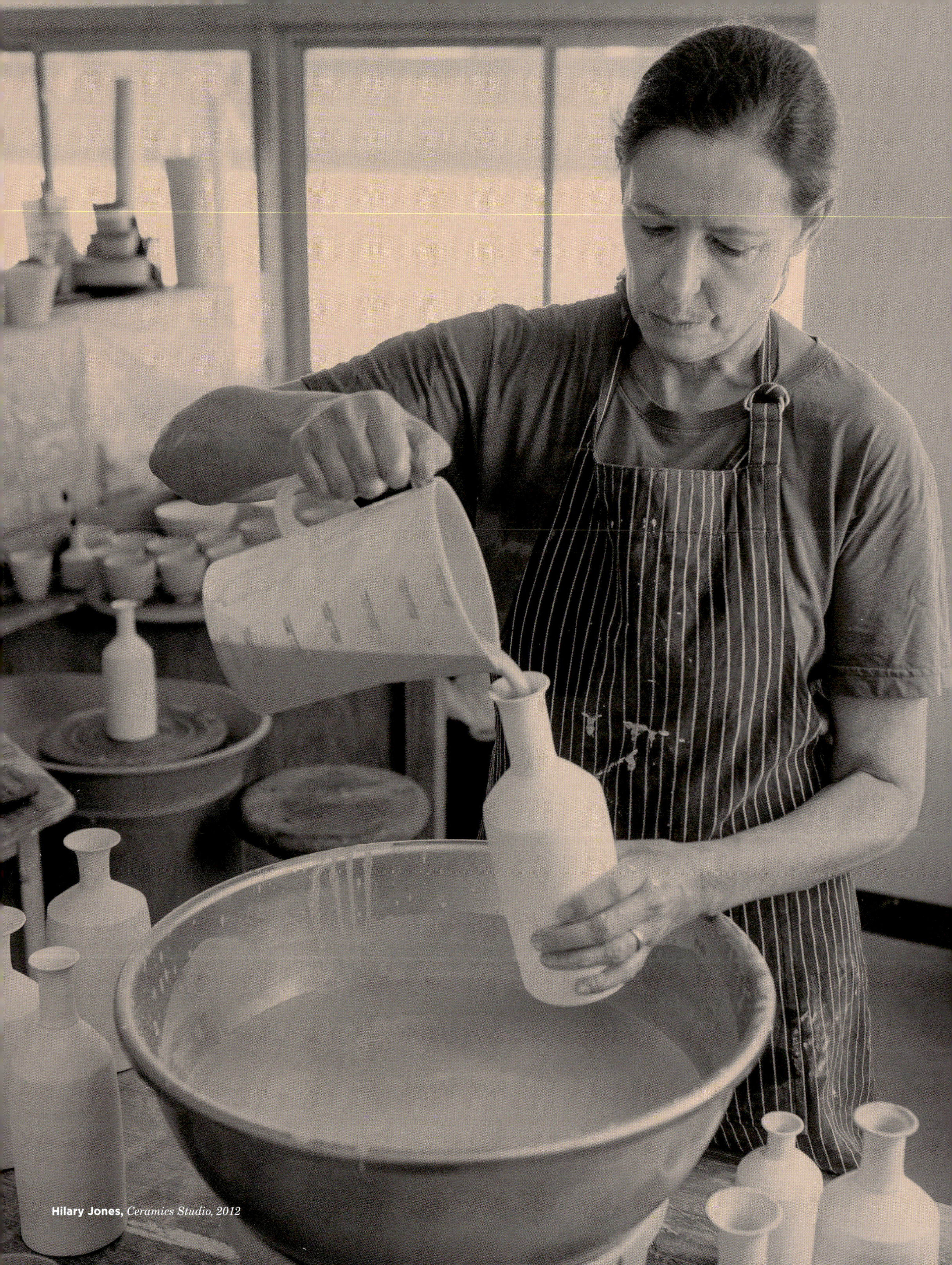

Hilary Jones, *Ceramics Studio, 2012*

IMPACT

"I found it very rewarding to see people respond to the opportunities JamFactory offered them. Responding to the idea and the reality of JamFactory – Associates, Studio Heads, colleagues, visiting artists, visiting appreciators of contemporary craft – all enhanced in some way by their association with JamFactory.

It was rewarding too, and satisfying, to see the very high level of achievement of a number of the Associates at JamFactory in winning awards including several Young Designer Awards at Talente*, in Munich; and regular awards for our Studios and individual Associates from the Design Institute of Australia."*

Mark Ferguson
Managing Director
1997-2004

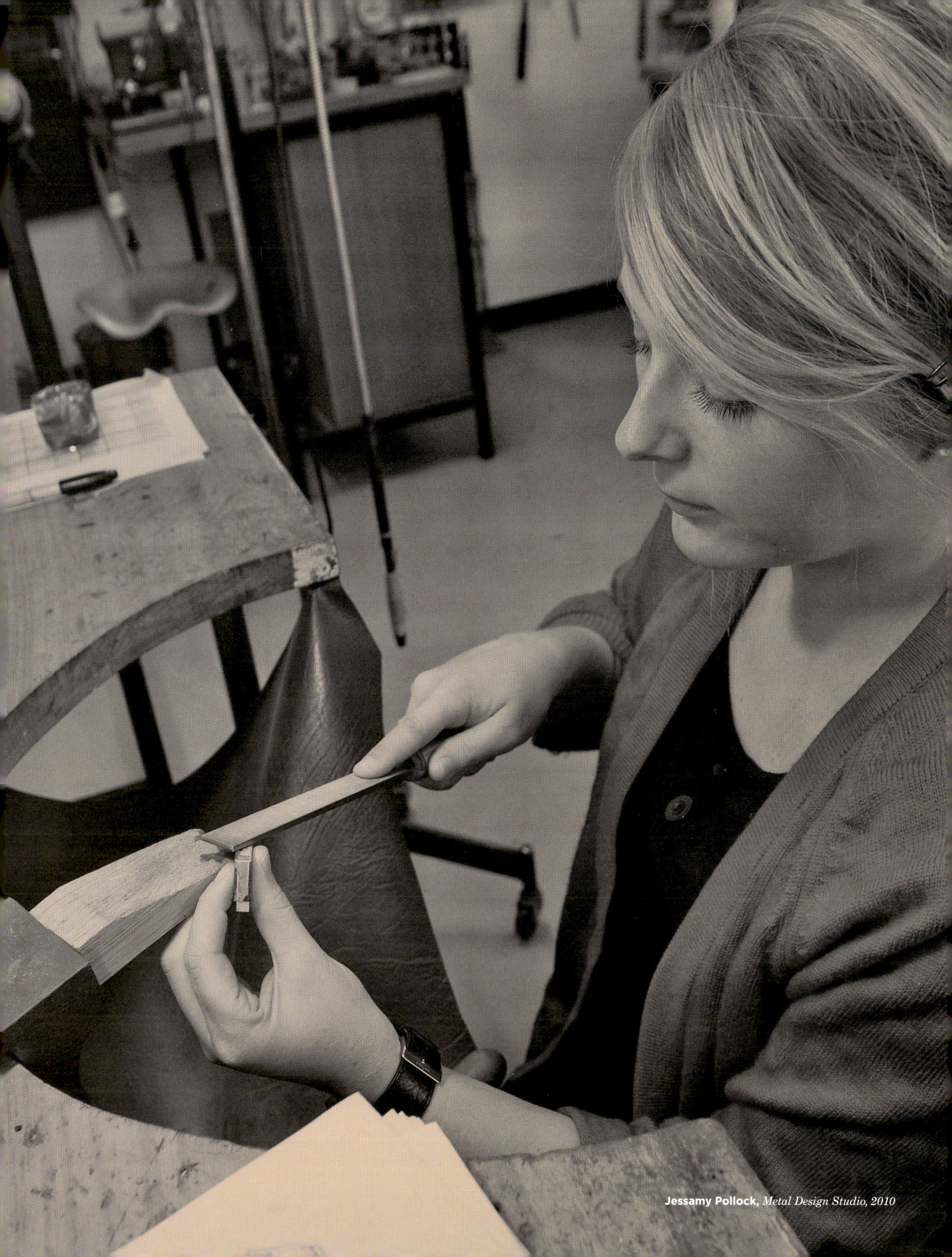

Jessamy Pollock, *Metal Design Studio, 2010*

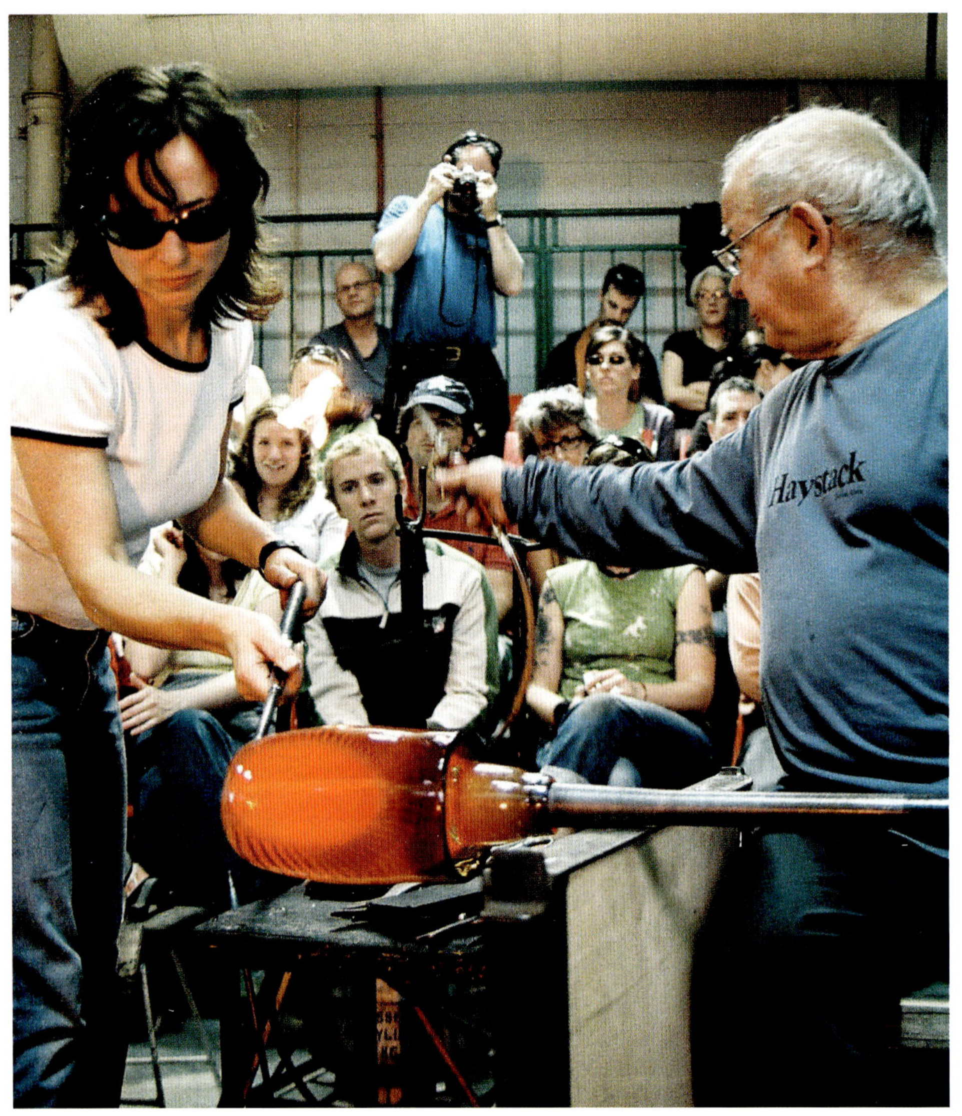
Haystack

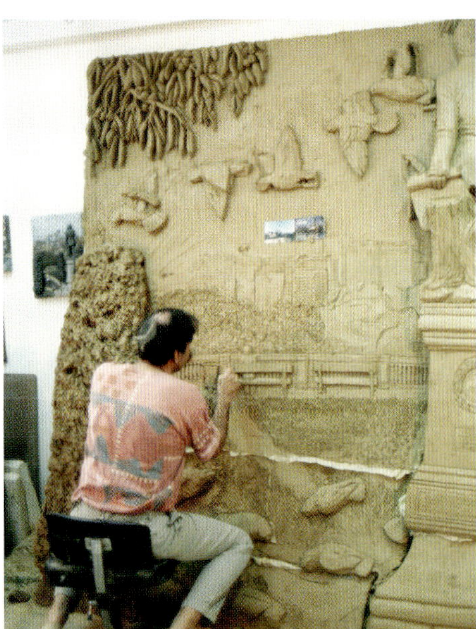

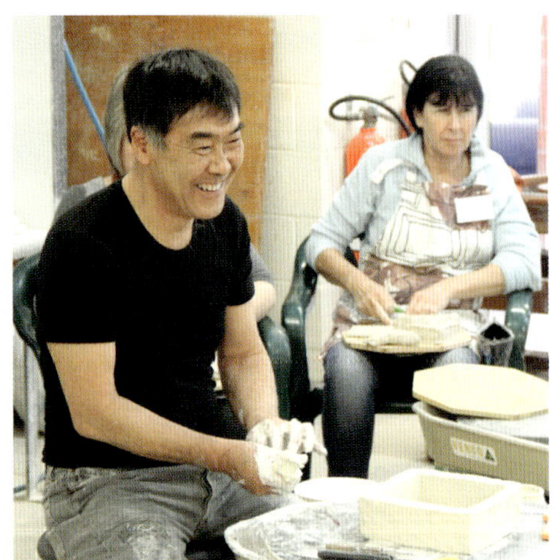

It's an international thing

Ian Were

By the time I returned to the city of my birth in early 1974—after several years working in the south-east of South Australia and followed by a year in Europe—Don Dunstan's government had been in power for three and a half years and the 'Dunstan decade', as it was later called, was in full swing. As part of my teaching experience in the small city of Millicent I drove a school bus, and Dunstan's strong deputy, Des Corcoran, who was born there, often gave a wave as he drove past early in the morning on his way to town and when Parliament wasn't sitting. A while before I arrived back in Adelaide word was out that Dunstan had already wrought substantial reform, both political and cultural.

In his 1969 election campaign, Dunstan had said that ' ... We'll set a new standard of social advancement that the whole of Australia will envy. We believe South Australia can set the pace ... We can do it'.[1] The last few words are somewhat prescient of Barack Obama's 'Yes we can' four decades later. At the 1970 election, Labor won 27 of 47 seats, and, after legislating a fairer seat and boundary system, the ALP won three more elections, in 1973, 1975 and 1977.

To set the scene: Dunstan's progressive administration saw a series of Australian firsts in the state including Aboriginal land rights recognised, homosexuality decriminalised, rape defined as a crime within marriage, a female judge appointed (Roma Mitchell), the first non-British governor, Sir Mark Oliphant and, later, the first Indigenous governor, Sir Douglas Nicholls. He abolished the death penalty, enacted consumer protection laws and anti-discrimination legislation, relaxed censorship and drinking laws and created a Ministry for the environment. Federally, together with Gough Whitlam, he helped remove the White Australia policy from the ALP platform. Dunstan also encouraged cultural exchanges with Asia, multiculturalism and a general increase in the state's culinary awareness and sophistication; and, importantly for many of us at the time, he encouraged a flourishing of the arts, with support for the biennial Adelaide Festival of the Arts, the State Theatre Company, the Art Gallery of South Australia and the establishment of a South Australian Film Corporation. In mid 1973, the Adelaide Festival Centre opened—Australia's first multi-function performing arts complex (although the Opera House opened in Sydney just a few months later). An impetus also grew, one not previously exercised, to encourage arts organisations to work together, 'to make major contributions to the Festival's programming every two years' and to be 'top professional companies'.[2] These reforms and developments were not hastily made but approached mostly with a calm, pragmatic determination on Dunstan's part, with strong support from his party colleagues and an enthusiastic team of advisors.

Over the first half-dozen years, government funding for the arts was increased by a factor of seven. The Film Corporation (begun in 1972 and still going) commenced production with acclaimed films such as *Breaker Morant* (1980), *Storm boy* (1976) and *Picnic at Hanging Rock* (1975), and Dunstan's commitment to and passion for the arts was credited by commentators with attracting artists, theatre people and writers into the

clockwise from left
Lino Tagliapietra, *International Workshop, Glass Studio, 2006 Photo: Mick Bradley*

Phil Schuster, *International Residency, Ceramics Studio, 1995 Photo courtesy Stephen Bowers*

Masamichi Yoshikawa, *International Workshop, Ceramics Studio, 2012 Photo: Brad Bonar*

state, helping to change its atmosphere. These were heady years and Adelaide seemed like the place to be and, at the time, I met a substantial number of artists and others who came to see what the fuss was about.

Dunstan wanted to promote South Australia as 'a place where the quality of life was good and the products distinctive'[3], so a proposal for the development of a world-class crafts and design facility fitted perfectly in this environment, and a Craft Authority was set up to make it happen. Dunstan was keen 'to broaden South Australia's industrial base from our tariff protected, limited manufacturing, and had looked at places in the UK [like Wedgwood] and others where industries are grown from small craft things ... ', said Graham Foreman, who worked in the Premier's Department in the '70s. 'The idea was to engage master craftsmen with whom budding craftspeople could work and that this should in the long term lead to industries that'd be based on craft and design.'[4] With these imperatives in mind it was the Scandinavian model that was considered as well as, and perhaps particularly, the Kilkenny Design Workshops in Ireland—begun in 1963, it was the first workshop of its kind to have been established by a nation's government. Right from its inception, JamFactory was international both in its perspective and in the craftspeople, artists and designers it attracted.

In 1971 Sam Herman—who'd been an early student of renowned US glass artist Harvey Littleton and had subsequently established the first studio glass course in Europe at London's Royal College of Art—agreed to come to Adelaide to set up a glass teaching and production workshop if the Jam Factory (as it was called then) eventuated. 'That was a very powerful thing for Don', says Dick Richards. 'I think if Sam hadn't committed very early the project may have faltered.'[5] By then Herman was aged 38 and an accomplished professional; he stayed for six years. (One of his students at the Royal College had been Jane Bruce, who went on to teach in the glass workshop at the Canberra School of Art from 1994 to 2004.) By 1973, the Jam Factory had been established at the old Mumzone facility on Payneham Road, St Peters, and Herman did come and Australia's first fully operational hot-glass workshop was soon up and running. Looking back, Herman is pleased that the Factory has prospered:

It was the first of its kind to create not only an apprenticeship scheme but also a chance for individuals to develop their artistic abilities in glass and other workshops ... as well as business acumen that is so necessary for survival ... Not only has it created and influenced Australian artists but they in turn have influenced other artists throughout the world.[6]

As it happened, Herman's glass was not Scandinavian in its sense of design but more spontaneous and freeform.

There was however a Scandinavian link with the first Head of the Jam Factory's Jewellery Workshop, Vagn Hemmingsen (1922–1990). After training (1935–41) at the Georg Jensen studio in Denmark, Hemmingsen had come to Adelaide in 1974 to set up the workshop, which ran for a short while.[7]

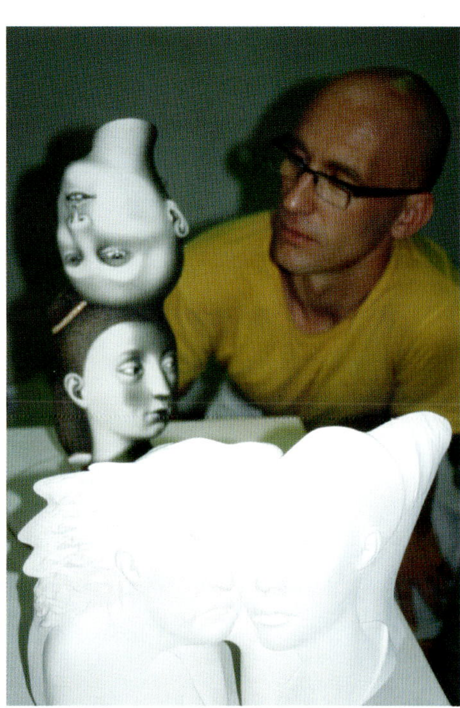

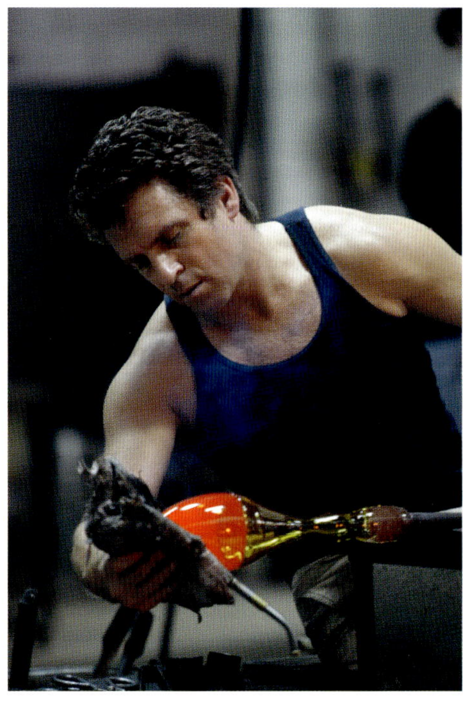

With his trainees, he developed a range of simple, well-designed objects before returning to Denmark; but his legacy lives on. Both Brian Wood and Susan Harle, for example—who established Harlewood Studio on Queensland's Sunshine Coast, where they design and manufacture one-off and limited edition jewellery pieces—acquired formal training at the Jam Factory under master craftsman Hemmingsen as well as designer and metalsmith Frank Bauer.[8] Bauer—who had arrived in Sydney from Germany in 1971 and worked there for five years—had also been invited to set up his own studio and do some teaching in 1975. He had trained in Germany and had worked at the Kilkenny Design Workshops.[9] The international links continued with the appointment in 1978 of fine leather designer Pietro Salemme from Calabria to run the Leather Workshop. He had worked in Florence as a fashion shoe designer and maker, for the firm Luciano Ricci, a manufacturer for Gucci.

By the mid 1970s I was living around the corner from the Factory, and visited the 'Jam' frequently for exhibitions and events. By now the vast building had been further colonised by the arts, with Noel Sheridan (recruited from Ireland by way of New York and Sydney) undertaking the setting up of the Experimental Art Foundation (EAF)—a proximity and relationship which continues today, with the EAF (now AEAF) and JamFactory sitting side by side at the Lion Arts Centre.

Later, in the early 1980s, I found myself at San Diego State University in Southern California. Celebrated metal artists Arline Fisch and Helen Shirk were heading the jewellery and metal studio with JoAnn Tanzer running the enamel studio. All three knew of the Jam Factory's growing international reputation, particularly Fisch, who had visited Australia a number of times and had close links with Australia's flourishing craft organisations. Why did and do so many people know about it?

Over the last four decades JamFactory has brought numerous international and Australian artists and designers to Adelaide to conduct workshops, give lectures, and show their work or to be part of major exhibitions. These people have returned to their home bases and subsequently invited artists from Adelaide and elsewhere to be involved in their programs. The organisation has also toured a number of exhibitions to venues around Australia and overseas. Reciprocity is always smart and mutually beneficial, particularly when it's tied to major events here or overseas, as has frequently been the case. At the Adelaide Festival of the Arts for example, the mix was nearly always rich.

For three years in the 1980s, CEO Lynn Collins consolidated the organisation with expanded exhibition venues and a changing character of exhibitions. He juxtaposed craft, design and fine art, Indigenous crafting, feral art and hobbyist activities, to prompt discussion. Interstate artists such as Alison Clouston brought fresh ideas into an extended residency, as did the series of exhibitions titled *Makers' Choice*—a national project presented inpartnership with the Crafts Council of South Australia—in which practitioners working in several media nominated muses or mentors as co-exhibitors and addressed work practices and thinking.[10]

top
Sergei Isupov, *International Residency, Ceramics Studio, 2006 Photo courtesy Stephen Bowers*

Dante Marioni, *International Workshop, Glass Studio, 2009 Photo courtesy JamFactory*

From 1989 to 1994, Frank McBride was the director. By late 1991 he had overseen the Jam Factory's move to first-rate facilities in Adelaide's arts hub at the Lion Arts Centre. This change pushed the organisation into the second stage of its life and, accordingly, McBride had 'design' added to its name and it became JamFactory Craft and Design Centre—the first of several craft organisations around Australia to do so. The architect-designed spaces, which included professional galleries, four fully equipped studios in ceramics, glass, furniture and metal as well as 10 independent rental studios, meant that public interest in JamFactory grew, and it was now more clearly visible on the national and international cultural scene. Increasingly, a larger percentage of trainees were attracted from interstate. During this period Don Dunstan returned as Chair of the organisation's board.[11]

The re-opening exhibitions (in February 1992) included *Real and Forged Contemporary Australian Metal*, curated by Janene Pellarin, followed by the *Tenth Anniversary Australian Glass Triennial* (touring from the Wagga Wagga City Art Gallery in April). For the first time JamFactory had appointed a curator (apart from the Artistic Director), with Pellarin coming from Canberra to take up the position. As a result, exhibitions became more substantial and thoughtful with more impact nationally. Some toured interstate and several had accompanying scholarly publications, for example: *Second Australian Contemporary Jewellery Biennial* (1993) and *Out of Canberra: an exhibition of contemporary kiln-formed glass from the ACT* (1994).

Then, from 1994, led by director Loene Furler, JamFactory moved strongly into an international program, presenting and promoting the best of Australian design and craft at key events in several countries. These promotions were mostly supported by an Australia Council program that subsidised participation in international art and design fairs, some via Craft Australia. The first event in 1994 was *SOFA (Sculpture, Objects, Functional Art + Design)* in Chicago, where the works of Nick Mount and the Glass Workshop were showcased along with Stephen Bowers' highly decorated ceramic plates. 'Nick was already reasonably well known in Seattle at Pilchuck Glass School', explained Furler, 'so it seemed a good basis to build upon'.[12] This promotion helped establish JamFactory as a leading glass studio in Australia, and resulted in a number of glass workshops coming to JamFactory, including an outstanding one by Lino Tagliapietra from Murano. Of such workshops, Adelaide writer and art critic, Wendy Walker, noted: 'I was present at an influential demonstration by renowned glass blower Lino Tagliapietra and, to cite a single example, I think this workshop had a significant effect on the work of Tom Moore, amongst other glass blowers.'[13]

The momentum continued in 1995 with JamFactory going back to *SOFA*. It also participated in the San Francisco International Gift Fair; the International Competition of Contemporary Ceramic Art in Faenza, Italy (promoting Stephen Bowers' work); and at *VicenzaOra* (a jewellery fair in Italy), organised in conjunction with Sylvano Toso, President of the Italian Chamber of Commerce, with

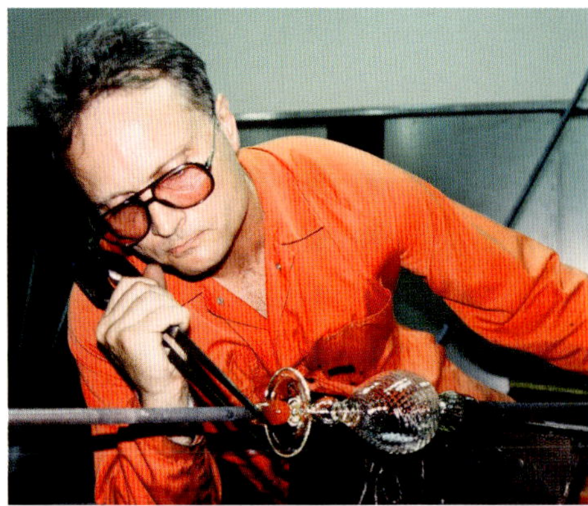

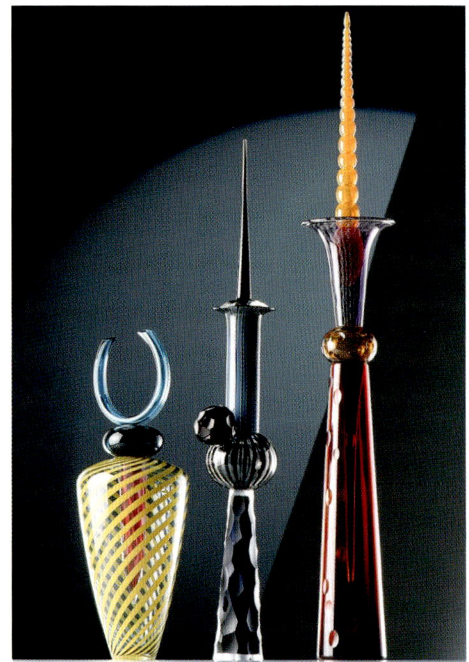

Furler noting that, 'The work of the JamFactory was refreshingly different in this exposition'.[14] The same year, Furler orchestrated JamFactory products to be on the shelves of a prestigious department store in Hong Kong and a shop in Paris. The careers and reputations of Nick Mount, Stephen Bowers and others have benefited substantially from these promotions.

Coinciding with the 1996 Adelaide Festival of the Arts, an exhibition at JamFactory focused on the skills of Finnish architect and designer Alvar Aalto, the types of materials he used and the similarity of landscapes in Australia and Finland. This is the kind of show that has the potential to get national attention and a broader audience, and it did.

By the early 2000s, and under Stephen Bowers as CEO, recurrent international projects were consolidated. JamFactory returned to *SOFA* each year from 2004 to 2008, for example, and fresh events were explored, including *Talente*, a Munich-based annual international applied arts, design and technology competition for younger practitioners, and *Collect*, a prestigious, invitation-only expo in London, presented by the UK Crafts Council and in its tenth year in 2013.[15]

Each year, from 2004 to 2008, JamFactory selected and promoted the best of Australian emerging talent at *Talente* and, at *SOFA*, it was in a position to present a series of four promotional shows and linked publications: *Luminous Surface—Under a Southern Light* (2004); *Lumière, Luxe and Volupté—luxurious light and seductive form* (2005); *Go Figure ...* (2006); and *New Ceramics from Ernabella, Hermannsburg and the Tiwi Islands* (2007). *SOFA*, in its 20th year in 2013, remains a major promotional event for craft and design.

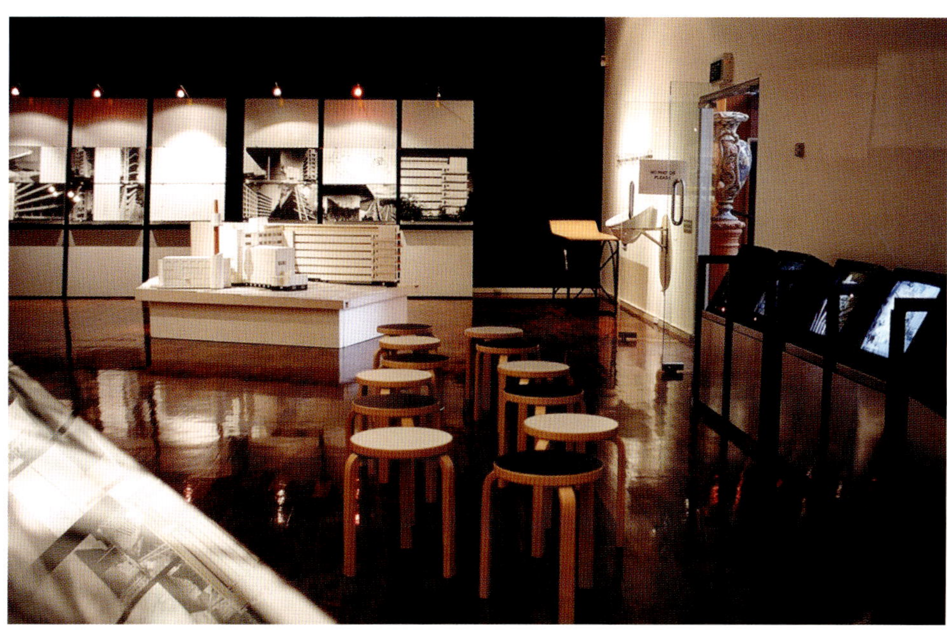

At *Collect* similar opportunities applied over four years, with the presentation of the following exhibitions (and publications) under the banner of 'Australian Contemporary': *A Survey of a Sense of Place* (2005); *Bare & Beyond* (2006); *Vito Bila, Scott Chaseling, Kirsten Coehlo, Sally Marsland* (2007); and *Tea Wares* (2008). The 2006 *Collect* was reviewed by Germaine Greer in The Guardian, where she praised the Australian contribution and excoriated almost everyone else. In part she said:

It was with some trepidation that I peeped round the partition of the Australian Contemporary stand ... What I found was the work of

above
Points of Contact, *Exhibition of Alvar Aalto, Gallery One, 1996*
Photo courtesy JamFactory

opposite top
Nick Mount, *Glass Studio, 1995*
Photo courtesy JamFactory

Nick Mount, *Scent Bottles, 2000*
blown and cold worked glass
dimensions variable
Photo: Grant Hancock

Julie Blyfield, who lovingly explicates Australian plant shapes, especially in her sequence of unusually wearable jewellery called Pressed Desert. Such gentleness and subtlety are not often associated with my birthplace. I so loved Prue Venables' pierced ladle (olives, for the draining of) ... because there were so few useful objects in the show.[16]

As a result of their participation, practitioners, such as ceramicist Kirsten Coelho, gained international representation and work was acquired for international collections, both private and public. Julie Blyfield was already represented by Galerie Ra in Amsterdam and Charon Kransen Arts in New York but, as a result of *Collect*, she was given a show at Galerie Hélène Porée in Paris, where two of her brooches were acquired by the Musée des Arts Décoratifs.[17] From 2004 to 2008, JamFactory presented over 120 artists at a dozen or so international events, as well as organising, in association with Asialink, *A Secret History of Blue and White* (2006–09), a ceramics exhibition and publication which toured to several venues in Asia and later, in Australia.

It's crucial to note that JamFactory's participation in all of these events, in Chicago, Munich and London, was made possible at the time because they were under the umbrella of the Australia Council's International Craft Initiative (part of an overall visual arts promotional strategy), a program that had, over the years, developed quite sophisticated funding arrangements. *SOFA* and *Collect* were seen to be priorities because they presented the best international craft and design, they attracted a large and predominantly informed audience—a combination of collectors, curators, gallery directors, artists, writers and publishers—and this environment provided an opportunity for Australian participants not afforded elsewhere. 'The Australia Council support for representation at *Collect*, *SOFA*, etc was an inspired initiative. It was important ... for Australian craft and design to be seen, and seen to excel, in that rarefied international context', says Wendy Walker.[18]

For 40 years JamFactory has been presenting outstanding exhibitions and public programs, along with nurturing the careers of artists, craftspeople and designers, both nationally and internationally, with gusto. Why has the Jam survived so well? Recurrent funding from the South Australian government over this period has been crucial, of course, combined with JamFactory's adherence to its original mission but with an ability to also be flexible in thinking and programming. The four main areas of its business—training, exhibiting, retailing and wholesaling—have been developed and fine tuned in accordance with Don Dunstan's original vision that training should be offered in tandem with production. With closures in specialist courses in art schools around Australia, I suspect that high quality training in areas to which JamFactory is committed has become increasingly important. Over the last four decades JamFactory has maintained a focus on training, production and promotion, closely linked to a growing emphasis on the role of design in crafts practice. As well-known artist and lecturer Kay Lawrence said, 'Dunstan realised [that] professional education is a crucial aspect of building quality in craft

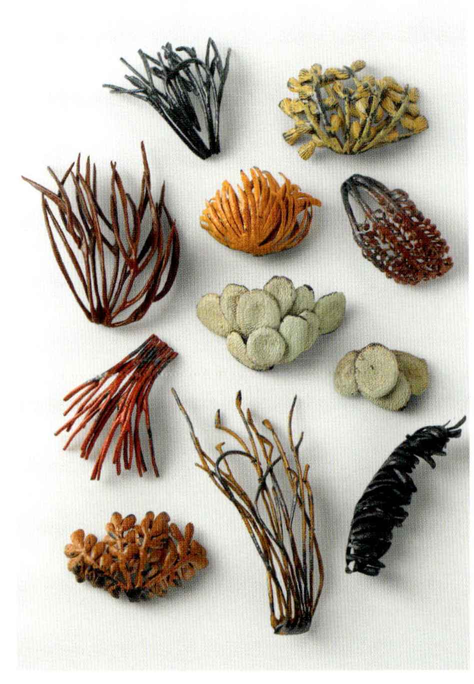

Julie Blyfield,
Pressed Desert Plant series, 2005
oxidised sterling silver, enamel
dimensions variable
Photo: Grant Hancock

and design practices, not just in technical skill but in design and conceptual depth'.[19]

1. Andrew Parkin, 'The Dunstan Governments: a political synopsis', in The Dunstan decade: social democracy at the state level, Longman Cheshire, Melbourne, 1981, pp 6–7.

2. Len Amadio, interviewed by Felicity Morgan for the Don Dunstan Foundation Oral History Project, 24 October 2007, about his contribution to the development of the arts in South Australia during Dunstan's Premiership, viewed August 2012, dspace.flinders.edu.au/jspui/bitstream/2328/8425/6/AMADIO_Len_Cleared.pdf.

3. Grace Cochrane, The crafts movement in Australia: a history, University of New South Wales Press, Sydney, 1992, p 282.

4. Graham Foreman, interviewed by George Lewkowicz for the Don Dunstan Foundation Oral History Project, 1 July 2008. Foreman worked in the Policy Division of the Premier's Department in the 1970s and, in the late '70s, the Public Service Board. Viewed August 2012, dspace.flinders.edu.au/xmlui/bitstream/2328/3235/3/FOREMAN_Graham_Cleared.pdf.

5. Dick Richards, interviewed by Felicity Morgan for the Don Dunstan Foundation Oral History Project, 29 August 2008, about his contribution to the visual arts and crafts in SA during the Dunstan decade, viewed August 2012, dspace.flinders.edu.au/jspui/bitstream/2328/25077/1/RICHARDS_Dick_Cleared.pdf.

6. Sam Herman, email to the author, 29 August 2012.

7. Grace Cochrane, op cit, p 223.

8. Harlewood Studio, web home page, viewed August 2012, www.harlewoodstudio.com.

9. After returning to Europe from 1979 to 1984, Bauer moved back to Adelaide to teach for a few years at the South Australian School of Art, and still works from his home studio in Adelaide.

10. Lynn Collins, email discussion with the author, 27 July to 2 August 2012.

11. Frank McBride, phone discussion with the author, 31 October 2012.

12. Loene Furler, email to the author, 8 October 2012.

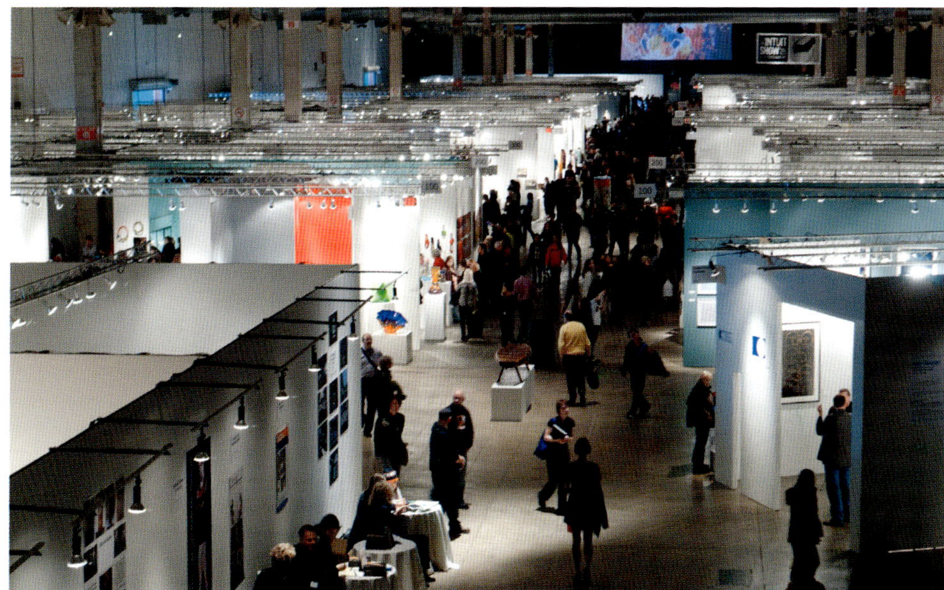

13. Wendy Walker, email to the author, 17 October 2012. Tom Moore is a past Associate of JamFactory's Glass Studio (1995–96), and now has a national reputation.

14. Loene Furler, op cit.

15. Stephen Bowers, email discussion with the author, 8 October 2012.

16. Germaine Greer, 'By design', The Guardian, 20 February 2006, viewed October 2012, www.guardian.co.uk/artanddesign/2006/feb/20/art.culture. The author thanks Wendy Walker for this link. Walker was guest curator for 'Australian Contemporary' at *Collect* 2006.

17. Wendy Walker, op cit.

18. ibid.

19. Professor Kay Lawrence, AM, opening speech for the exhibition Freestyle: new Australian design for living (developed by Object, Sydney in partnership with the Melbourne Museum), Art Gallery of South Australia, 17 August 2007, viewed August 2012, w3.unisa.edu.au/artarchitecturedesign/communityindustry/art.asp.

SOFA, Chicago
Photo: Cheri Eisenberg

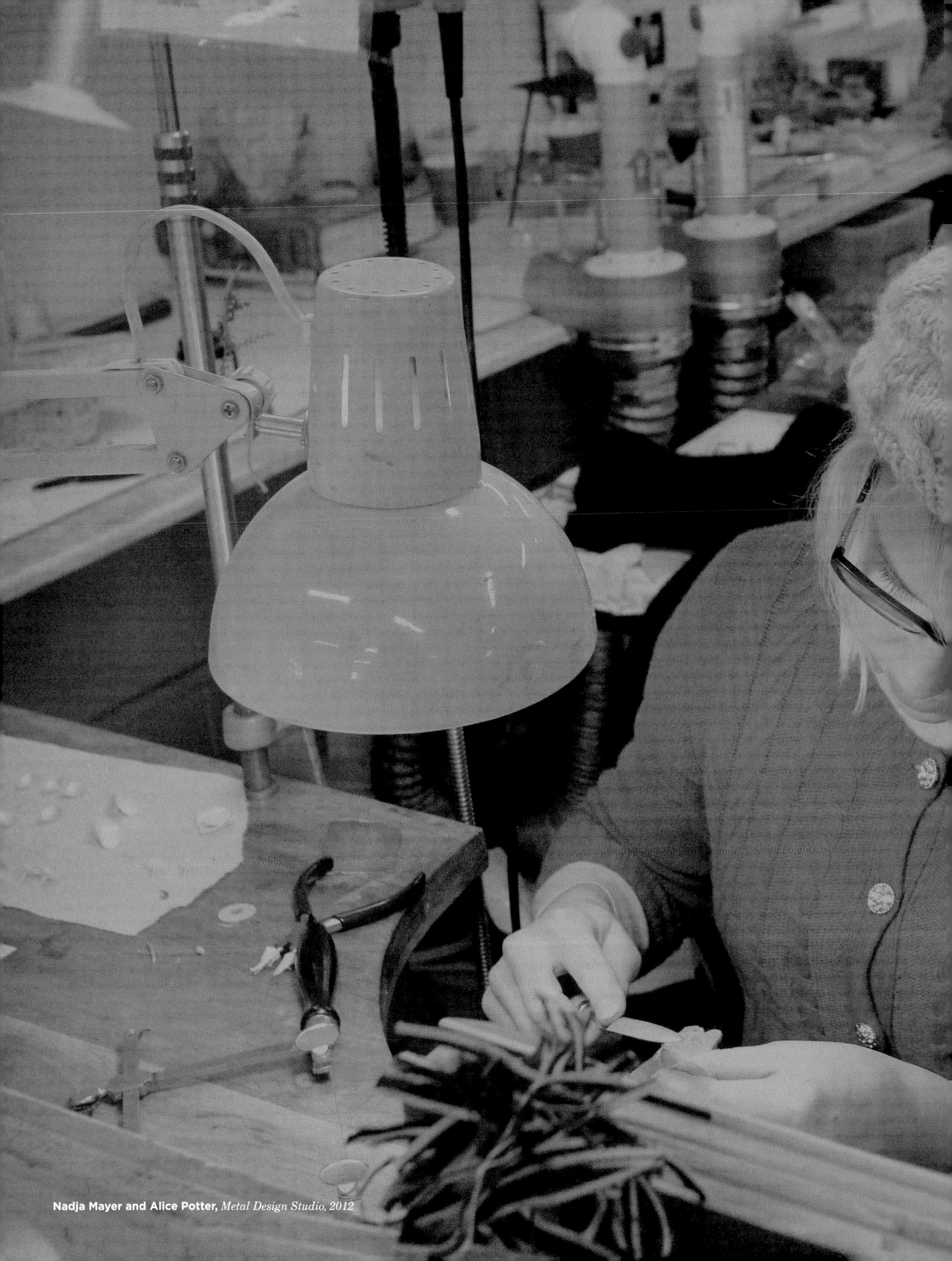

Nadja Mayer and Alice Potter, *Metal Design Studio, 2012*

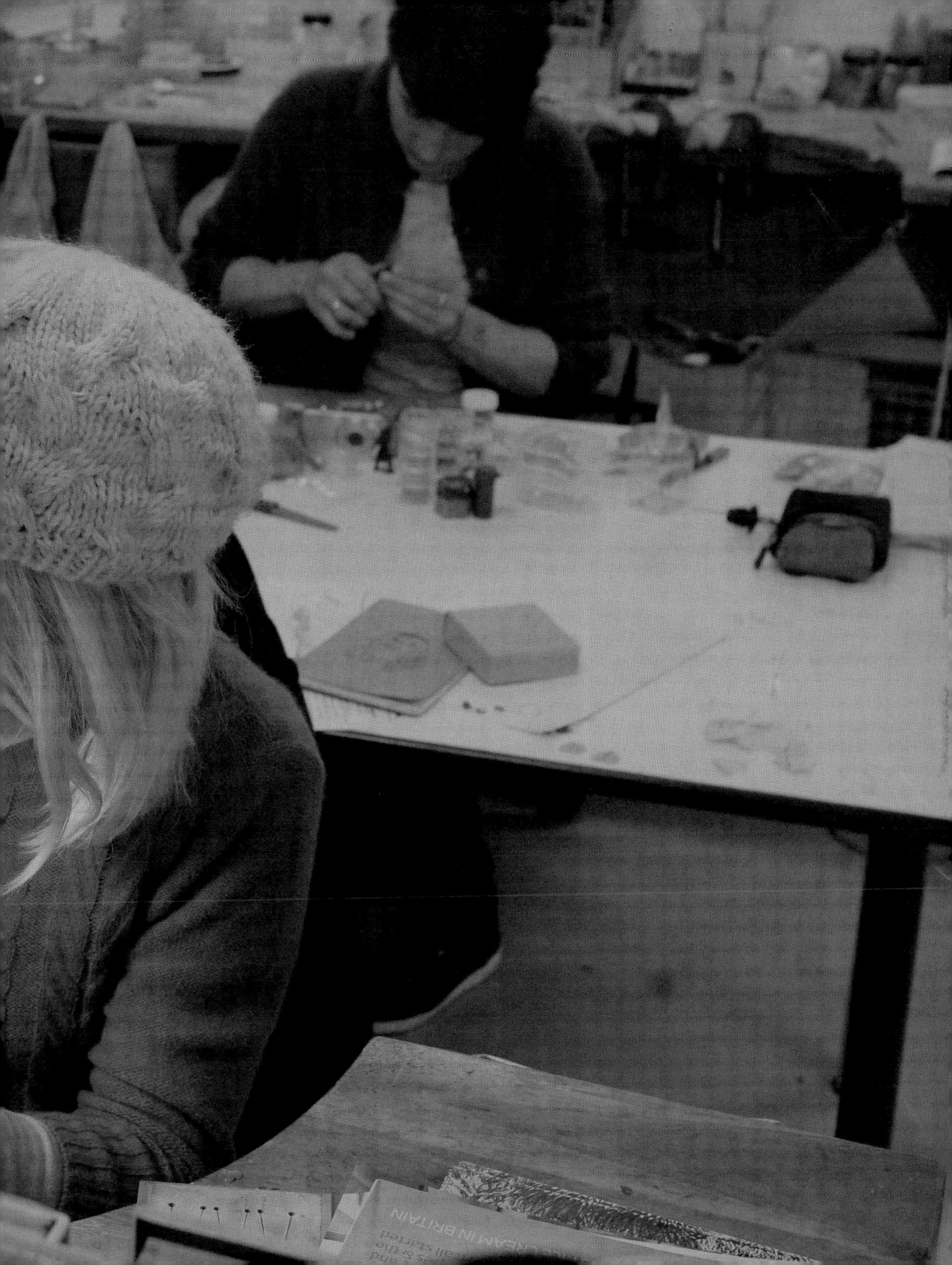

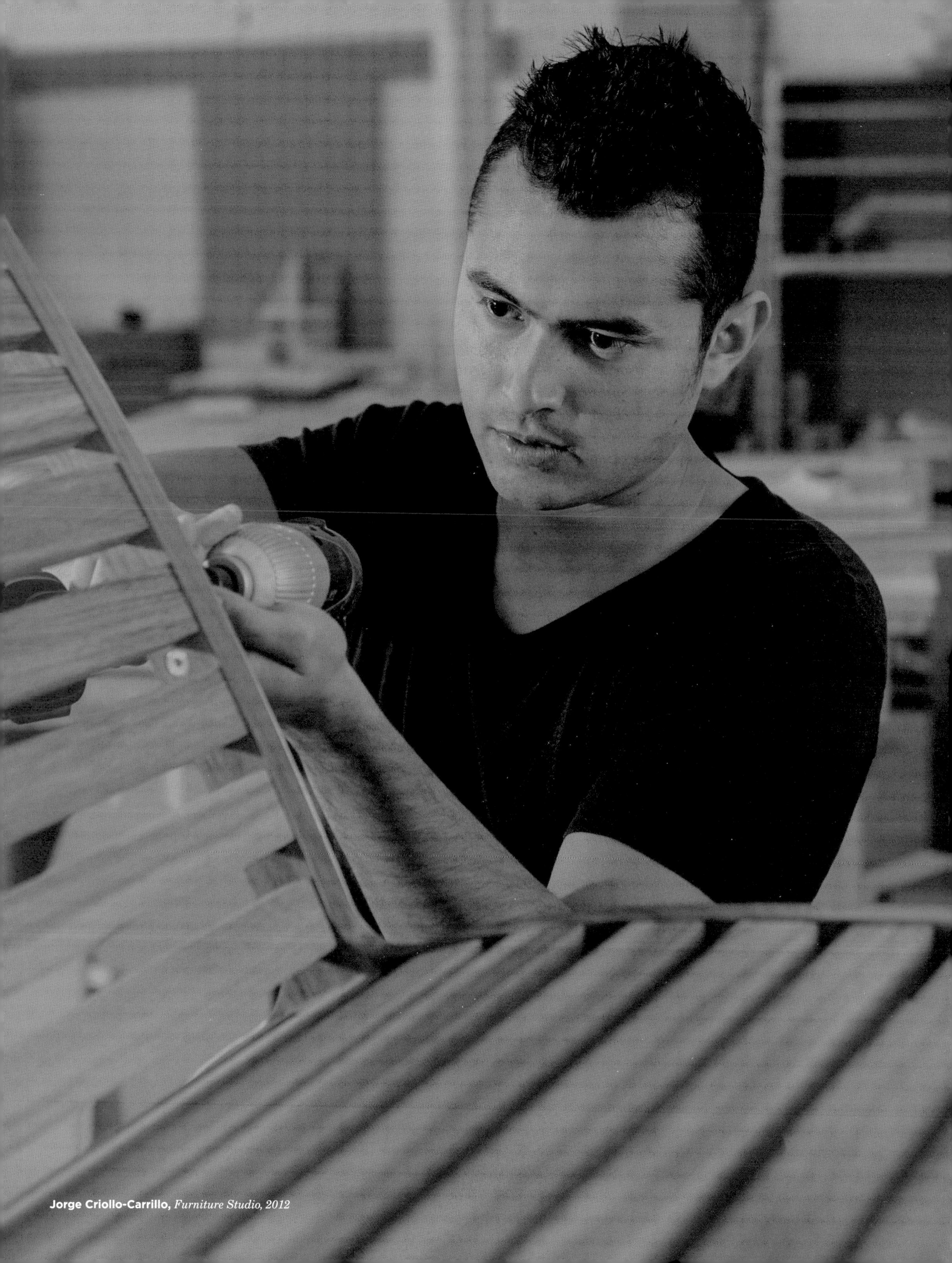

Jorge Criollo-Carrillo, *Furniture Studio, 2012*

NOW AND THE FUTURE

“Khai Liew dramatically transformed the look and feel of the entryway and retail shop at JamFactory in 2009/10. He wowed everyone – even winning over the critics – when he incisively drilled down through years of comfortable familiarity and indifference to re-engage the eastern entry of the building with the vision of the original architect (Steve Grieve) for light and accessibility. Khai created a sense of vista and discovery on a miserly budget that would have barely covered the cost of paint and surface treatments in comparable spaces.”

Stephen Bowers
Managing Director
2004-2010

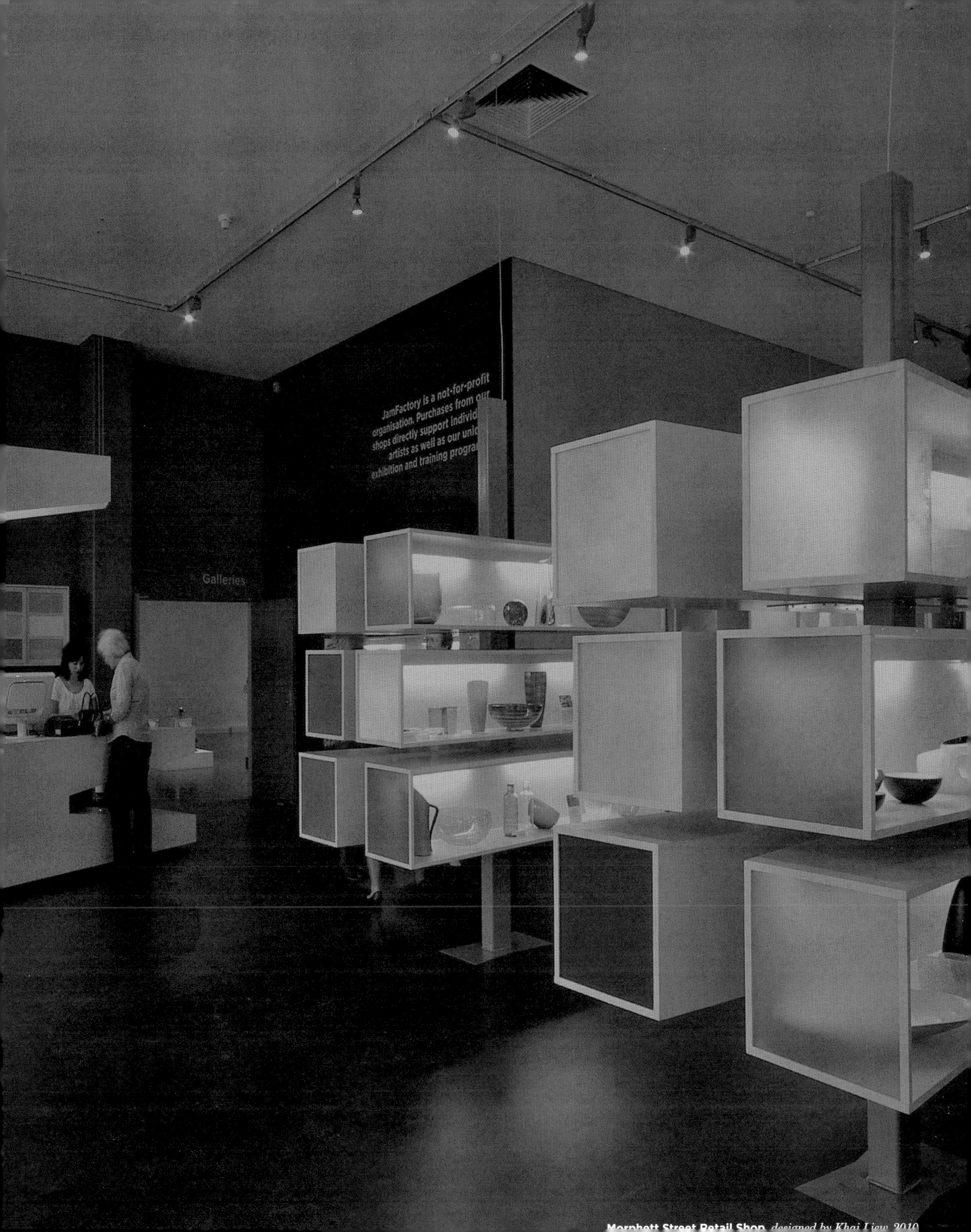

Morphett Street Retail Shop, *designed by Khai Liew, 2010*

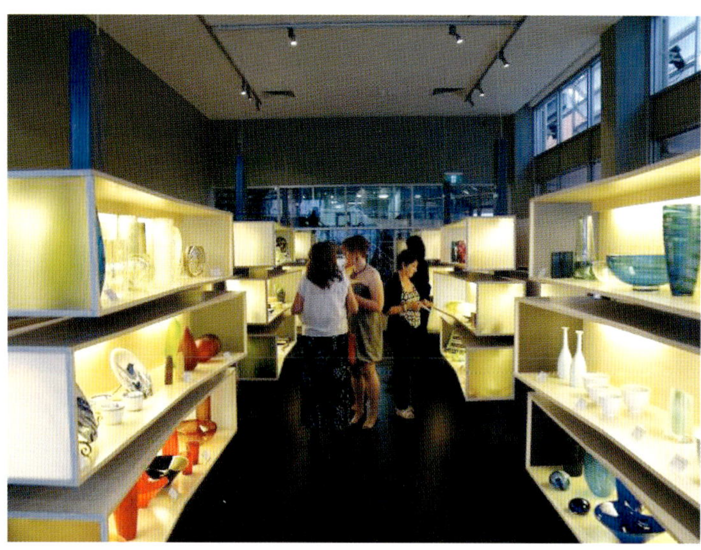

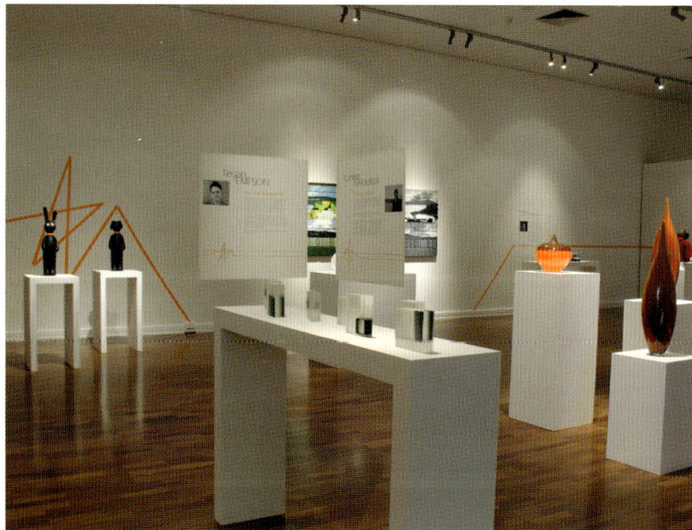

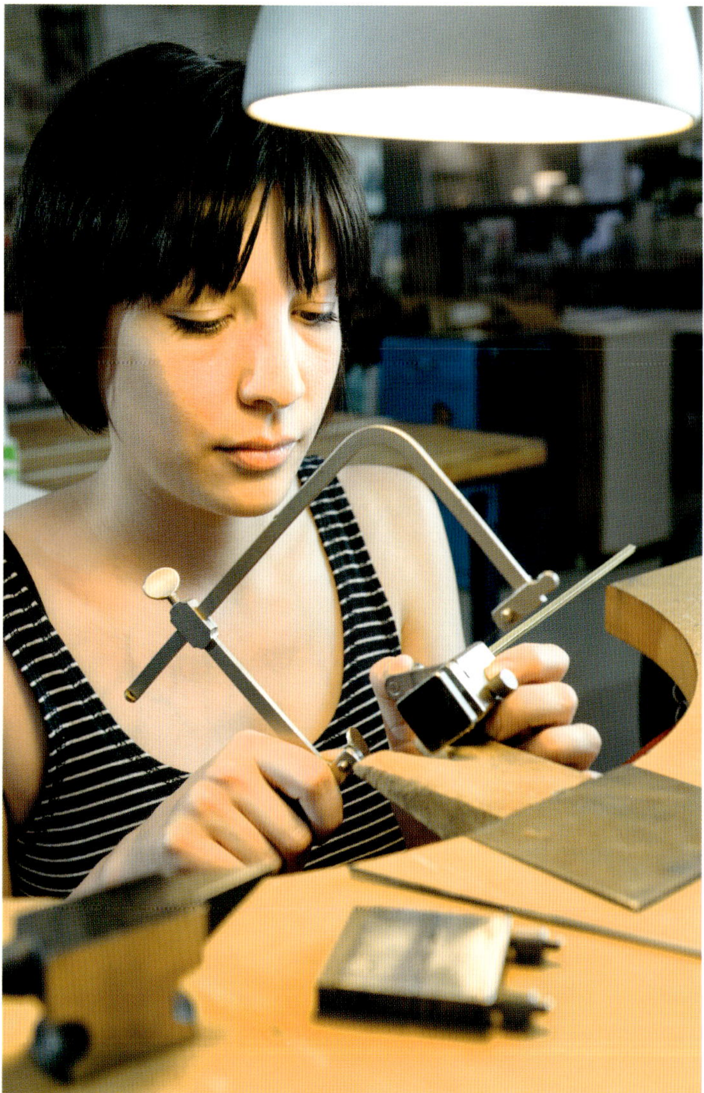

JamFactory Now

Brian Parkes

JamFactory is so many things to so many people. I am often asked to describe or define it in the most simplistic terms and, of course, I have a range of standard lines: 'it's a not for profit organisation supporting craft and design'; 'it supports and promotes artists, craftspeople and designers through its purpose-built studios, galleries and shops'; 'it's a unique training organisation dedicated to enhancing the creative and entrepreneurial skills of emerging designer–makers', and so on.

None of the standard lines ever do it justice—JamFactory is diverse, complicated and ever evolving. There's nothing else like it in Australia and nothing that has quite the same range or combination of activities and facilities anywhere in the world. JamFactory's complexity is part of what makes it so wonderful. This is what attracted me to the role of CEO in early 2010.

For me, JamFactory is much more than the purpose-built three-storey building in Morphett Street, Adelaide. It is a community of creative people, both within the building and well beyond. It is a powerful vehicle to engage audiences in the social, cultural and economic value of both good design and the maintenance and refinement of craft skills.

JamFactory's business model is extraordinary and dynamic. Its current business activities include: offering training to emerging practitioners in ceramics, glass, furniture and metal design; developing and presenting exhibitions with a specific emphasis on contemporary craft and design; leasing studio space and hiring out facilities; undertaking commissions (from trophies and awards to large-scale interior fit-outs and public artworks); running workshops and short courses; venue hire; publishing; manufacturing; wholesaling; and retailing.

When I arrived in April 2010, the organisation was in good shape financially, with steady income from sales and commissions. It was well governed by its Board and enjoyed strong state government support. The thing that struck me most, having moved from Sydney to Adelaide to take up the job, was the enormously high regard that JamFactory was held in by so many people I met in the cultural, political and business sectors in South Australia.

With a strong personal interest in the intersections between craft, design and industry, I was excited to learn (while enquiring about the job) about the policy debate in South Australia relating to the value of integrating design and design thinking across government and into the private sector, which led to the establishment of the Integrated Design Commission[1] and other initiatives. I was confident that there was a key role for JamFactory to play in the development of these ideas. Combined with this, my predecessor Stephen Bowers provided an extraordinary parting gift in the form of the freshly refurbished shop designed by Khai Liew. The sensibilities that Liew and Bowers brought to this new space seemed to symbolise the organisation's potential to open up to the new audiences and opportunities related to the community's growing interest in design, while respecting and drawing on JamFactory's strong history in the crafts.

clockwise from left
Morphett Street Retail Shop, *2011*
Photo: Brad Bonar

Minnette Michael, *Metal Design Studio, 2012*
Photo: Tom Roschi

Transparency, *Gallery One, 2012*
Photo: Brad Bonar

I saw no need to dramatically reinvent the organisation, but I wanted to build on existing strengths, raise the profile and unite the Board and staff around a shared vision. A process of strategic planning and re-branding began, not with the intent of creating a new logo—though this did eventually happen—but rather to get clarity and consensus around what we stood for and what aspirations should drive the next phase of the JamFactory story. We began by discussing and agreeing on a set of core values. Among the ten final dot points, we described JamFactory as 'committed to the skills, ideas and values of artists, craftspeople and designers, and to promoting their place in a vibrant culture', and as an organisation that, 'promotes design, innovation, craftsmanship and creative thinking as vital to a healthy society'.

Since then—with these values as a guide—we have undertaken a complete re-brand of the organisation, including the development of a new website and graphic identity, upgrades to various parts of the building, the launch of several new print and online marketing tools and of course, the adoption of a new strategic plan.

I was aware of various attempts in JamFactory's past to develop a range of JamFactory-branded products—some quite successful and others surprisingly short-lived. Having spent over a decade researching and writing about many of Australia's most successful designer-makers and design entrepreneurs, I was well aware of the models that worked and those that could be applied to JamFactory's particular capacities. The design and manufacture of JamFactory products is now a key focus within each of the four studios. The design development process, prototyping and costing of each new product and its ongoing manufacture are vital parts of the Associate training experience. Each product involves a different skill or technique in production and direct exposure to the process—from conception through to distribution—provides invaluable learning for the Associates who are encouraged to utilise similar approaches in the development of their own products.

JamFactory-branded products, which include the *KINK oil bottle*, designed by Deb Jones, the *PRESS salad servers*, designed by John Quan and the *AIRCRAFT lamp*, designed by Christian Hall, all reflect the values of the organisation. They sit on the shelves of our own shops and in highly regarded design stores and gallery shops around Australia, promoting JamFactory and the individual designers. The sales support our training program and hopefully provide delight to consumers who appreciate Australian design and craftsmanship.

In late 2011 we employed Emma Aiston, one half of the acclaimed South Australian design duo Daniel Emma, to assist in the development of these products and to manage the sales and distribution. We also invited other leading Australian designers such as Robert Foster, Simone LeAmon, Trent Jansen and Elliat Rich to undertake cross-disciplinary design workshops with Associates from all four studios to promote new approaches to thinking about design and studio production.

The four studios are the life force of JamFactory, and the current

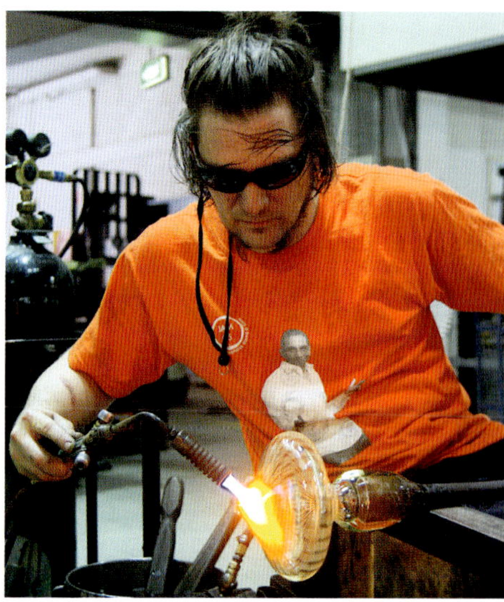

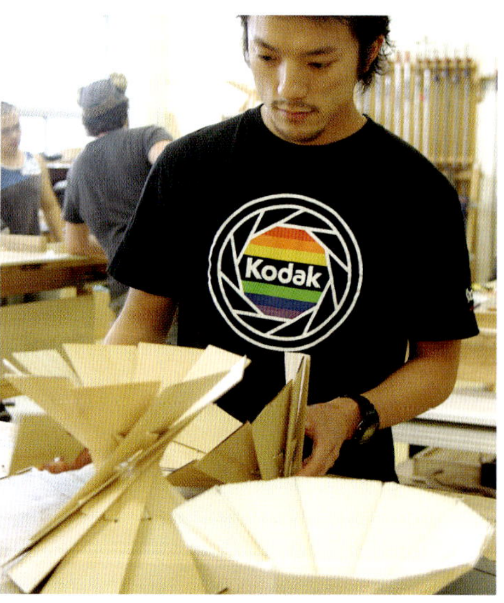

top
Tom Moore,
Glass Studio, 2009
Photo: Mick Bradley

Takeshi Iue,
Furniture Studio, 2009
Photo: Mick Bradley

Creative Directors—Karen Cunningham (Glass), Tom Mirams (Furniture) Christian Hall (Metal Design) and Prue Venables (Ceramics- until December 2012)—bring a range of technical expertise, entrepreneurial experience and vast professional networks to the organisation. In 2012 we revised the staffing structure in the studios and introduced a Program Manager to assist the Creative Director in each studio.[2] All of the studio staff work part time (three or four days per week) and maintain significant independent practices, most of them making their work or components of it within JamFactory's studios.

JamFactory has always provided studio space for independent makers—mostly emerging artists and designers who have completed the Associate training program or who see the opportunityto accelerate their professional development through being based at JamFactory. When I arrived, there were 16 rental tenants and I was eager to reclaim and reconfigure spaces in the building to increase this number. We now comfortably accommodate 24 individual tenants who each make a valuable contribution to the building's community.

For the Associates who undertake JamFactory's two-year training program, there are significant benefits from being exposed to so many successful practitioners (creative staff, studio tenants and visiting artists/designers in residence) with whom they can share ideas, seek advice from and form important long-lasting friendships with.

JamFactory's exhibition program provides important opportunities for local artists, craftspeople and designers and for others from around Australia and elsewhere. The exhibitions are valuable not only for engaging the general public but also for inspiring and stimulating JamFactory's creative community.

During 2011–12 we tested several approaches to exhibition development and a particularly successful project was *Prototyping: Making Ideas* (2011), curated by our Curator and Exhibitions Manager Margaret Hancock Davis. This show explored the idea of the 'prototype' as a meeting place for design and craftsmanship, and featured leading designers and

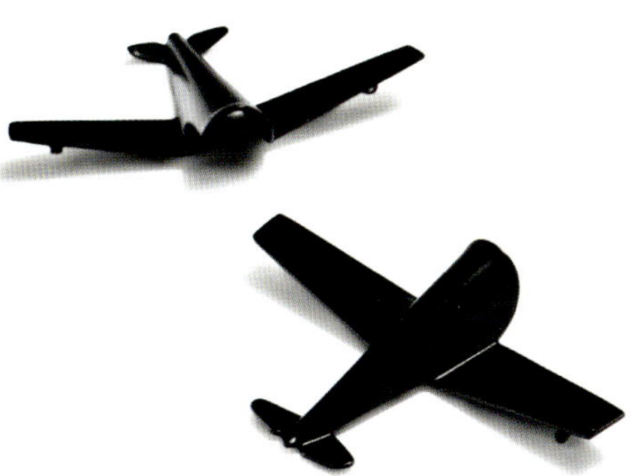

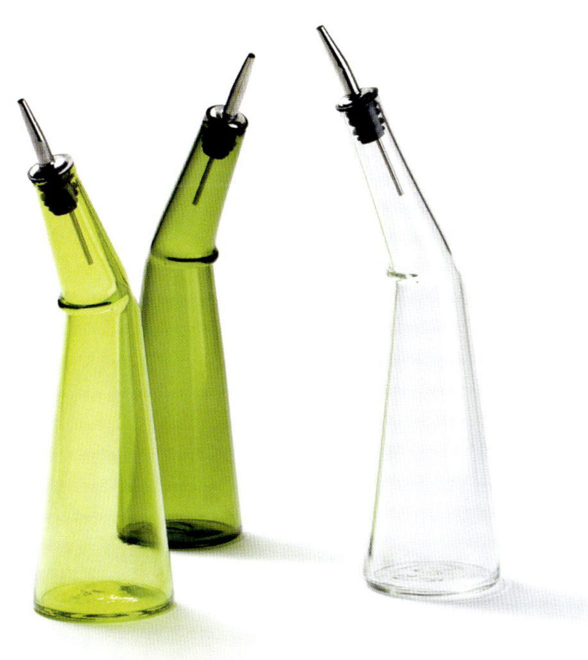

top
AIRCRAFT Brooch, *2012, designed by Christian Hall powdercoated stainless steel 14 x 75 x 50mm each Photo: Tom Roschi*

KINK Oil Bottle, *2010 designed by Deb Jones, blown glass, pourer 320 x 700mm dia. each Photo: Tom Roschi*

makers from around the country including several associated with JamFactory. Through the inclusion of sketches, models, early prototypes, informative wall texts and digital video content, along with the presentation of a symposium (in partnership with UniSA) and the production of a substantial catalogue, the exhibition reached new audiences and exposed the process behind the product.

In 2013 JamFactory will have three major exhibitions touring nationally, including *WOOD: art design architecture*[3] in collaboration with the Botanic Gardens of Adelaide, and the exhibition that accompanies this catalogue *Designing Craft/Crafting Design: 40 years of JamFactory*. These exhibitions have attracted significant grant funding and sponsorship, are accompanied by major publications and will be seen by somewhere between 100,000 and 200,000 people beyond Adelaide.

The opportunities that currently exist for JamFactory in relation to sponsorship and philanthropy are exciting and our long-term growth will be dependent on our success in this area. Against a backdrop of constrained public funding and escalating running costs, we created the role of Development Manager in August 2012 and appointed Emily Troon. Emily has since worked with the staff and Board to build corporate and individual support for JamFactory.

There have been many significant changes to the craft and design sector in Australia in recent years. We are seeing something of an upheaval in the area of craft skills training. High costs of delivery and relatively low enrolments have led to closures of ceramics, glass, furniture, jewellery and textiles courses at many universities, with many more under pressure to reduce in scale or amalgamate. The TAFE system, too, is facing similar pressures across the country and graduates from both programs are emerging with less technical proficiency than in previous decades. At the same time, enrolments in design courses have been steadily increasing—though most preference computer-aided design over workshop skills.

Post Global Financial Crisis we have also witnessed a flattening of the art market and the subsequent closure of several commercial galleries that specialised in or supported craft-based work. Countering this to some extent is the increased consumer interest in 'design and the handmade',[4] and artists and designers now have access to larger and/or more targeted niche markets through the Internet.

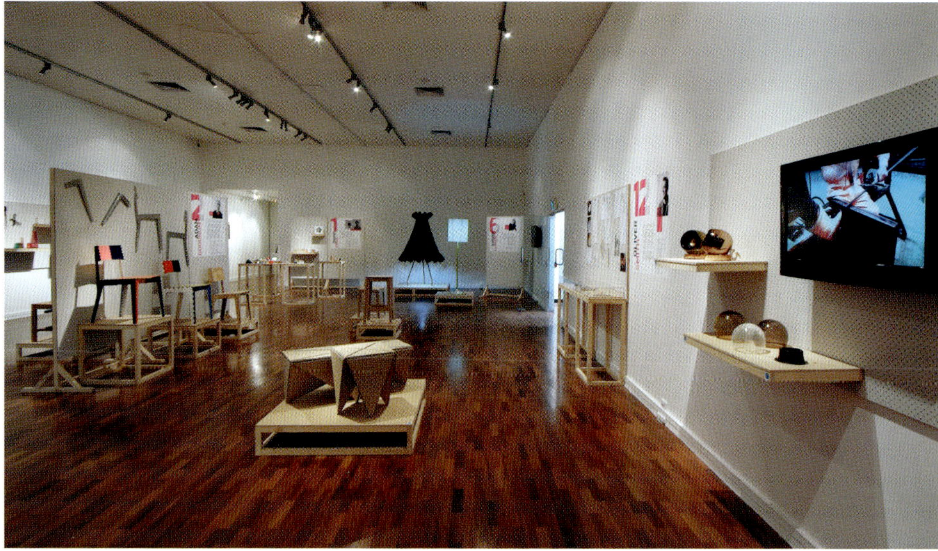

above
Prototyping: Making Ideas, *Gallery One, 2011*
Photo: Mick Bradley

opposite top
Glaze Testing, *Ceramics Studio, 2010*
Photo: Mick Bradley

Blackwood Display Case, *designed and made by the Furniture Studio for the Art Gallery of South Australia, 2012*
Photo: Don Brice

These are just a sample of the current issues likely to affect the future of JamFactory and those whom we support. Moving forward it seems critical to maintain a strong skills and business focus in our training program. To help our Associates build sustainable practices we need to expose them to a broad range of experiences, from developing products for retail, to undertaking private commissions, creating work for exhibitions and teaching skills to others. We need to equip them with skills to adapt to circumstances in an unpredictable future.

JamFactory at 40 is more confident and financially secure than at any point in its history. But, like our Associates, we must continue to evolve in response to the constant changes around us. We have identified a number of opportunities for growth that build on our existing strengths. Our ambitions over the coming decade include establishing a Textiles Studio, expanding our Indigenous artist mentoring program, broadening our engagement in public art, building on our innovative work with local schools, delivering more programs to regional centres, expanding our retail operations nationally and promoting outstanding work internationally.

An ambition that we look forward to achieving during our 40th year is the opening of a new satellite campus of JamFactory at Seppeltsfield Village in the heart of the Barossa Valley. This will be the most significant development for JamFactory since the organisation moved from Payneham Road to Morphett Street in 1992, and will see a new JamFactory shop, gallery and group of studios housed in the refurbished stables building at the historic Seppeltsfield Winery.

In order to thrive in the future, JamFactory will need to reach out in new ways to new audiences and continue to build and diversify its income base. In spite of the financial pressures that will no doubt continue to intensify, the organisation must remain a vibrant hub for the local creative community, providing benefit to the general public and to the professional artists, craftspeople and designers it exists to support.

---

1. The Integrated Design Commission (IDC) was established by the South Australian government in early 2010 as Australia's first multidisciplinary design agency to provide strategic advice across government. Replaced to a large extent in 2013 by the Office for Design and Architecture, the momentum built by the IDC continues to grow.

2. In 2010 the Ceramics, Furniture and Metal Design Studios each had a single full-time Creative Director with no additional staff, and a group of six part-time individuals managed the Glass Studio. In 2011–12, David Pedler (Ceramics), Kristel Britcher (Glass), Lex Stobie (Furniture) and Alice Potter (Metal Design) were appointed to the new Program Manager roles, and Glass continues to have a higher number of staff, with Production Manager Tom Moore and Studio Technician Dale Roberts.

3. *WOOD: art design architecture* showcases innovative and outstanding uses of wood by 28 contemporary Australian artists, designers and architects and is touring nationally throughout 2013–14.

4. This was the subject of the seminal exhibition *Smart works: design and the handmade*, curated by Dr Grace Cochrane for the Powerhouse Museum in 2007.

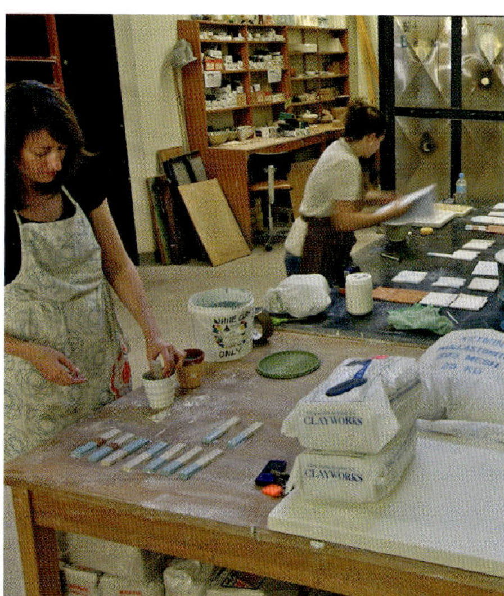

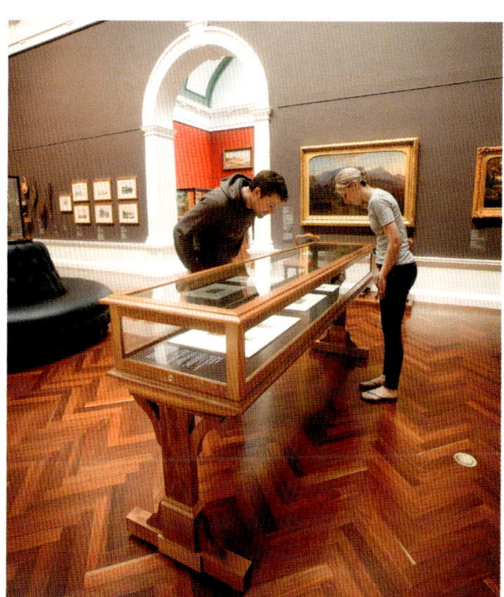

DESIGNING CRAFT/ CRAFTING DESIGN: 40 CONTEMPORARY ARTISTS FOR 40 YEARS

Frank Bauer
Clare Belfrage
Robin Best
Gabriella Bisetto
Stephen Bowers
Gareth Brown
Scott Chaseling
Kirsten Coelho
Lesa Farrant
Honor Freeman
Brenden Scott French
Christian Hall
Jim Hannon-Tan
Greg Healey
illumini
Kath Inglis
Takeshi Iue
Stephanie James-Manttan
Deb Jones
Elizabeth Kelly
Bronwyn Kemp
Erin Keys
Peta Kruger
Sue Lorraine
Leslie Matthews
Jeff Mincham
Tom Mirams
MONO
Tom Moore
Nick Mount
Belinda Newick
Julie Pieda
Lauren Simeoni
Vipoo Srivilasa
Christopher Thomas
Michelle Taylor
Prue Venables
Janice Vitkovsky
Peter Walker
Gerry Wedd

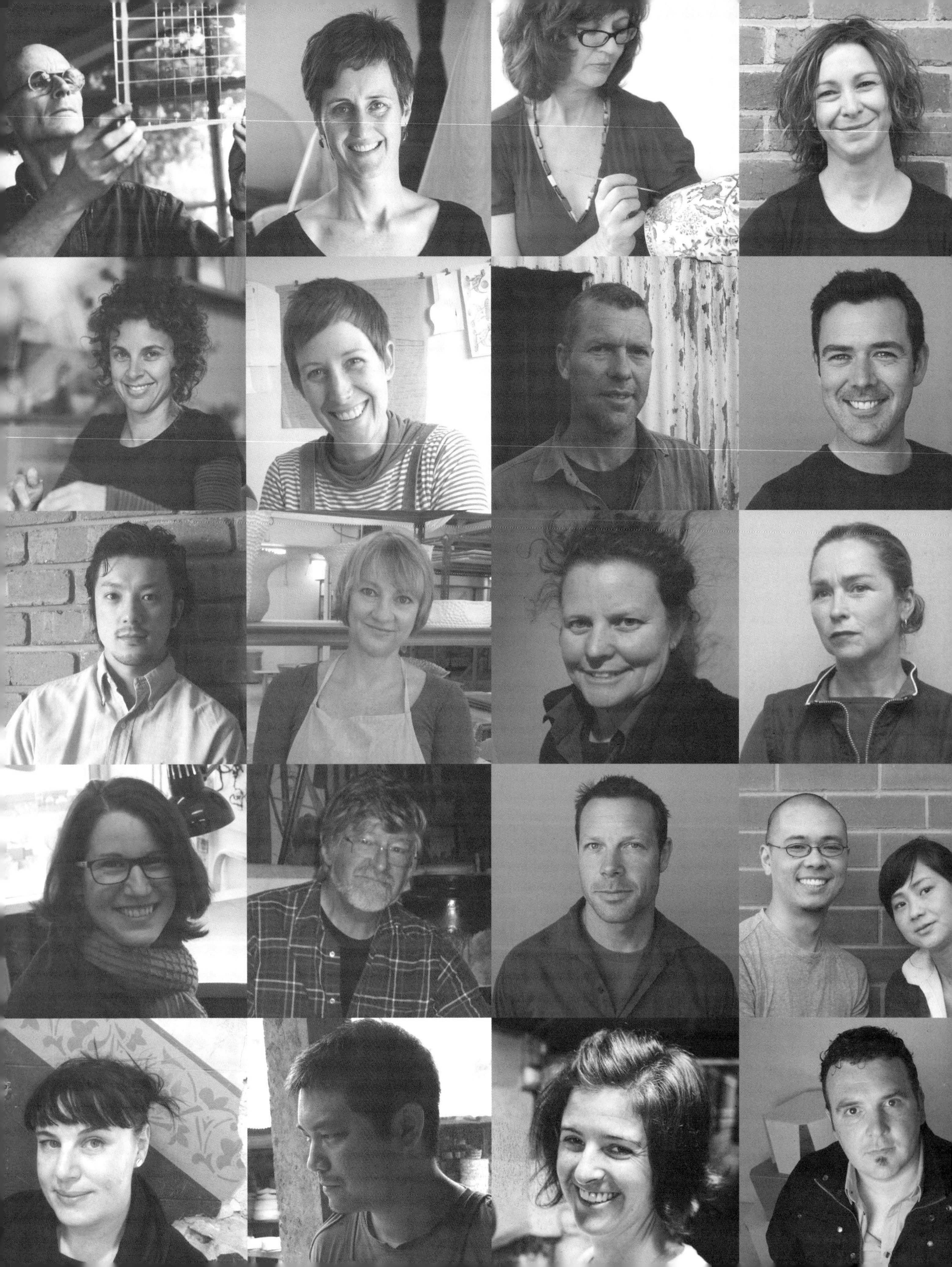

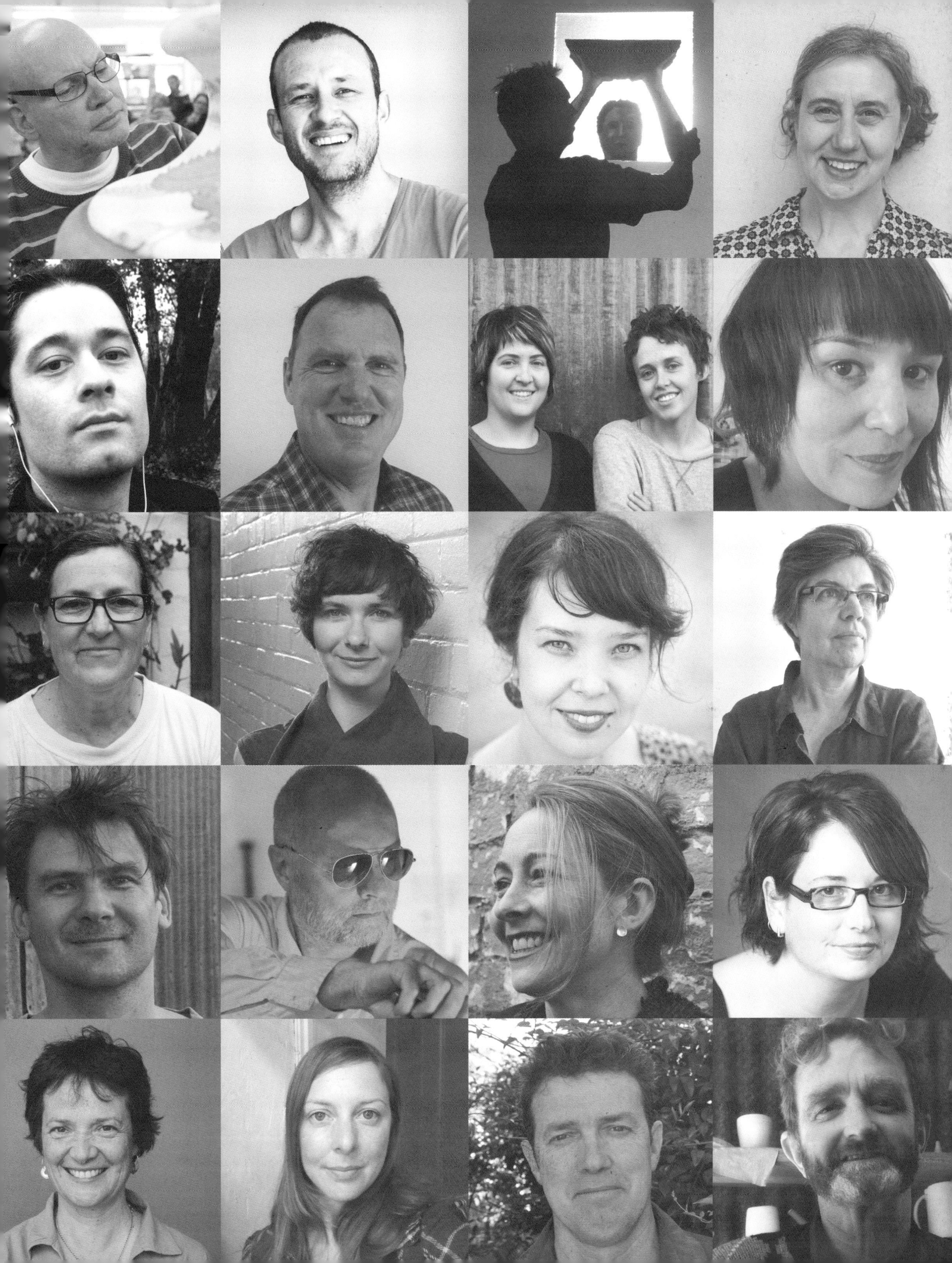

FRANK BAUER

born 1942, Hannover, Germany
lives in Adelaide, SA

The esteemed designer and metalsmith, Frank Bauer, has a prodigious record of achievement in Australia and Europe. Over the years he has won acclaim for his jewellery, sculpture, furniture, spectacles and lighting. One of his silver teapots is represented on an Australian postage stamp (1989). His work is held in major public collections in Australia, including the National Gallery of Australia, the Art Gallery of South Australia, the National Gallery of Victoria and the Powerhouse Museum. Internationally his work is in collections of the Bauhaus Archive, Berlin, Schmuckmuseum, Pforzheim, Stadtmuseum, Munich and the Victoria and Albert Museum, London.

Bauer undertook rigorous training in industrial design and metalsmithing in his native Germany, and also worked at Ireland's Kilkenny Workshops and in the studio of renowned architect Frei Otto. He migrated to Australia in 1971 and moved to Adelaide in 1975, at the invitation of Dick Richards, to establish a private practice within the Jewellery Workshop of the South Australian Craft Authority (later renamed the Jam Factory Workshops) at St Peters. The workshop was run by Danish silversmith Vagn Hemmingsen. Bauer taught evening classes in the Jewellery Workshop for two years, and received one of the first master/apprentice grants from the newly established Crafts Board of the Australia Council to train two apprentices, Chris Wells and Peter Cunningham. During this period Bauer's silver teapot with an olive-wood handle was acquired for the collection of the Art Gallery of South Australia.

His memories of those years are of the people he met and with whom he worked. He recalls his friendship with English glass artist Sam Herman, who had established the Glass Workshop in a shed out the back. Sculptor Bert Flugelman was working there at the time, as were young ceramicists Jeff Mincham, Liz Williams and Margaret Dodd. Japanese weaver Jun Tomita was working with Pru Medlin in the Textile Workshop. Bauer and Tomita formed a lasting friendship, leading some 30 years later to their shared exhibition of lighting and textiles, *Colour Boundary* at JamFactory in 2008.

After leaving Adelaide in 1979, Bauer worked in London for several years, where he was highly regarded as being at the forefront of innovative jewellery design. He returned in 1984 to teach metalsmithing in the School of Design, at the former South Australian College of Advanced Education (now University of South Australia). In 1989 he left to establish his own studio and to concentrate on developing his unique lighting grid system, which he patented in 1992. The FB Grid Light System is an ingenious low voltage meccano-like system that can be assembled in a range of configurations—the power is carried through slim metal-rod connectors, and the light is diffused through layered metallic mesh filters. These elegant light sculptures evince Bauer's finely honed sensitivity to the interplay of colour and form.

In 1993 Bauer was honoured with a three-year creative fellowship from the Australia Council. In 2000 JamFactory in association with the Powerhouse Museum presented an ambitious retrospective survey of his career, *Frank Bauer: designer—jewellery, metalwork, lighting 1975–2000.*

Margot Osborne

Grey Lichtbild #063, *2012*
perforated anodized aluminium sheets, stainless steel, light fitting
1100 x 1100 x 150mm

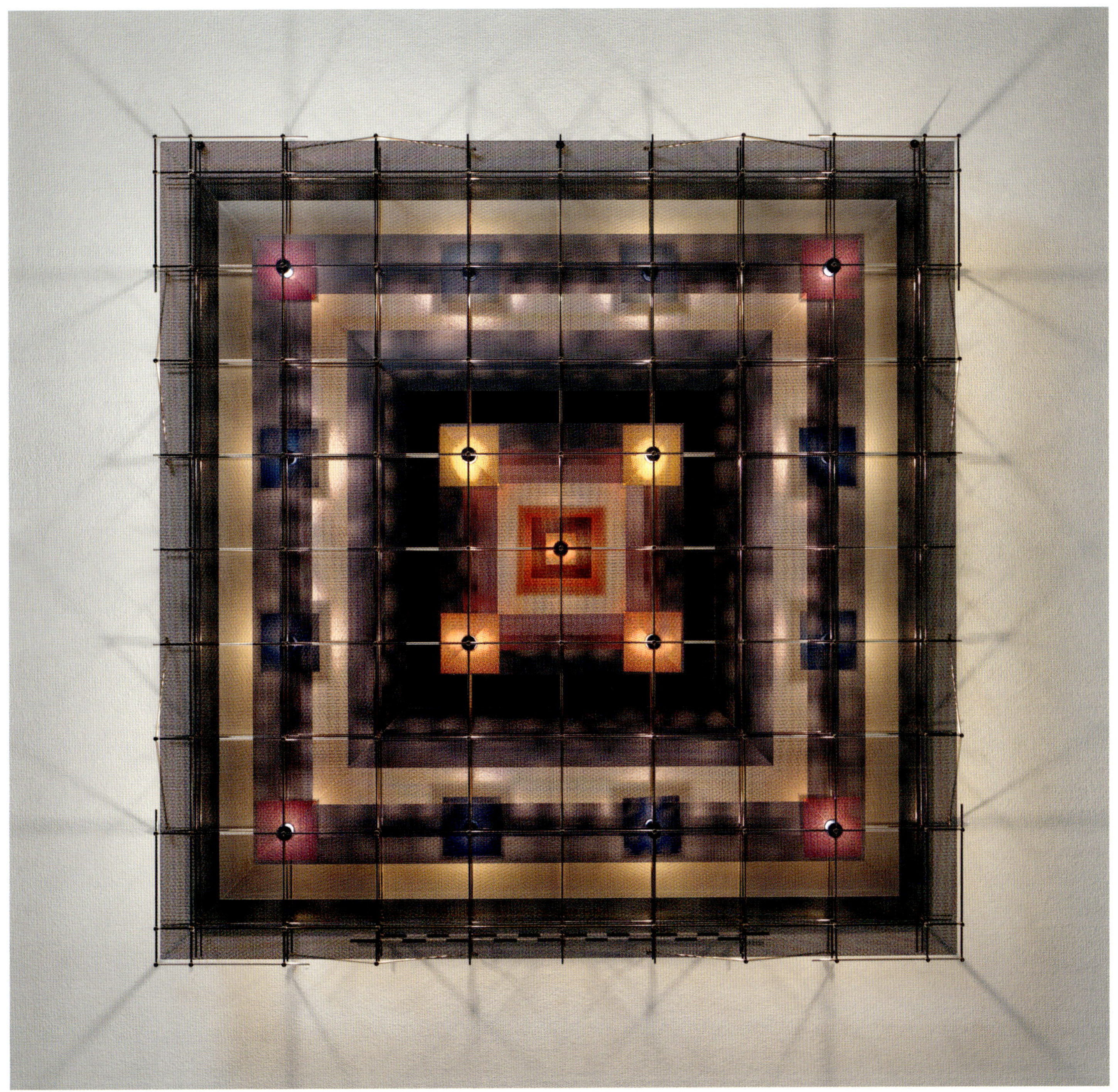

CLARE BELFRAGE

born 1966, Melbourne, Vic
lives in Canberra, ACT

Clare Belfrage balances her studio practice as one of Australia's leading glass artists with her role as Creative Director of Canberra Glassworks. Despite the pressures of these dual roles, she has continued to produce an ongoing body of work for galleries in Australia and overseas, with her most recent solo exhibition at Sydney's Sabbia Gallery in November 2011. Her work has been selected for the major exhibition *Links: Australian glass and the Pacific northwest* at Tacoma Museum of Glass, Washington State, USA, from May 2013. She has twice won the Art Gallery of Western Australia's prestigious Tom Malone Prize for glass, in 2005 and 2011.

After graduating with a Bachelor of Fine Arts degree from Monash University in 1988 and working for two years as a glass blower, Belfrage came to JamFactory's Glass Workshop as a trainee in 1991, when it was headed by Peter Tysoe. However it would be Nick Mount, Head of the Glass Workshop from 1994 to 1997, who would become a key mentor. She formed enduring friendships with fellow trainees, including Gabriella Bisetto and Matthew Larwood. Belfrage remembers her time as a trainee as 'the hardest I've worked in my life physically—that was fantastic, it was training through production'. She was a founding member of Adelaide's renowned Blue Pony glass artists cooperative (1997–2011) but continued her connection with JamFactory at the same time, working at least once a week in the Glass Studio over the next 16 years until she left for Canberra in 2009. In 2008 she and her partner, fellow glass artist Tim Edwards, held a joint exhibition, *Duologue*, in JamFactory's main gallery.

Belfrage has developed a distinctive body of work using fine glass threads, known as stringers, to create organic linear designs across the body of her flattened blown forms. For many years she applied these after blowing and hot-forming was complete, to create alluring textured surfaces with allusions to natural vegetation. In her most recent work she has applied these stringers at an earlier stage, so that the linear markings lie beneath the surface and respond to further blowing to create subtle fluid patterns. In her catalogue for the Sabbia Gallery exhibition in 2011 she stated: 'In this body of work ... I am working with pattern and rhythm expressive of life, growth and the passing of time, the weave of fabric and the qualities of drawing.'

Belfrage's work is held in Australian and international public collections, including Tacoma Museum of Glass, USA, Museo do Vidro, Portugal, the National Gallery of Australia, the National Art Glass Collection (Wagga Wagga), Artbank and the state galleries of Western Australia, South Australia, Tasmania and the Northern Territory.

Margot Osborne

left
Fluence #020711, *2011*
blown glass
350 x 390 x 80mm

Fluence #010711, *2011*
blown glass
380 x 500 x 80mm

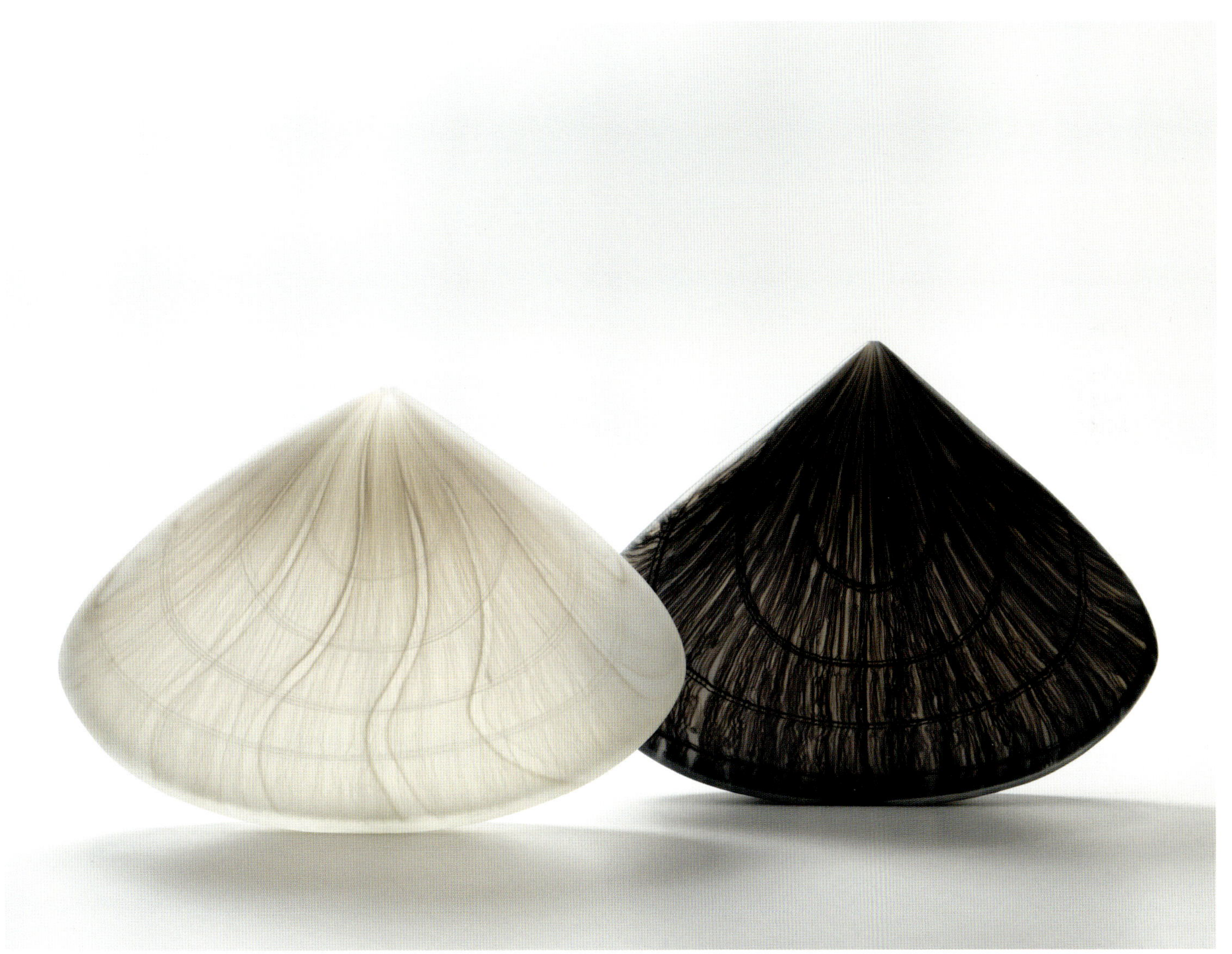

ROBIN BEST

born 1953, Perth, WA
lives in Jingdezhen, China

Robin Best's long association with JamFactory goes back to the early 1980s, when she was a studio tenant in the original Jam Factory Workshops at St Peters. After working in Melbourne for several years, she returned to Adelaide as coordinator of JamFactory's CADCeram Industrial Ceramics Project (1994–2002) and Design Lab Project (2000–01), funded by the Australia Council. One outcome of this project was that the *Concertina bowl*, designed by Best, received the Design Institute of Australia's product design award in 2000.

Between 1998 and 2004 she coordinated the Ernabella Ceramics Project for JamFactory. Under her supervision, the Ceramics Studio produced jigger-jollied, bisque-fired plates. These were sent to Ernabella, in the Aṉangu Pitjanjatjara Lands, for Indigenous women artists to decorate with their traditional walka (designs), and were then returned to JamFactory for a final firing. They were first exhibited at JamFactory in late 1998, to great acclaim. During this period, Best held a solo exhibition of her *Marine Forms* series in Gallery Two (2001) and exhibited work from this series in two of JamFactory's major touring exhibitions, *Wild Nature* (national tour, 2002–04) and *Light Black* (Asialink tour to Japan, 2003). The final chapter of Best's relationship with JamFactory was as Creative Director of the Ceramics Studio (2008–10).

Best left Adelaide in 2010 to relocate to the ancient Chinese ceramic centre of Jingdezhen. Here she teaches at the university, and works with Chinese potters who create the porcelain blanks for her to hand-paint. Her current body of work features fine on-glaze painting and cobalt-blue drawing. It is a sophisticated realisation of thinking about cross-cultural pollination that has been long present in her work in differing manifestations. Best references, on the one hand, the history of transmission of cultural influences along the Silk Route, in particular through textile and ceramics designs; and, on the other, the early representations of flora and fauna resulting from the first contact of Europeans with Australia. These dual concerns are apparent in her exquisitely fine on-glaze painting on the translucent, cast egg-shell porcelain, *The Arcana Bowl*, 2011, of which she states:

The Arcana *by George Perry was published in 1811, and is a record of the observations of the first naturalists who journeyed to Australia between 1770 and 1805. The patterns are derived from beautiful hand-printed Indian chintz cotton textiles, some of which are held in British museums. The chintz patterns are taken from fabrics that were made on the Coromandel Coast of south-eastern India, home to a flourishing textile industry that supplied England, France and Holland with hand-printed cottons. The import of these extravagant cottons was later banned by English law, to protect the local cotton printing industries that had emerged during the Industrial Revolution.*

The move to China has enabled Best to expand her international career. She has a strong presence in London, exhibiting at *Collect* and other major art fairs through her dealer, Adrian Sassoon. In 2013 she has exhibited in *Blue and White* at the Boston Museum of Fine Arts. In Britain her work has been acquired for the Norwich Collection and the National Museum of Scotland.

Margot Osborne

The Arcana Bowl, *2011*
eggshell porcelain, on-glaze decoration
300 x 500mm dia

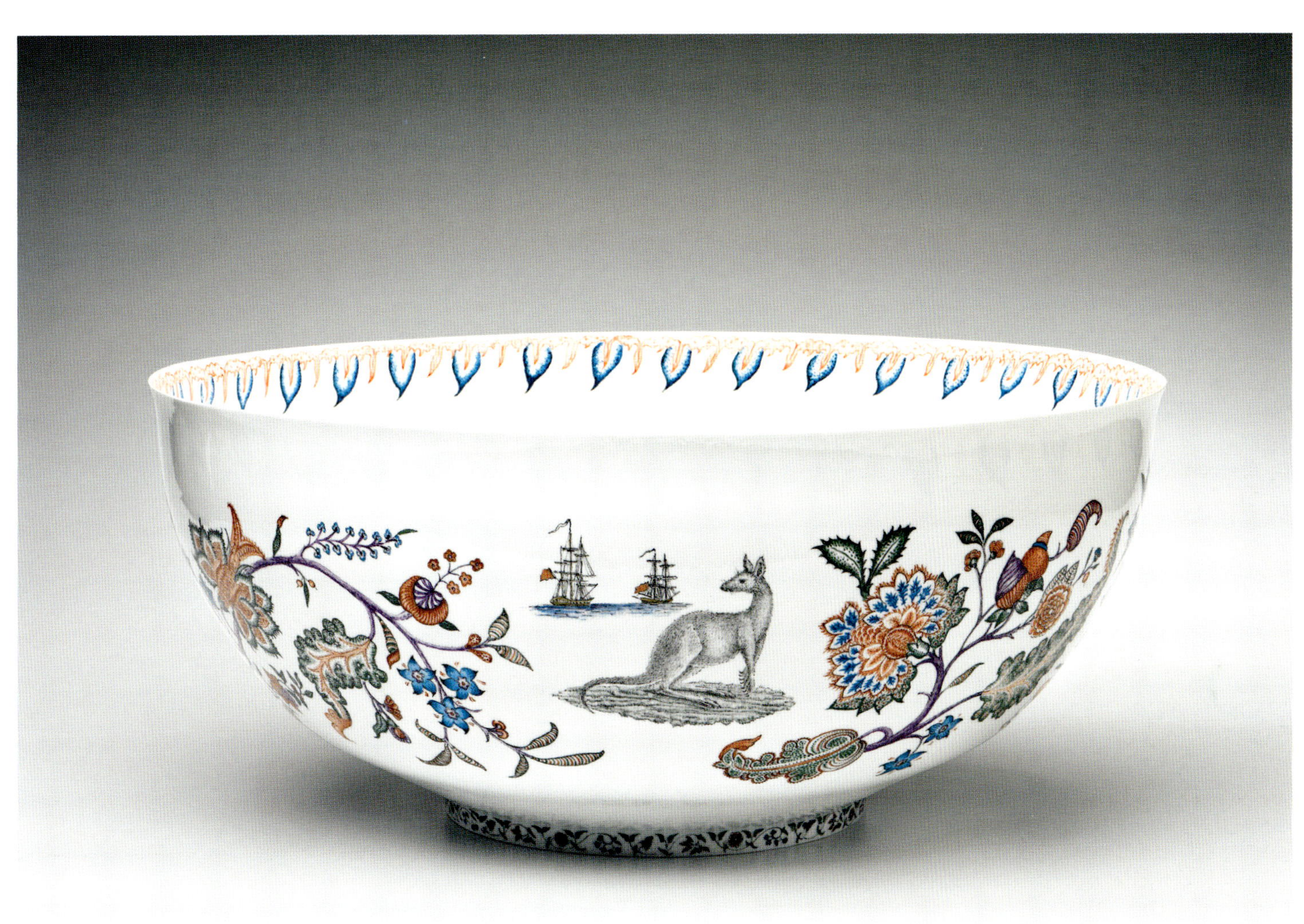

GABRIELLA BISETTO

born 1968, Griffith, NSW
lives in Adelaide, SA

After graduating from the Glass program at Canberra School of Art, Gabriella Bisetto came to JamFactory as an Associate in the Glass Studio from 1991 to 1992. She returned as Production Manager from 1996 to 1999, before leaving to become a lecturer in glass and subsequently Head of the Glass Workshop at the University of South Australia. Together with other former Associates, including Clare Belfrage, Tom Moore and Deb Jones, she was a founding member of Adelaide's long-running Blue Pony glass artists cooperative (1997–2011). She comments:

I believe that the JamFactory was a crucial element in my ability to have an ongoing career as an artist and is the reason I still live in South Australia. Not only did the traineeship give the mandatory grounding and technical skills required to have the confidence to initiate a career in the early days as a production artist, but it was a place where I met my lifetime friends and colleagues, with whom I went on to set up a studio, to exhibit with, and to work with on boards such as Ausglass, facilitating future conferences and opportunities for glass artists. JamFactory is the incubator for careers in the arts and 20 years on I still appreciate the vital role it played in my career.

Bisetto's distended abstract forms in blown and hot-worked glass explore metaphorical notions of embodiment and bodily awareness. They allude to an unseen world within us: the internal vessels and organs of the human body, our blood and breath. In 2006, as an artist in residence at Alberta College of Art and Design, Canada, and Alfred University, USA, she first experimented with creating forms based on the amount of air that passes through the human body over a measured period. This resulted in a video performance titled *Three Minutes of Breathing*. In 2007 Bisetto was invited to present a lecture about her work at the multi-disciplinary conference, 'Take a Deep Breath', at the Tate Modern in London. In 2009 she was awarded the Australia Council Rome Residency.

Her piece for this exhibition, *All the Breath Inside of Me*, 2012 is a further extension of her blown forms, which are created by her attempt to exhale all the air in her body and to measure the physical space occupied by this air. There is a poetic simplicity to this idea that is realised in the clarity of the transparent asymmetric form. It contains both nothing and something. This existential container for the artist's breath evokes the mysterious ineffability of life.

Margot Osborne

All the Breath Inside of Me, *2012*
blown and solid glass
580 x 640 x 320mm

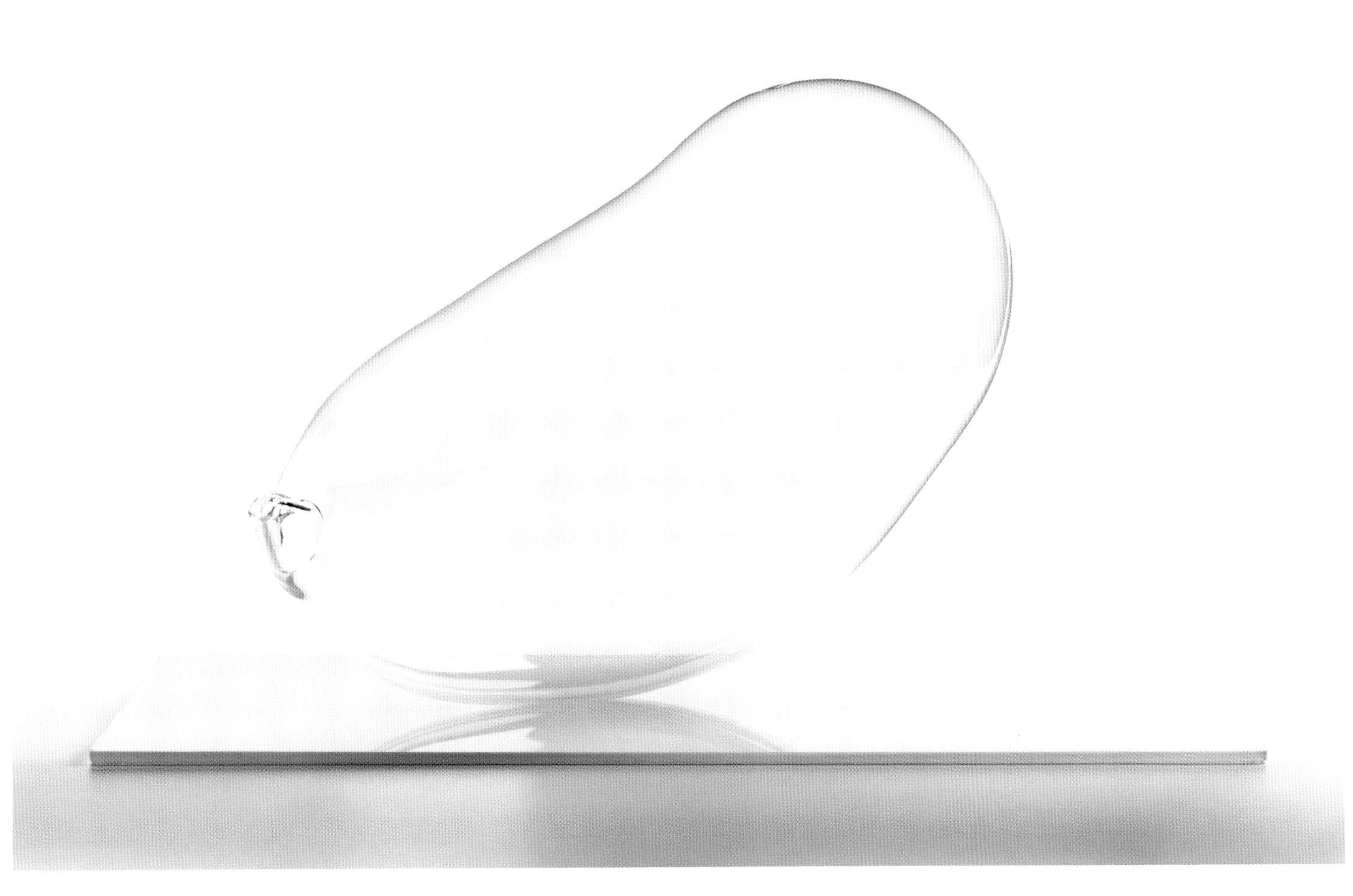

STEPHEN BOWERS

born 1952, Katoomba, NSW
lives in Adelaide, SA

Stephen Bowers started his long relationship with JamFactory in the early 1980s as a trainee in the Ceramics Workshop under Jeff Mincham. He then became a studio tenant for a further two years. He held his first exhibition at JamFactory in 1983, jointly with Robin Best. At that time, Bowers met another JamFactory studio tenant, Mark Heidenreich. Over the ensuing years the two have formed a complementary working relationship, with Bowers commissioning Heidenreich, who is a master thrower of ceramics formed on the potter's wheel, to provide the blanks for him to decorate. Bowers is a virtuoso exponent of hand-painted, multi-fired underglaze decoration, displaying great expertise in handling layers of colour, glaze and lustre. His large plates and vases are lavishly embellished with his distinctive interpretation of blue willow pattern references, cockatoos and Australian flora, set against a montage of intricate patterns and idiosyncratic imagery.

As Head of the Ceramics Studio from 1990 to 1999, he left his mark through facilitating a range of innovative projects. These included public artworks, a jigger-jolly production workshop, the CADCeram Industrial Ceramics project and the partnership with Ernabella. He changed the model for the studio's operations, forming a production team to create his successful *Andamooka* product range for retail and wholesale, and enabling Associates to work on their own projects or contribute to the studio range.

In 2004 Bowers returned, this time as Managing Director. During his six years at the helm he invigorated the organisation, and delivered many important projects. These included artist residencies, the GAS (Glass Art Society Conference, 2005), the Australian international presence at *Collect*, London and *SOFA*, Chicago, (2004-2008) and the fit-out of the retail space by Khai Liew. He also curated several important ceramics exhibitions in the gallery, including most notably *A Secret History of Blue and White*, which toured Australian and Asian galleries under the auspices of Asialink and Object (2006-2009) He returned to private studio practice in 2010.

Bowers was awarded the National Ceramics Acquisitive Award, Perc Tucker Regional Gallery, Queensland in 2001, and the National Craft Acquisition Award, Alice Springs Art Gallery in 1996. His work is held in major national public collections including the National Gallery of Australia, Canberra, Art Gallery of South Australia and Powerhouse Museum, Sydney, as well as international collections including the Museum of International Ceramic Art, Denmark, Los Angeles County Museum of Modern Art, USA and the National Museum of History, Taipei, Taiwan.

Bowers is the recipient of the 2013 South Australian Living Artists (SALA) Monograph. His major solo show *Stephen Bowers: Beyond Bravura* will tour nationally, as the first exhibition in JamFactory's new ICON series.

For this exhibition Bowers is represented by the large plate *White Cockatoos*, 2010. Of this work he states:

Along with the totemic and slightly minatory figures of two white sulphur-crested cockatoos, the key element in this work is the intensely detailed botanical study of luxuriantly interlocked and intertwined eucalyptus leaves, branches and gum nuts. With their marks of growth, decay and attack by insects, the writhing eucalyptus forms represent the complexity and inextricably linked relationships of the natural world. Beyond the bordered section that contains them, they are contrasted with the atomised, fragmentary shard elements of human design—referencing wallpapers, textiles, ceramics and construction—that float in the atmospheric void of the chaotic background.

Margot Osborne

White Cockatoos, *2010*
earthenware,
underglaze colour,
clear earthenware glaze
70 x 670mm dia.

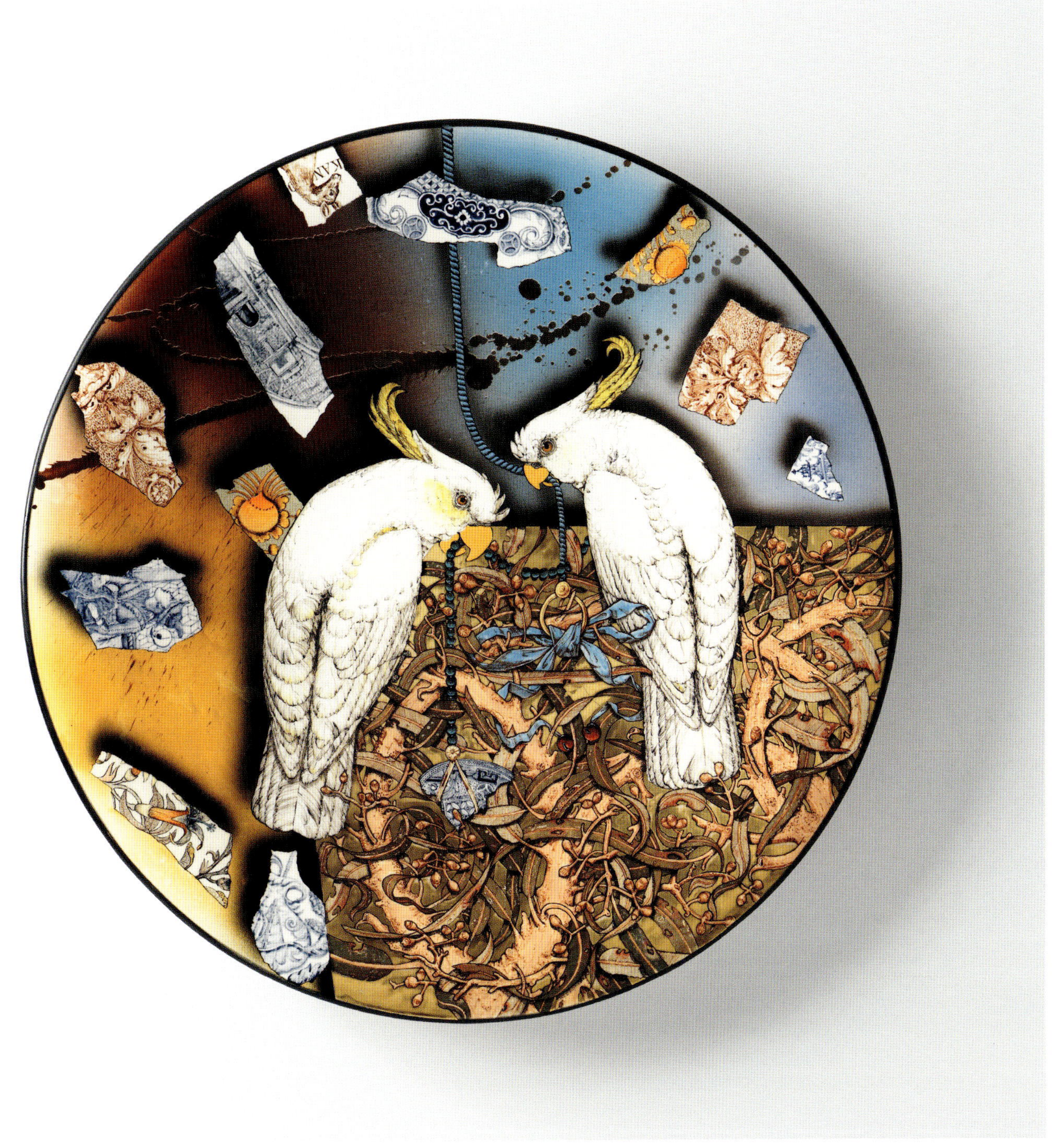

GARETH BROWN

born 1976, Belfast, Northern Ireland
lives in Adelaide, SA

Gareth Brown originally studied handcrafted furniture making at the City of Bristol College in the United Kingdom before undertaking the two-year Associate training program in JamFactory's Furniture Studio from 2007 to 2008. He has expertise in working with solid hardwood and veneers, and now runs a successful practice out of a large, well-equipped studio workshop in the industrial suburb of Hindmarsh in Adelaide.

Brown specialises in the production of one-off and limited edition handmade pieces for exhibition and commission, but has in recent years concentrated on the design and production of a collection of furniture for Agostino & Brown, a business he set up in 2010 with interior designer Samantha Agostino. The Agostino & Brown range includes the *Fig Table* 2010, *Fig Bench*, 2012 and *Plum Stool*, 2012 featured in this exhibition, and are all made using sustainable methods and materials wherever possible. Brown says:

The products we make are unique, time efficient, cost effective and constructed one by one with minimal wastage. We develop the best methods of construction, making sure products can be maintained over time, while minimising the need for replacement.

Designing efficiency of manufacture into the pieces has enabled the business to grow through a consistent stream of commercial and residential interior commissions. The designs can be made in custom sizes and finishes, and are produced quickly to order in the workshop as each client requires them. These pragmatic design concerns sit well with Brown's preference for simple forms, honest materials and a bold splash of colour. The Agostino & Brown collection is sold and distributed through Insitu Furniture in Sydney and Melbourne, Design Farm in Perth and 1000 Chairs in Adelaide.

During his time as an Associate at JamFactory Brown was involved in several significant commission projects, including a major job for Forestry SA consisting of a suite of board and meeting room tables and a large bespoke reception counter. He also began successfully undertaking his own commissions—a practice strongly encouraged by the Studio—including the fit-out of a private study in an inner-city apartment.

Brown's JamFactory experience provided important opportunities to build professional networks. He says that one of the key things he gained was 'inspiration from the culture of the JamFactory and the opportunity to work with a diverse range of talented artists'. He adds, 'this inspired me to move forward and achieve my own business goals'.

JamFactory has an established tradition of building business skills in Associates through active involvement in real commercial projects, but Brown feels fortunate to have gained additional assistance in this regard through a program that JamFactory supported at the time: *the Springboard Projec*t, a structured, creative-entrepreneur mentoring program run by the Australian Design Unit's Heidi Dokulil and Ewan McEoin.

I received a grant from Craftsouth and financial support from JamFactory to participate in stages one and two of the program, which taught me key business, branding, legal and financial skills, which I find I am using more and more at this stage of my career.

Brian Parkes

top
Plum Stool, *2012*
solid Hoop pine, 2pac lacquer
650 x 400mm

Fig Table, *2010*
solid American white oak
750 x 1800 x 900mm

bottom
Fig Bench, *2012*
solid Hoop pine, 2pac lacquer, steel
450 x 1200 x 400mm

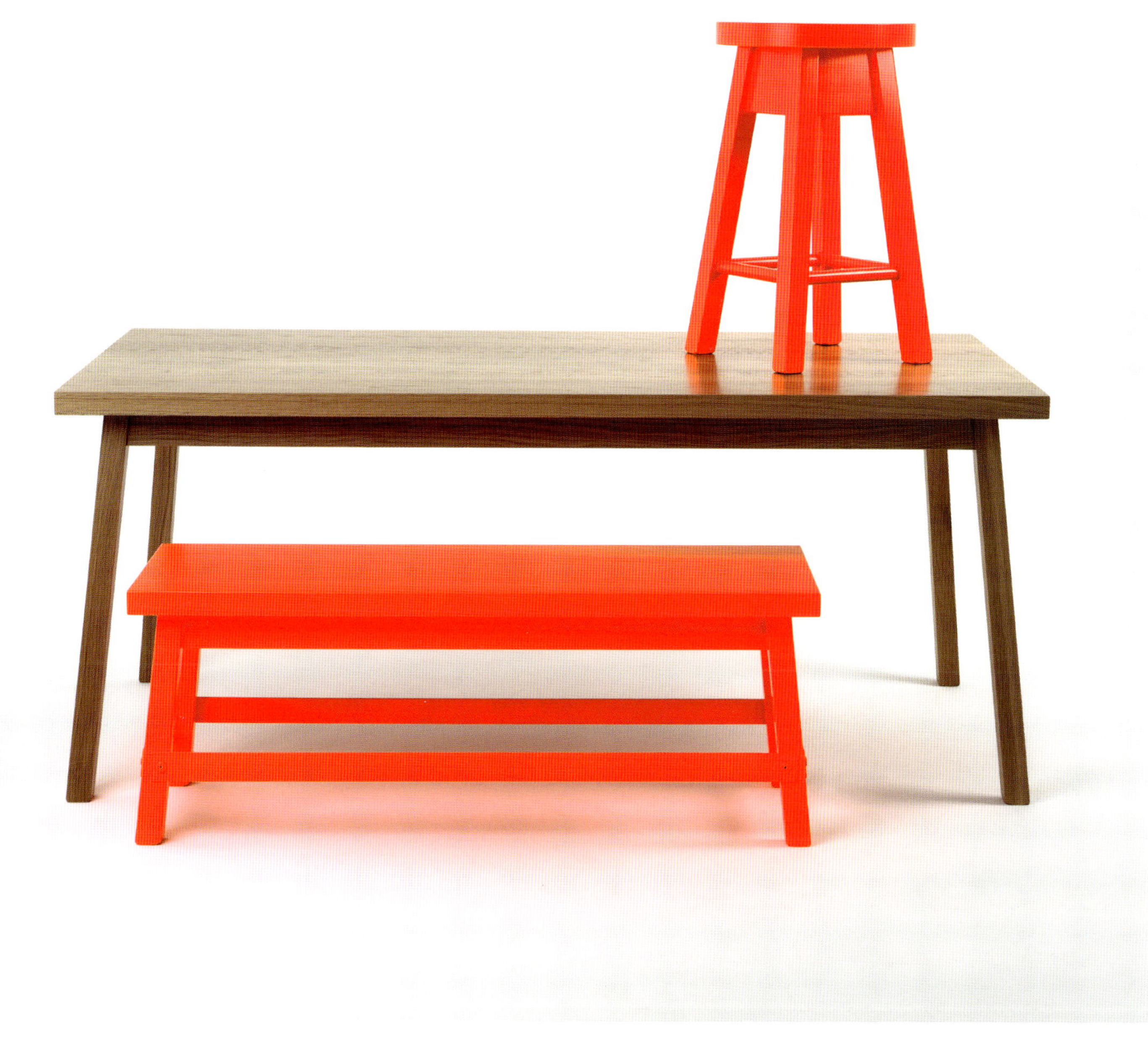

SCOTT CHASELING

born 1962, Tamworth, NSW
lives in Canberra, ACT

Scott Chaseling was a trainee in the Glass Workshop under Stanislav Melis and Peter Tysoe from 1982 to 1985. This was the beginning of a creative journey spanning more than 25 years' involvement with glass—first as a master blower, then as an internationally recognised exponent of the Australian 'roll-up' in fused glass, and now as a sculptor of 'readymade' sculptures using glass from recycled bottles. He recalls his time at the former St Peters JamFactory:

We spent a lot of time together, not just in the studios, socialising into the nights and weekends. In the first year as a trainee I assisted in the morning production team under Stan Melis. This involved a lot of mould blowing and repetitious bit work. The Jam's glass production at this time was a broad domestic utilitarian series. In the afternoon we were able to build upon our skills and develop a personal aesthetic through individual work.

After leaving Adelaide in the late 1980s, Chaseling went to Canberra to take up a position as the first hot-glass teacher at the Canberra School of Art glass workshop. Klaus Moje became a mentor, introducing him to Dante Marioni. In 1989 Chaseling attended Pilchuck Glass School, USA and gained experience assisting for Marioni, Chihuly and Tagliapietra. He spent the next ten years 'going back and forth' between Canberra and Pilchuck.

The next phase of Chaseling's career grew out of his introduction to the possibilities of Bullseye Glass Company's kiln-compatible fusing glass at the now legendary *Latitudes* workshops at Canberra School of Art in 1995 and 1997. Chaseling worked with Kirstie Rea and Moje to perfect the technique of rolling the fused glass, then picking it up and blowing it. Over the next decade he and Rea travelled the world demonstrating the roll-up technique. He created a body of fused and blown work, incorporating *murrine* and hand-painting, to create narratives circling both the exterior and interior of the vessel.

Chaseling's glass received international acclaim. He exhibited at major US galleries Leo Kaplan Modern, New York and Habatat, Chicago. In 2004 he won the prestigious Ranamok Glass Prize and in 2005 he won an award of excellence from Toledo Art Museum. His work is held by international collections, including: Pergamon Museum, Berlin, 21st Century Museum of Contemporary Art, Kanazawa, Japan, Museum of American Glass, New Jersey, and Palm Springs Art Museum. In Australia his work is held by the National Gallery of Australia, the Queensland Art Gallery, Australian National Art Glass Collection, Wagga Wagga and Canberra Museum and Art Gallery.

In 2007 Chaseling moved to the UK as senior research fellow at the University of Sunderland. He then moved to Berlin, where he lived for the next three years as Director/Curator of Parkhaus Projects and then as Artistic Director of Berlin Glas. He returned to Australia in 2012 as artist in residence at Canberra Glassworks and now maintains a nomadic existence moving between Canberra and Berlin. In Europe his work underwent a transformation as he returned to his original passion, sculpture. Moving on from making glass, he turned to readymade conceptual sculptures utilising found objects.

The recurring feature of this body of work is his assemblage of forms using glass rings cut from recycled bottles and then connected using plastic ties. This approach references his interest in low-tech, low-skill making processes. To cut the bottles into crude rings he works with two 're-purposed' record turntables and a small 'crème brulée' blow torch. The rejection of skilled making shifts the focus more fully on the conceptual basis for his work.

The Conqueror, 2012, is a life-size figure of a man, assembled from glass rings, standing on a trolley with one leg ending in a plastic bucket. For Chaseling, the trolley makes the work portable and stands as a signifier of the nomadic ethic that has become one of his driving existential concerns, while the bucket alludes to domesticity. Does the sculpture represent the artist as torn between this nomadic existence and the domestic, or is the domestic being rejected as an impediment? Either reading seems possible.

Margot Osborne

The Conqueror, *2012*
glass, plastic, wood
2100 x 700 x 700mm

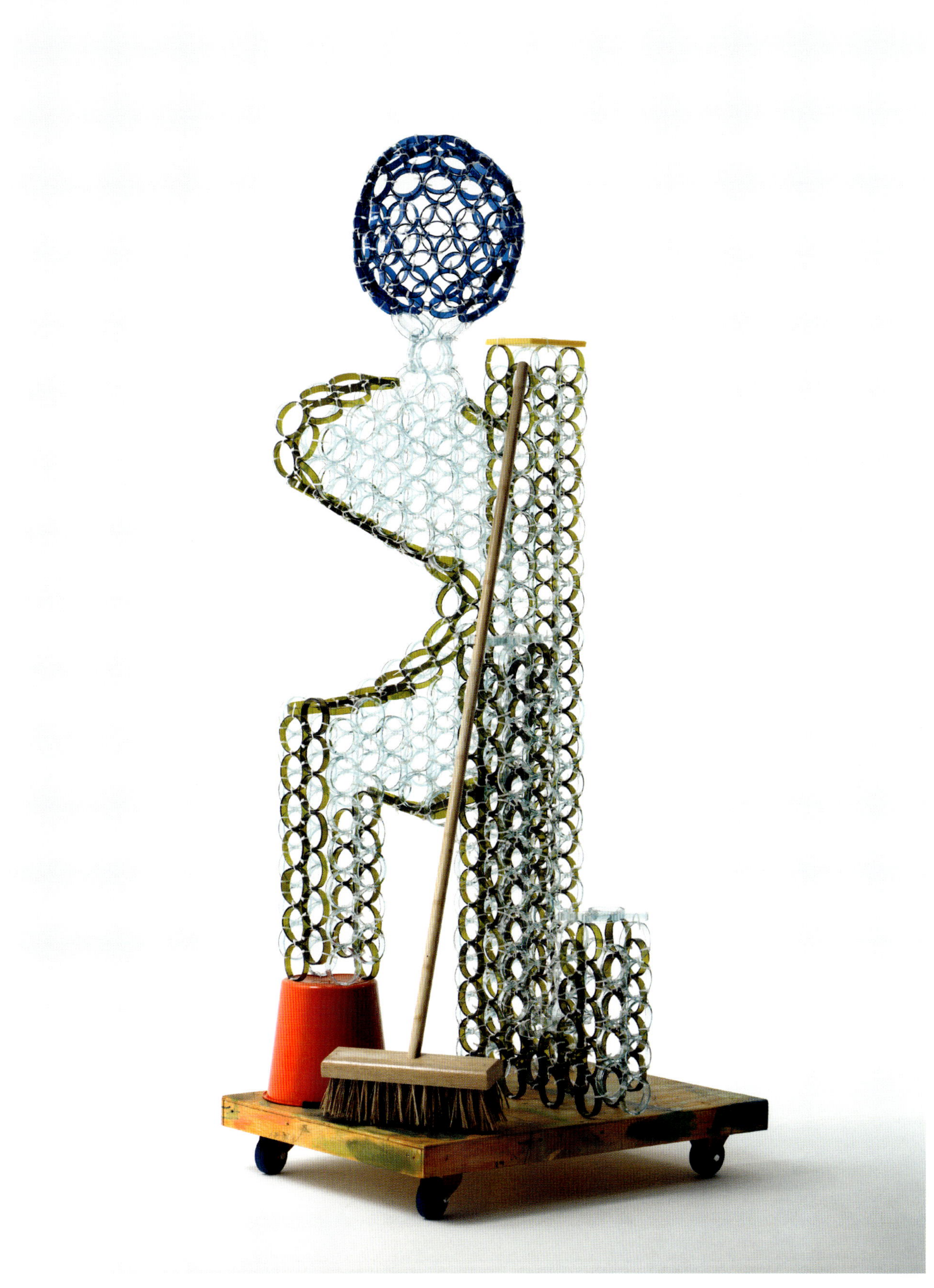

KIRSTEN COELHO

born 1966, Copenhagen, Denmark
lives in Adelaide, SA

When Kirsten Coelho came to JamFactory as an access tenant in 1999, she was at a more advanced stage in her professional development than most Associates, having spent eight years working as a potter in England after she graduated in ceramics from the University of South Australia. She continued as a tenant at JamFactory for three years, sharing a studio with Stephanie Livesey, while also lecturing at the University of South Australia and completing a Master of Visual Art degree in 2004.

Coelho's time immersed in the British studio pottery tradition of Leach, Cardew, Batterham and others has left an enduring though subtle legacy. It is revealed in her fascination with reduction-fired glazes and 'humble' forms derived from domestic pottery, although her current body of porcelain forms reveals only a residual debt to functional ware. However, during her time at JamFactory, she was making teapots, bowls and cups while experimenting with traditional Oriental glazes, including a pale-blue celadon and the rich, viscous black/browns of tenmoku.

For Coelho, JamFactory provided a supportive incubator environment. She received advice on glazes from Livesey and Stephen Bowers and fired her work there until 2006, when she built her own studio. She says, 'I wouldn't have been able to do anything without the JamFactory ... It's about professional development and skills. There is no other place where you could have that opportunity. If you work hard you can really benefit.'

The creative breakthrough for Coelho came when she started her continuing series of reduction-fired porcelain vessels and containers coated in a milky off-white glaze with a rim of iron oxide. The diffusion of the iron oxide through the glaze has resonances with the weathered, rusted enamel of old-fashioned jugs and storage containers. The rust staining the purity of the milky white invokes the Japanese notion of *wabi-sabi*—an unintentional, imperfect beauty perceived in humble objects bearing the marks of time. Her porcelain is imbued with a refined quietude, a sense of perfectly calibrated harmony between subtle glaze surfaces and simplified forms.

In 2007 Coelho undertook a residency in the Australia Council's London studio, and exhibited at *Collect*, Victoria and Albert Museum, as part of the Australian Contemporary International Craft Initiative organised by JamFactory on behalf of the Australia Council. An outcome of this was that she was picked up by the highly regarded decorative arts dealer Adrian Sassoon, London and by Matin Gallery in California. Her work has since been exhibited internationally at art fairs through Adrian Sassoon, as well as at Ann Linnemann Studio Gallery, Copenhagen and in the USA with the Philadelphia Art Alliance.

In 2010 Coelho took part in the Indigenous Mentorship Program initiated by Robin Best during her time as Creative Director of the Ceramics Studio. This involved helping Indigenous artists to realise their ideas, and giving them technical advice. As a result of this project, two of Coelho's students had work accepted for the Sidney Myer Indigenous Ceramic Award.

In 2011 she was part of the acclaimed collaborative exhibition, *Collectors*, first shown at Khai Liew Design, Adelaide and then at the Design Museum, London for the *Brit Insurance Designs of the Year Awards*. In 2012 *Collectors* was acquired by the Art Gallery of South Australia. Coelho won the Sidney Myer Fund Australian Ceramic Award in 2012. Her ceramics are held by public collections including the National Gallery of Australia, Samstag Museum of Art, University of South Australia, Art Gallery of South Australia, Art Gallery of Western Australia and the Gold Coast City Gallery.

Margot Osborne

left
Oil Can and Tea Can, *2012*
wheel thrown porcelain, matte white glaze, banded iron oxide
Oil Can 290 x 100mm
Tea Can 280 x 90mm

Bowl, *2012*
wheel thrown porcelain, matte white glaze, banded iron oxide
150 x 250mm

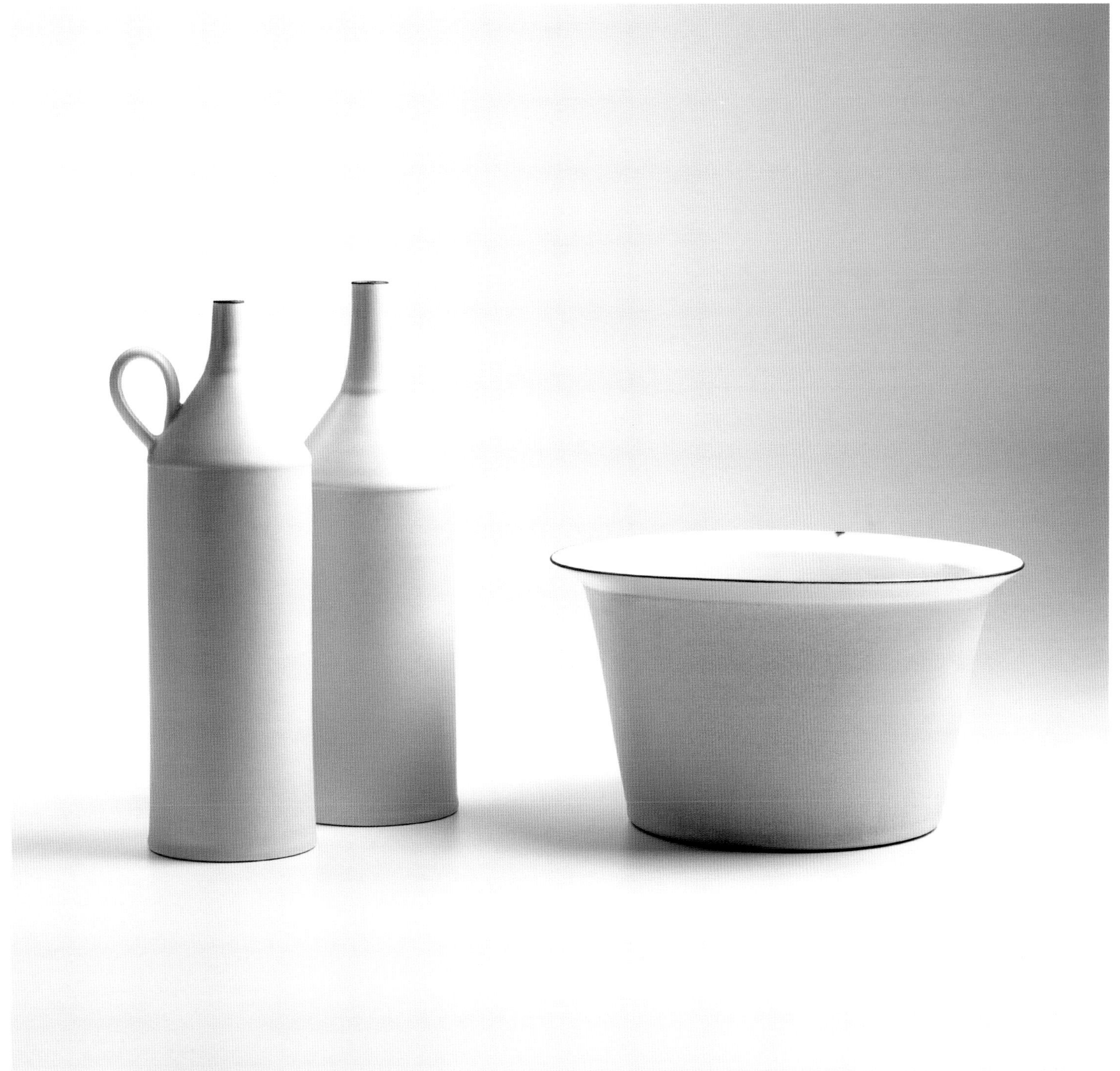

LESA FARRANT

born 1970, Cohuna, Vic
lives in Port Willunga, SA

In 1995 Lesa Farrant, like many fellow JamFactory Associates, moved to Adelaide to pursue the program, after finishing her Bachelor of Visual Arts at La Trobe University, Bendigo. Farrant says:

JamFactory was a significant stepping stone from university to the real world of being a professional craftsperson. My time as an Associate with Stephen Bowers was such a crucial facility and facilitator into the professional craft world. It was a conduit, linking me with national and international craftspeople, artists and designers, as well as being a hub where I developed long-lasting friendships with craftspeople from many disciplines, and provided vital links with prominent arts associations.

Farrant stayed at JamFactory for two years until she joined the team of dedicated ceramic artists at Jamboree Clay Workshop in 1997.

Jamboree was established in 1991 when four potters—Gerry Wedd, Peter Johnson, Jo Crawford and Phil Hart—decided to form a collective studio in what was once a scout hall in Welland, hence the name Jamboree Clay Workshop. All four artists had been either Associates or tenants of JamFactory while Bronwyn Kemp was Head of the Ceramics Workshop. Kemp was keenly aware of the synergies in their practices, work ethic and, some may even say, taste in music, and she actively encouraged their move to an independent studio collective. Much like Adelaide's long-running collective-based jewellery studio Gray Street Workshop, Jamboree Clay Workshop saw the flow to and from JamFactory of many of its tenants, including artists such as Lincoln Kirby Bell, Leo Neuhofer, Marie Littlewood and Liz Williams. Farrant remained a tenant of Jamboree Clay Workshop, on and off, until it closed in 2003. Throughout this time she undertook national and international residencies and work placements, including the Banff Centre, Canada, and as the tutor in wheel-thrown pottery at CAE (Council of Adult Education), Melbourne.

Since 2002 Farrant has been a sessional lecturer at the South Australian School Art, University of South Australia. In 2008 she received a Masters of Arts from the same institution.

Farrant's work is inspired by the detritus she collects along the South Australian coastline and the charming botanical watercolours of Charles Alexandre Lesueur (1778–1846). Lesueur travelled to Australia in 1801 as part of the French journey of exploration and discovery led by Nicolas Baudin on the *Géographe* and *Naturaliste*. Baudin's journey played a unique role in South Australia's history—on 8 April 1802, *Géographe* met up with Matthew Flinders in his ship, *Investigator*, in Encounter Bay, near Victor Harbour.

There are enchanting synergies between the collecting, sampling and botanical investigations of Lesueur's watercolours and Farrant's contemporary porcelain sculptures, *Flotsam and Jetsam, 2012*. Farrant scours her local beach, Port Willunga, for a range of natural and man-made debris, from which she creates her slip-cast components. These delicate porcelain casts are then constructed to produce specimens of both the indigenous and introduced plant forms of the region. For the native plant specimens, Farrant includes casts of organic material such as sticks, shell and cuttlefish bone; and for the noxious species, she collects what she describes as the 'jewel-like beach rubbish' of brightly coloured plastic bottle lids, children's confectionery containers and tennis balls.

Margaret Hancock Davis

Flotsam and Jetsam,
2012
slip cast porcelain
420 x 120 x 100mm

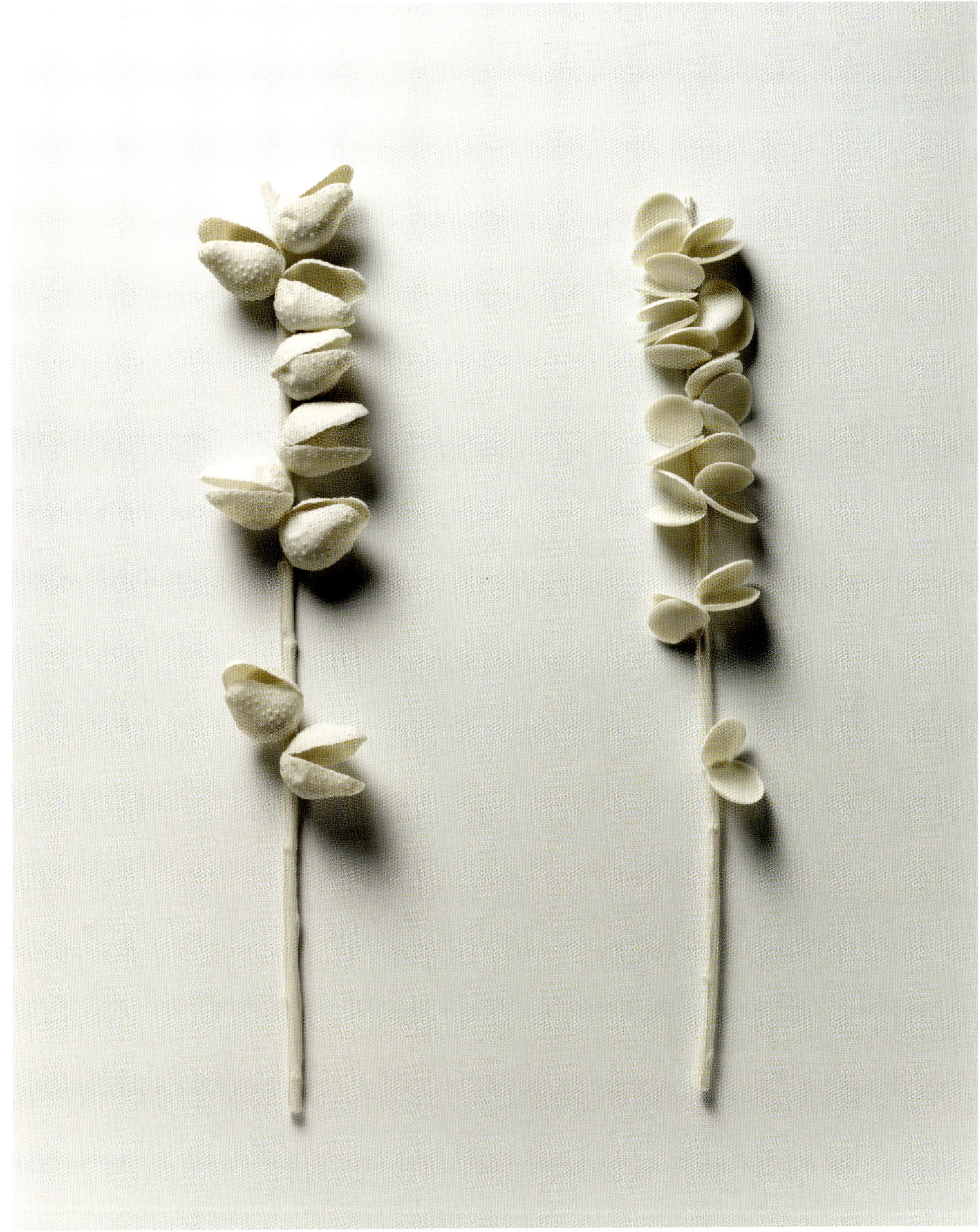

HONOR FREEMAN

born 1978, Glenelg, SA
lives in Adelaide, SA

Honor Freeman joined the Associate training program in 2002 after completing a Bachelor of Applied Arts (Honours) at the University of South Australia. She is an accomplished ceramic artist whose work has been consistently recognised for its skill and poetic observations of the everyday. On graduation, her work was selected for *Hatched* (the national graduate exhibition at Perth Institute Contemporary Art, 2003), and has been presented in leading exhibitions, including *Primavera* at the Museum of Contemporary Art, Sydney (2007), and *Snap freeze: still life now*, at Tarrawarra Museum of Art, Victoria, (2007).

While Freeman was an Associate at JamFactory, Neville Assad-Salha was the Ceramic Studio's Creative Director. Honor describes Assad-Salha as 'energetic and enthusiastic, he bounced about the studio doing high kicks and gesticulating wildly and passionately ... I really appreciated and benefited from the freedom he gave the Associates to find their own way to run their practice.'

On completion of her Associateship, Freeman became an access tenant of the studio for two years. The Ceramics Studio is designed to provide dedicated studio spaces for a mix of artists. Ranging from emerging to established artists, these access tenants form a valuable peer-to-peer support network. Freeman believes that this unique opportunity, working alongside artists she had long admired, helped her improve her skills and extend her ceramic knowledge.

The continual making and handling of kilns full of ceramics over her four years at JamFactory gave her a level of material understanding—of the weight of an object, the balance of form, the lusciousness of glaze, the relationship of the foot and the lip to form—which would have taken her a lifetime to build up and acquire if working from her own independent studio.

Working exclusively in porcelain, Freeman's practice includes both production and exhibition pieces. Her limited-run production ranges, *Half full/half empty* and *Warp + weft,* have evolved subtly over time. She may have given them different forms and glazes, but essentially they remain the same as the work she produced as an Associate.

Much of Freeman's work continues to explore the still-life tableau, utilising unpretentious objects to celebrate the overlooked daily moments. Her current body of work also incorporates well-worn phrases and idioms, playfully engaging with metaphors for hope and optimism, ideas of half full and half empty ever present. These one-off exhibition works capitalise on the mimetic qualities of slip-cast porcelain to create objects that shrewdly play with our perception of materiality and making. What once was liquid is now solid, and what is solid may look like liquid or at least refers to liquid. Replicated surfaces and textures are enhanced by Freeman's subtle mix of polished matte finishes, satin glazes and coloured clay bodies, and the recent addition of lustre in works such as *Every Cloud has a Silver Lining*, 2012.

Margaret Hancock Davis

Every Cloud has a Silver Lining, *2012*
slipcast, handbuilt porcelain, silver lustre
280 x 500 x 400mm

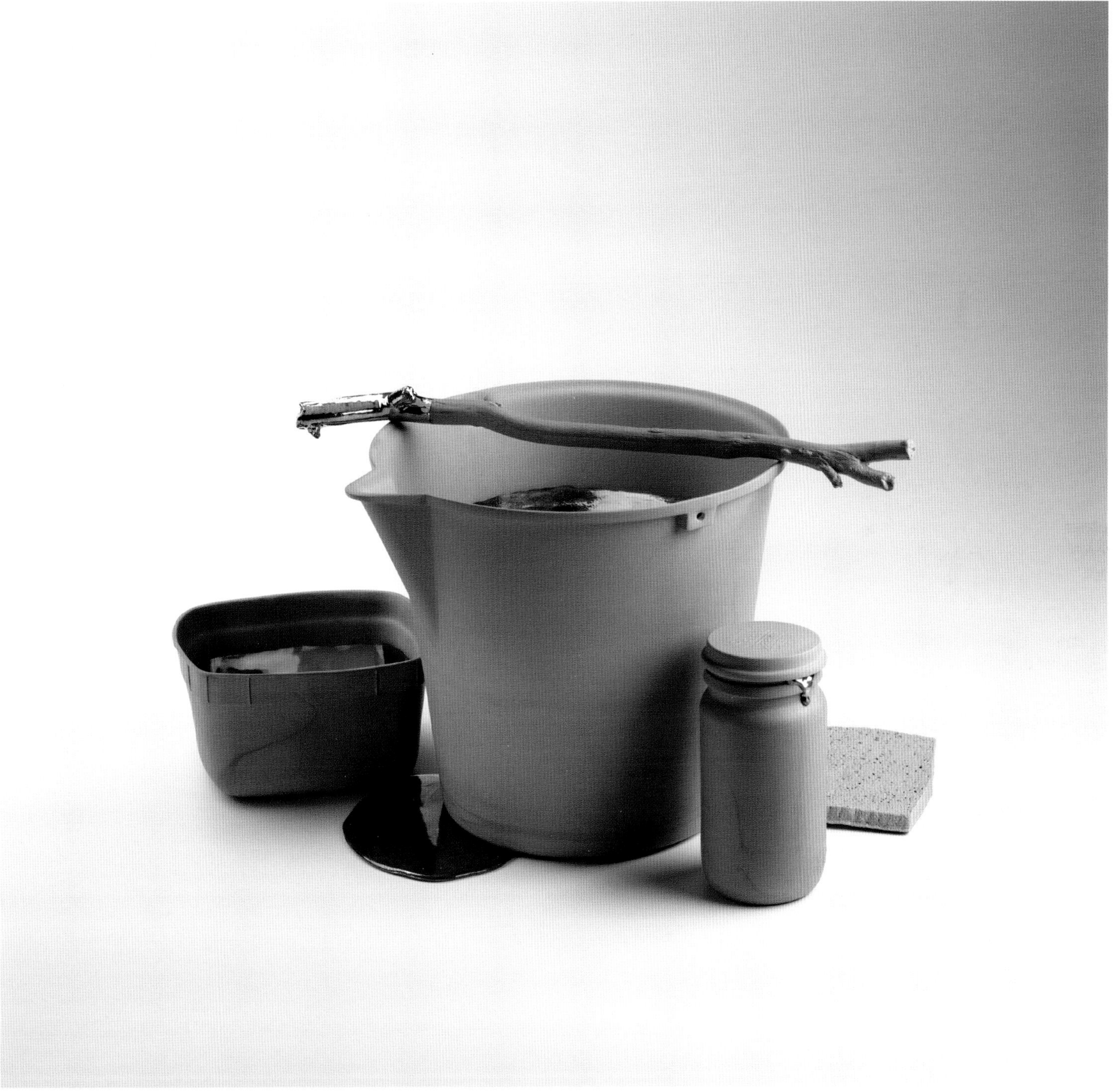

BRENDEN SCOTT FRENCH

born 1969, Toowoomba, QLD
lives in Adelaide, SA

On completion of his Bachelor of Visual Arts at Sydney College of the Arts, in 1998 Brenden Scott French was offered an Associateship in the Glass Studio joining the community of 'glassies' who regularly use JamFactory's hot-shop and cold-working facilities.

Under the creative direction of Elizabeth Kelly, the Associate training program during French's time was not only about working on the hot-shop floor, but also incorporated teachings about the chemistry and capabilities of glass. During this period, Associates regularly experimented with coloured glass pots and a range of new processes in glass manufacture. French remembers:

Liz was visionary. She has a strong design intellect in both product placement and manufacture. Twelve years ago Liz tried to install a lot of the things that are going on now in the studio.

Kelly introduced large-scale manufacturing processes into the studio. Working closely with designers, in particular Robert Foster at F!nk & Co, the Glass Studio developed a range of hydraulic-pressed products. As well as making Studio product, Associates worked on their individual production ranges. French adds:

I had numerous developmental production works while an Associate, one of which, the Meridian range, *has been very successful and I am still making today. Establishing a successful production line gave me a reason to continue blowing glass, to improve my skills and allow my practice to evolve. It provided time to explore technique through repetition and adventure.*

A key part of the Associateship program is the access Associates have to leading international practitioners, through JamFactory's artist- and designer-in-residence program. French credits residencies by German jeweller Karl Fritsch in 1998 and the USA-based Russian ceramic artist Sergei Isupov in 2006 as providing a new level of optimism in his practice. He became keenly aware that his practice was not limited to a studio practice within Australia, and that opportunities were possible internationally.

In recent years, French has focused on developing work for exhibition. This, in part, has been informed by his return to study in 2003 for an Honours degree at Canberra School of Art, and a number of subsequent residencies throughout 2007, including the Stephen Procter Fellowship at Canberra School of Art, and others at North Lands Creative Glass, Scotland, and Canberra Glassworks.

Unlike many glass artists, French is seduced by the opacity and density of colour of the material, rather than its transparency. An innovative glass artist, he uses multiple kiln firings to create his striking painterly effect. Discussing his process, French notes:

I pre-fuse coloured pieces in a kiln. I look at how the glass moves, the flow of it. Then I reassemble it. I construct foreground and perspective by picking out key colours, then I put the pieces back in the kiln and re-fire them. The process is intuitive, something like a mosaic.

Paralleling this layered technique, *Tectonic Trace - Binary #6,* 2012 presents a geological profile of an imagined landscape. Oscillating between a desolate, then pristine, environment, this work references both natural forces and man's impact on our surroundings.

Margaret Hancock Davis

Tectonic Trace – Binary #6
2012
kiln formed glass
1200 x 960 x 40mm

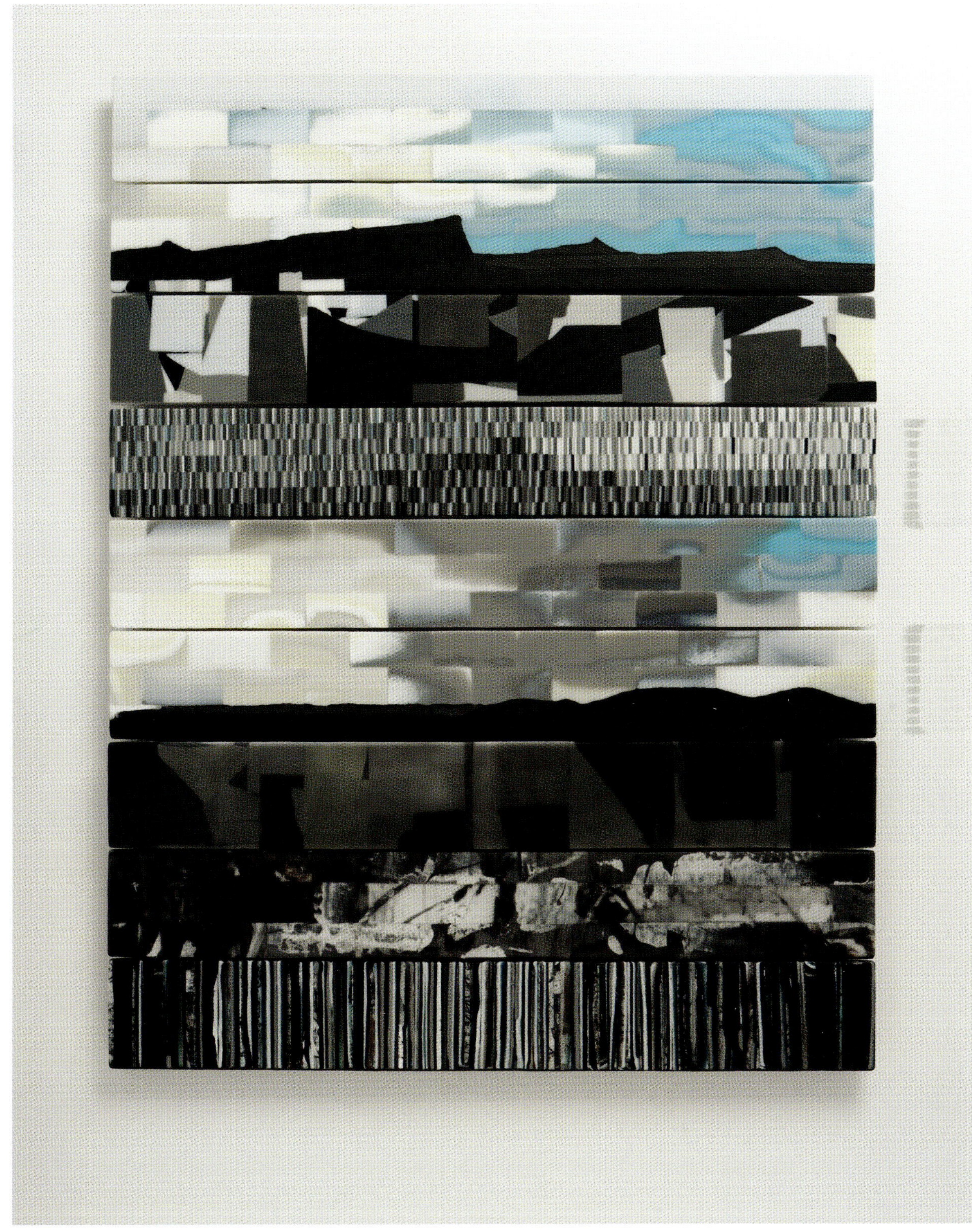

CHRISTIAN HALL

born 1973, Mona Vale, NSW
lives in Adelaide, SA

Christian Hall is an accomplished designer–maker with a particular interest in jewellery and lighting design. Over the past ten years he has exhibited widely in Australia and overseas, including five solo shows in Sydney and Adelaide. He has taught at Sydney College of the Arts, the University of South Australia and TAFE SA and is the current Creative Director of JamFactory's Metal Design Studio.

Hall was a student at Sydney College of the Arts in the mid 1990s when its Object and Jewellery Studio was run by Helge Larsen, Margaret West and Rowena Gough. This formidable trio possessed a deep and extensive knowledge of the history and current state of the jewellery and object scene within Australia and abroad. Hall remembers:

What we were taught was informed not only by academic context, but also a direct personal involvement in a living community. We were taught about the broad range of opportunities that were open to us, and the careers of past students were often offered as examples.

This is how I first became aware of JamFactory, as the Head of the Metal Design Studio at that time was Greg Healey, a graduate of Sydney College of the Arts and former student of Margaret West's. Even as a first year student I was aware of JamFactory and the Associate program as one of a range of options open to graduates.

Some years later, in 2003, while Hall was setting up his Masters Degree exhibition for examination in Sydney, he met with Sue Lorraine, who was then Creative Director of the Metal Design Studio. He recalls:

Sue was looking for potential resident artists. The meeting was brief but important as the following year I was to win my first Australia Council grant to pursue a self-developed residency in JamFactory's Metal Design Studio.

This residency proved to be a pivotal time for Hall personally and professionally—he saw new opportunities for his practice in Adelaide and also met his life partner, Sally Mahony, who was an Associate in the Metal Design Studio from 2004 to 2005. Hall relocated to Adelaide and became a tenant in one of JamFactory's independent studios from 2005 to 2007, and was appointed Creative Director of the Metal Design Studio in 2009.

Under Hall's leadership the studio has delivered challenging commissioned works, conducted innovative educational programs, designed and produced products that contribute to training and revenue generation, and helped solidify the careers of some outstanding Associates. One of the stand-out achievements is the Creative Education Partnership, Artists in Schools project, which Hall ran throughout 2010–11 with members of the Metal Design Studio and Gilles Street Primary School, with significant funding through the Australia Council. This project has been lauded by state and federal bureaucrats within arts and education as an exemplary model.

For this exhibition Hall has specifically developed a dynamic new lighting piece, about which he states:

Spectrum One and Two is a work that continues my interest in metal craft and object making, specifically as it relates to light and the built environment on a domestic scale. The underlying motive for this work was to begin to approach the question of how one might build a rainbow, hence the development into colour. Made from hand-machined and anodised aluminium, the work explores the potential for simple domestic forms, such as shelves, to function as sculptural objects. One key challenge in the work was to develop a light-driven piece that could exist in all levels of domestic light, from full daylight to darkness, without compromising its sculptural qualities. The language of box and louver answered this as well as producing a formal intrigue of inside and out.

Brian Parkes

top
Spectrum One and Two, *2012*
machine milling, anodized aluminum, light fitting
80 x 680 x 180mm each

Spectrum Two *(detail)*

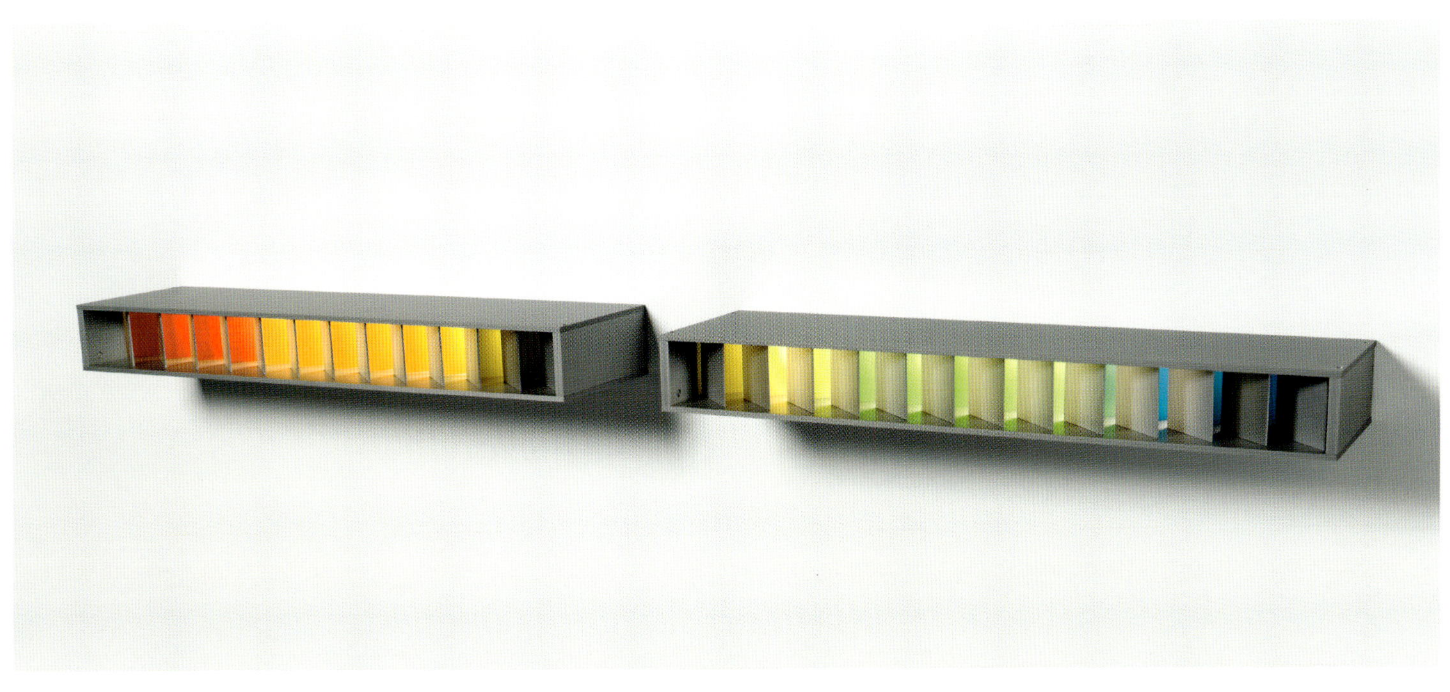

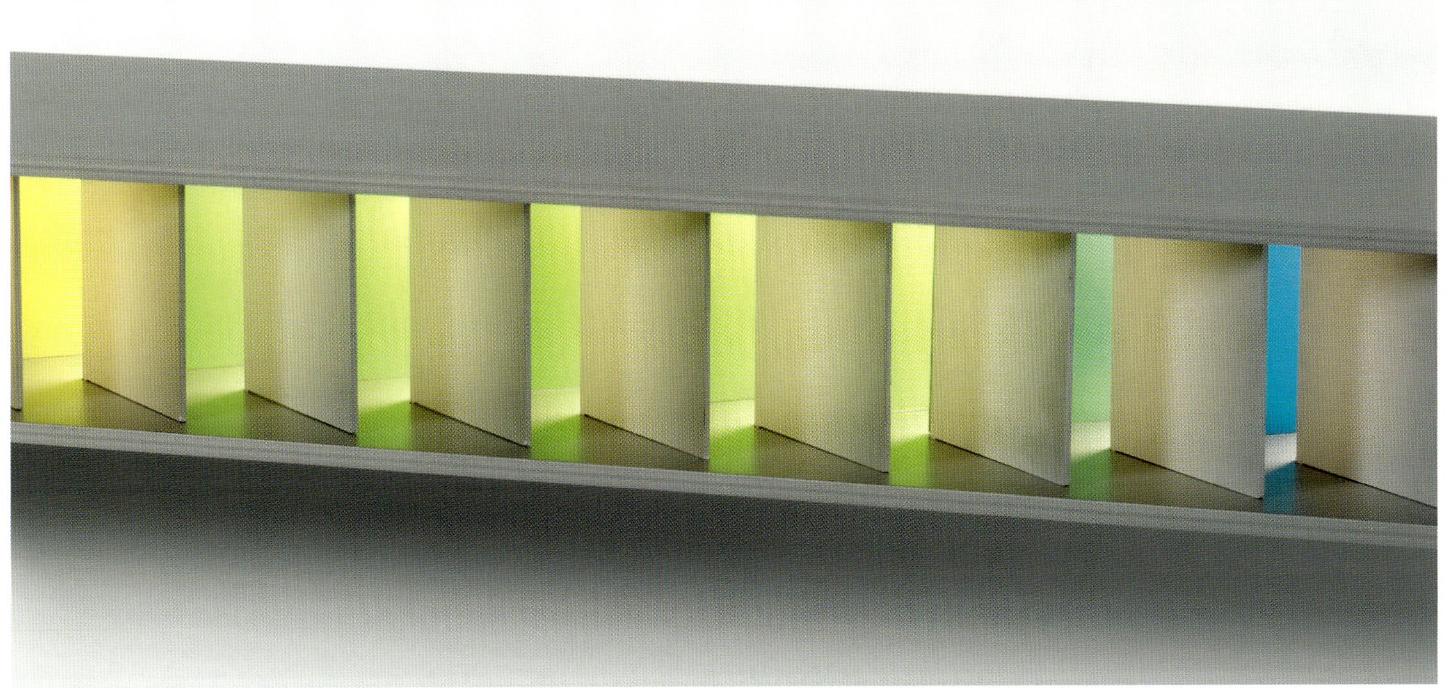

JIM HANNON-TAN

born 1975, Santiago de Compostela, Spain
lives in Amsterdam, the Netherlands

On graduating from RMIT with a Bachelor of Industrial Design, product designer Jim Hannon-Tan packed his bags and headed to Milan. Immersing himself in this hub for industrial design, he developed designs for Magis while working at Jozeph Forakis Design, before returning to Australia to join the Furniture Studio's Associate training program in 2003.

Hannon-Tan quickly made an impression in the studio with his clever designs, such as *Hinge*, 2003. Finding inspiration from an everyday door hinge, Hannon-Tan magnified the mechanism and employed the use of veneered plywood to create a dual-purposed chair/table. The work showcased at *London's 100% Design* as one of the 30 finalist in the international *Designboom, 100% Design Folding Chair Competition*. The Art Gallery of South Australia subsequently acquired the work.

Reflecting on his time at JamFactory, Hannon-Tan notes :

JamFactory gave me hands-on knowledge of materials and processes early in my career, which gave me confidence and enabled me to approach design problems in a more rounded way. It also gave me a chance to experiment with process.

Antarctica bowl, 2004 another of his designs from this time, earned significant attention when it was exhibited at *Salone Internazionale del Mobile di Milan*, 2004. Moving from the hands-on approach employed in *Hinge, Antarctica* manipulated rapid prototyping and mathematical algorithms. Its success encouraged Hannon -Tan to return to Milan, and from 2004 - 2007 he collaborated with designer Sebastian Bergne.

With a goal of one day designing for the famed Alessi brand, Hannon-Tan attended one of its 'ethics in design' workshops in 2007. During this workshop, his inspiration came from unique behaviours he had experienced in his travels. As he recalls:

I was sitting at the kitchen table with some friends in front of a bowl of walnuts, with no nut cracker. I went off to invent an improvised solution and finally returned with a hammer, amazed to find my Italian friend effortlessly splitting the walnuts open with his dinner knife.

Further research revealed that farmers and foresters open walnuts with both hands, using a small hole punch. His version of a hole punch was the elegant, investment cast *Nut Splitter*, 2008. This low-cost gift is now part of the Alessi range and has proven to be highly successful, with over 60,000 units selling in its first year of manufacture.

During the development of his design, Hannon-Tan was able to meet with some of Alessi's leading designers, and as a result he worked in the studio of Stefano Giovanni from 2007 to 2010 on designs for both Alessi and Magis.

Hannon-Tan's second product for Alessi, the *Piccantino Chilli Scruncher*, 2009, again drew upon his keen observations of daily rituals.
He notes:

Italians tend to crumble dried whole chillies into their pasta sauce. I found whenever I did this I would always get burned by the residual chilli on my fingertips. With this clear problem in mind, I set about conceptualising a solution.

The flexibility of the chilli scruncher's rubber enables one to crush chillies without contact. The prototype testing created quite a stir:

At one point in the project I visited Alessi at their factory in Crusinallo, Italy to review the prototypes. They had supplied a bag of dried chilli with which we could test the different models sitting on the table in front of us. We discussed various aspects of the design ... the form, the colour, the usability, the hardness of the silicon ... but very quickly the meeting disintegrated into sneezes and burning eyes as the chilli diffused itself across the room. It was hilarious, people just went off in different directions with no explanation, just to get away from the pain ... thus completely validating the functionality of the product.

In 2010, Hannon-Tan moved to Amsterdam to join leading Dutch designer Marcel Wanders' studio.

Margaret Hancock Davis

top
Piccantino Chilli Scruncher, *2010*
silicon rubber, stainless steel
90 x 30mm dia.

Nut Splitter, *2008*
cast stainless steel
35 x 40 x 4mm

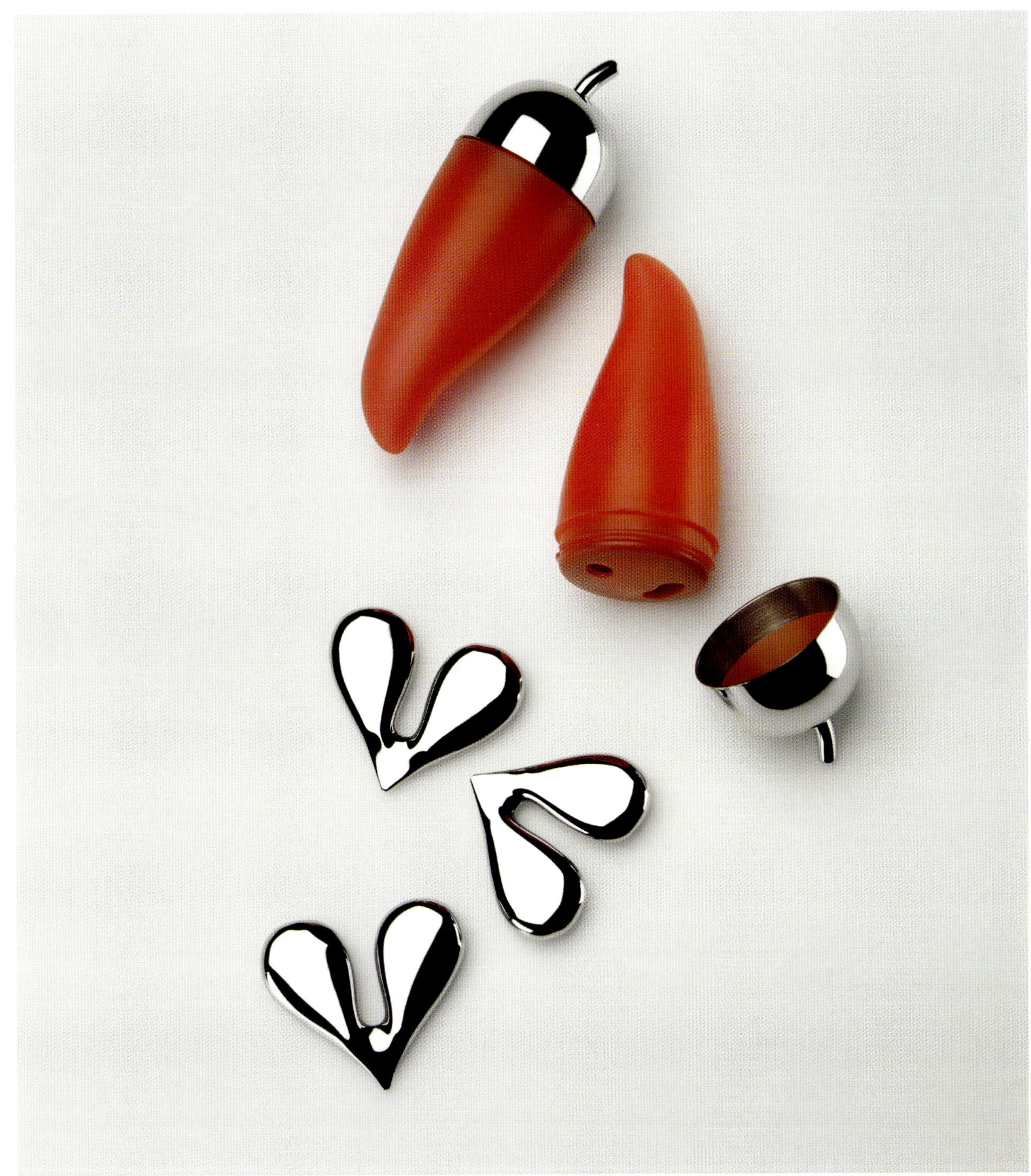

GREG HEALEY

born 1963, Washington DC, USA
lives in Adelaide, SA

Like so many of the artists associated with JamFactory's Metal Design Studio, Greg Healey originally trained as a jeweller and small-object maker. After studying at Sydney College of the Arts, he maintained a solid independent studio practice in Sydney.

Having grown up in the Adelaide Hills and Clare Valley, Healey recalls visiting the Jam Factory on Payneham Road as a young teenager with his mother. He says he 'grew up in a house where we ate from Milton Moon plates and drank from Jam Factory glass tumblers'. Healy's re-acquaintance with JamFactory more than a decade later would be as the founding Creative Director of the Metal Design Studio.

In mid 1991, Frank McBride [JamFactory CEO] visited my studio in Sydney out of the blue. I was wondering why, until he mentioned that the Jam had sold all of the equipment in the Leather Studio in order to get enough funds to establish a Metal Design Studio in time for the 1992 move to the new building in the city. Despite being quite settled in Sydney, I applied for the job. When it was offered to me the next day I told Frank I needed some time to think about it, but the next day flying back into Sydney, I thought 'why not?' and I am still in Adelaide to this day!

Setting up the Studio from scratch allowed me to determine the direction it would take, and I had $30,000 to spend on whatever equipment I thought would be the best to achieve this. With a bit of clever second-hand bargain hunting and attendance at various auctions, the money went a long way at the time. After a frantic six months or so setting up, we then had to start producing income for the studio.

Healey describes the early days of the Metal Design Studio's operation as a baptism of fire, and a great deal was achieved during his three years at the helm. A number of significant large-scale commissions were undertaken, including the magnificent tabernacle at Our Lady of the Sacred Heart Church at Henley Beach and a retail fit-out for Arco shoe shop at Burnside Village. The Studio also developed products for wholesale and retail sale, including picture frames, plate stands and clocks.

Healey's experience at JamFactory had a dramatic impact on his life. It was where he met his wife Belinda Powles—a former Associate of the Metal Design Studio—and where he gained the confidence to up-scale his own practice:

The extraordinary range of activities that I was directing gave me the self-belief to return to my own practice and take on similar commission-style projects, working with other design professionals such as architects and landscape architects—something that I had not done during my ten years in Sydney.

His involvement with JamFactory continued with his appointment to the Board of Directors from 2004 to 2011 including four years as Deputy Chair.

Today, Healey's practice focuses primarily on commissioned works for the public realm. Much of this is undertaken through the art and design consultancy Groundplay, which he established with graphic designer Gregg Mitchell in 2009. The *Link Figure* featured in this exhibition was designed by Groundplay, as part of a suite of 21 galvanised steel figures and interpretive graphic panels for a section of the Mike Turtur bikeway (a shared path running alongside the tramline from the Adelaide CBD to Glenelg). Responding to the public art commission brief, the work evokes themes of playfulness and energy.

Brian Parkes

Link Figures (Child and Dog), *2012*
Public artwork for the Mike Turter bikeway, galvanised steel, painted acrylic
child 1375 x 850 x 260mm (each)
dog 730 x 800 x 290mm

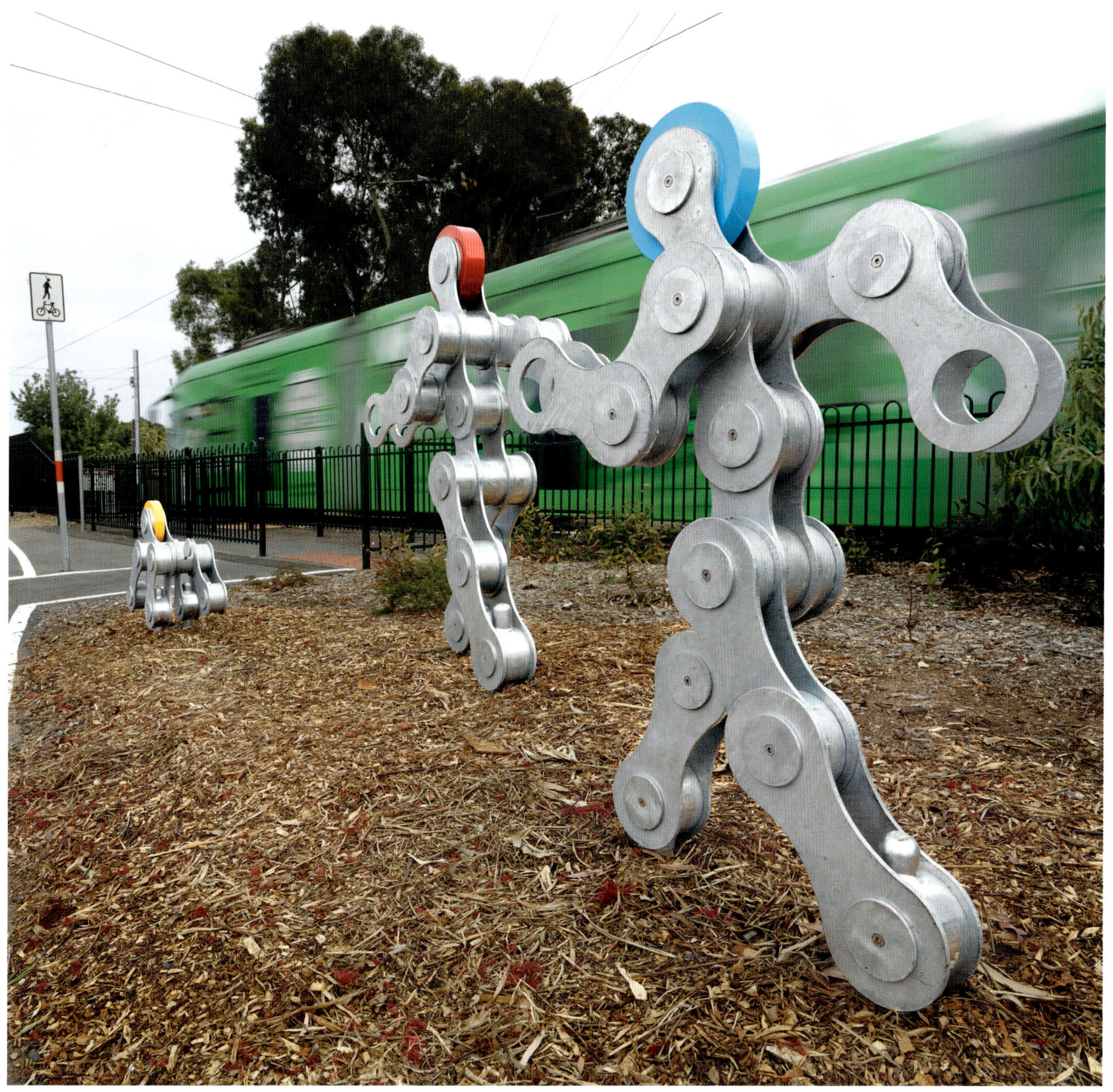

ILLUMINI

Karen Cunningham, born 1978, Adelaide, SA
Mandi King, born 1982, Columbus, Ohio, USA
both live in Adelaide, SA

illumini is a design and business partnership between glass artists Karen Cunningham and Mandi King, who are both alumni of JamFactory's Associate training program. illumini evolved from a Glass Studio special project in early 2010, in which Cunningham and King were experimenting with the potential of collaborative design in finding new markets for studio glass. Since then, illumini products have been exhibited nationally and internationally and are now stocked by high-end retailers in Melbourne, Sydney and Adelaide. They have said that:

It is our strong belief that we are part of a movement of young artists who are actively re-imagining the bridge between the worlds of design and craft through our work. Our wares demonstrate successful balances of the best sensibilities that both approaches of making have to offer: intimate and intuitive understanding of material combined with fluency in the clean visual language of contemporary design.

Both artists have been committed weekly users of JamFactory's hot-glass facilities since commencing their Associateships in 2006. King originally found out about JamFactory while researching Australian glass artists during her final year of college in New York. She noticed that many of her favourite artists, such as Clare Belfrage, Gabriella Bisetto and Deb Jones, had been through the JamFactory program, and soon after committed to moving to Adelaide to become an Associate herself.

For Cunningham, JamFactory had been a highly visible option for her as a student majoring in Glass at the University of South Australia, and she regularly visited JamFactory to watch and learn from the community of artists that utilise the Glass Studio. As an Associate at JamFactory, she received JamFactory's Pilchuck Scholarship (which took her to Seattle to the world-renowned Pilchuck Glass School where King had also attended on a scholarship from New York the previous year) and had the opportunity to undertake a master class with Gijs Bakker (co-founder of Droog) as part of the Xperiment Design Symposium in Adelaide. This latter experience opened Cunningham's eyes to the broader world of design, and in 2008 she won the Qantas Spirit of Youth Award, enabling her to undertake a mentorship with expatriate Australian designer Marc Newson in London in 2009. At the beginning of 2012, Cunningham was appointed Creative Director of JamFactory's Glass Studio.

In addition to bridging notions of craft and design, illumini is also underpinned by a philosophy of sustainability—both minimising the environmental impact of studio glass production (through, for example, finding creative ways to offset rising energy costs involved with manufacture), and creating work for local emerging craft artists and designers. The material selection and production process for the illumini lights featured in this exhibition reflect these particular interests:

The Holey lights *were first prototyped in early 2011 as a part of the Glass Studio's Special Projects program. We challenged ourselves to experiment with the use of glass as a strictly compositional element within a new design. We hoped to create different contexts of thinking about studio glass outside of the traditional categories of vases, decorative sculpture and tableware.*

The resulting ambient nightlights are composed of hand-sculpted, recycled scrap plywood and water-jet cut glass. The lights strike a distinctive balance of form and material with contour and light, achieved through an innovative combination of traditional and high-tech fabrication techniques in woodworking and computer routing. The intricately textured layers of laminated plywood and the soft diffusion of cool LED-light through etched glass, give the lights an extra-dimensional quality, while remaining deceptively simple in functionality.

Brian Parkes

left
Holey light 1, *2012*
laminated plywood, etched and sandblasted float glass, light fitting
160 x 240 x 80mm

Holey light 2, *2012*
laminated plywood, etched and sandblasted float glass, light fitting
360 x 360 x 80mm

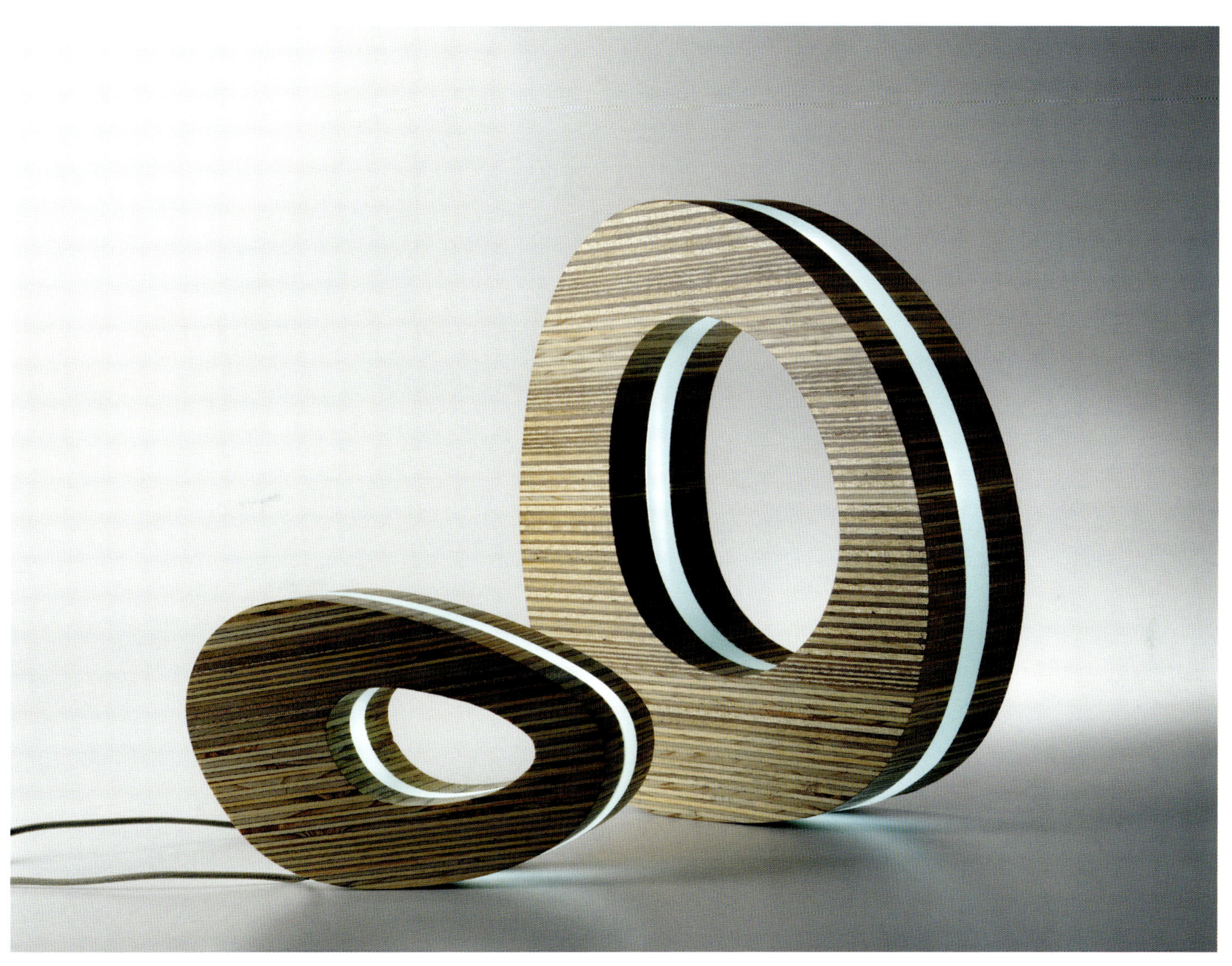

KATH INGLIS

born 1975, Adelaide, SA
lives in Adelaide, SA

After graduating from the South Australian School of Art, University of South Australia in 2000, Inglis spent a year at the renowned Gray Street Workshop before starting an Associateship with JamFactory Metal Design Studio in 2002.

Inglis relished her time in the Metal Design Studio, working on large-scale public art projects such as the Lyell McEwin Hospital *Dandelion Garden* with fellow Associates Sim Luttin and Katrina Freene. When working on such projects, Associates are involved in all areas of the project from the concept development, budget consultations, project presentation, through to manufacture and installation of works. Working on projects of this scale gave Inglis the confidence to undertake public artwork projects post JamFactory, such as the Glass Doorknobs and Wall Brooches on the Adelaide Botanic Gardens Amazon Waterlily Pavilion, with Naomi Schwartz.

Inglis exhibits regularly with her work showcased in leading national touring exhibitions including *Tinker Tailor Soldier Sailor* (2011- 2013) as well as three of JamFactory's international exhibitions *Two Degrees South* held at Fingers Gallery, Auckland, New Zealand (2004), *Flipside* at Velvet da Vinci, San Francisco, USA (2008) and *Southern Stars : Northern Lights* at Bluecoat, Liverpool, UK (2009).

Alumni of JamFactory regularly highlight the benefits of meeting likeminded and committed practitioners, many of whom became lifelong friends, collaborators and mentors. One connection for Inglis was the relationship developed between her and fellow jeweller Naomi Schwartz. Schwartz was a tenant in Studio 7 with Lauren Simeoni while Inglis was an Associate. Having similar courage, ambition and a shared work ethic, Inglis and Schwartz took a leap of faith and established their own studio and gallery space in North Adelaide. Opening soda and rhyme in 2005 was one of the greatest achievements flowing from her time at JamFactory. The space ran successfully until 2010, when it was wound up due to the committments of young families.

Inglis's signature material is the prosaic polyvinyl carbonate (PVC), which she skilfully manipulates into patterned and faceted jewel-like brooches, earrings, bangles and necklaces. The inspiration for her jewellery initially came from a chance encounter in 2001, during a trip to her local supermarket, where she noticed the beautiful way in which the sunlight reflected on the surface of a roll of PVC. Instantly it provoked her to explore this plastic as a potential material for jewellery.

Dyeing and cutting the PVC, Inglis has created a language of production that defies the suppleness and flexibility of the plastic. Her works seem static, even hard, like cut glass—the optical illusion is enhanced by the play of light through the work. Her deft ability to cut the PVC sheets, removing only the smallest amount of material, creates surface textures on which light plays, creating brilliant prisms of colour when worn.

Having a production range was one Inglis's aims while at JamFactory, and her *Skin Deep* bangles, originally developed for an exhibition at Zu Design in 2001, have been in production ever since. In subsequent bodies of work, She continues to push the material, creating works that form a self-portrait of concerns and issues.

In describing the work for the exhibition Inglis notes :

Damn It, *2012 is a play on words... To dam a river and to damn a river. In this work I am referencing the South Australian Government's proposed course of action to construct a weir at Wellington during the height of the drought to limit the flow of water into Lakes Alexandrina and Albert.*

Margaret Hancock Davis

Damn It, *2012*
hand-cut and coloured PVC
3 x 400 x 150mm

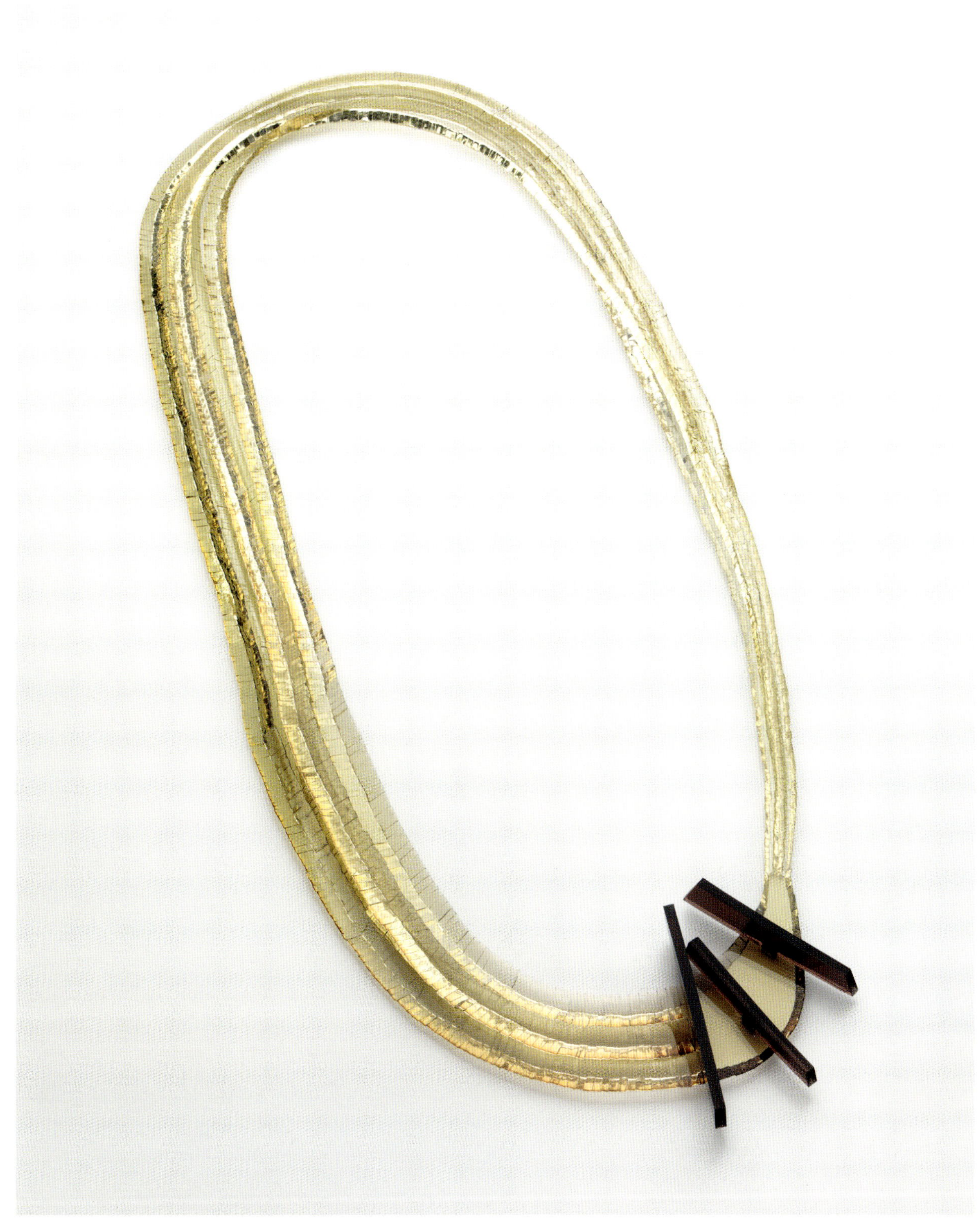

TAKESHI IUE

born 1980, Osaka, Japan
lives in Adelaide, SA

Takeshi Iue is a South Australia-based furniture maker and product designer. He came to JamFactory as an Associate in the Furniture Studio in 2006, after gaining a Diploma of Art (Furniture Design) at TAFE SA, and Bachelor of Visual Communications (Graphic Design) from the University of South Australia.

With simplicity as a guiding principal, Iue creates pared-back designs that contradict the complexity of their construction. Working from sketches, models and prototypes, each of his designs undergoes an exacting series of iterations. Slowly refining angles, shape and shadow lines, his thoughtfulness allows him to create sophisticated, timeless furniture.

Many of Iue's designs hint at his Japanese heritage, employing techniques reminiscent of origami folds and traditional packaging. However, in *East* chair, 2012 and its precursor *Habit* chair, 2007, Iue was intent on designing a Western-style dining chair. Realising the design potential of the back of a dining chair, Iue has shaped a series of intersecting subtle curves and angles that when placed around a table, create a harmonious screen.

During his Associateship, Iue was involved in studio commissions, including a suite of furniture for Forestry SA's head office in Mt Gambier. This was the first major commission for the newly reopened studio, and consisted of a boardroom table, meeting-room tables and a reception counter. Reflecting on the process, Iue notes:

Forestry SA was my first involvement with such a large-scale commission. My fellow Associates and I were all part of the team, working together on all stages of the project, from the first concept drawings, through construction, delivery and installation of the works. As part of the studio I was able to work on projects that were of a scale unachievable if I was simply working as an independent practitioner. The ability to share ideas, and to discuss concepts and processes with a group of designers was one of the great benefits of being an Associate at JamFactory.

On completion of his Associateship, Iue continued to work from JamFactory's independent studios for a further four years. During this period he participated in a number of exhibitions, including three group exhibitions; *Resource Re-Source* (2009), and *Credenza Credentials* (2010), at JamFactory and the 2010 Australian Design Museum exhibition at Shapiro Gallery, Sydney.

Acknowledged by his peers and industry, Iue was awarded the 2008 VIVID competition Green award at Furnitex for his *Bamboo* nesting table, 2008, and his *Autumn* stool, 2007 was selected as part of the Matilda presentation of Australian design at *London Design,* 2011.

In 2009 leading South Australian furniture designer Khai Liew invited Iue to join his team of talented cabinet-makers. With a shared passion for a minimalist aesthetic and attention to detail, working for Liew has enabled Iue to further hone his skills as maker of furniture of a refined beauty.

Margaret Hancock Davis

East chair, *2012*
American white oak
800 x 450 x 600mm

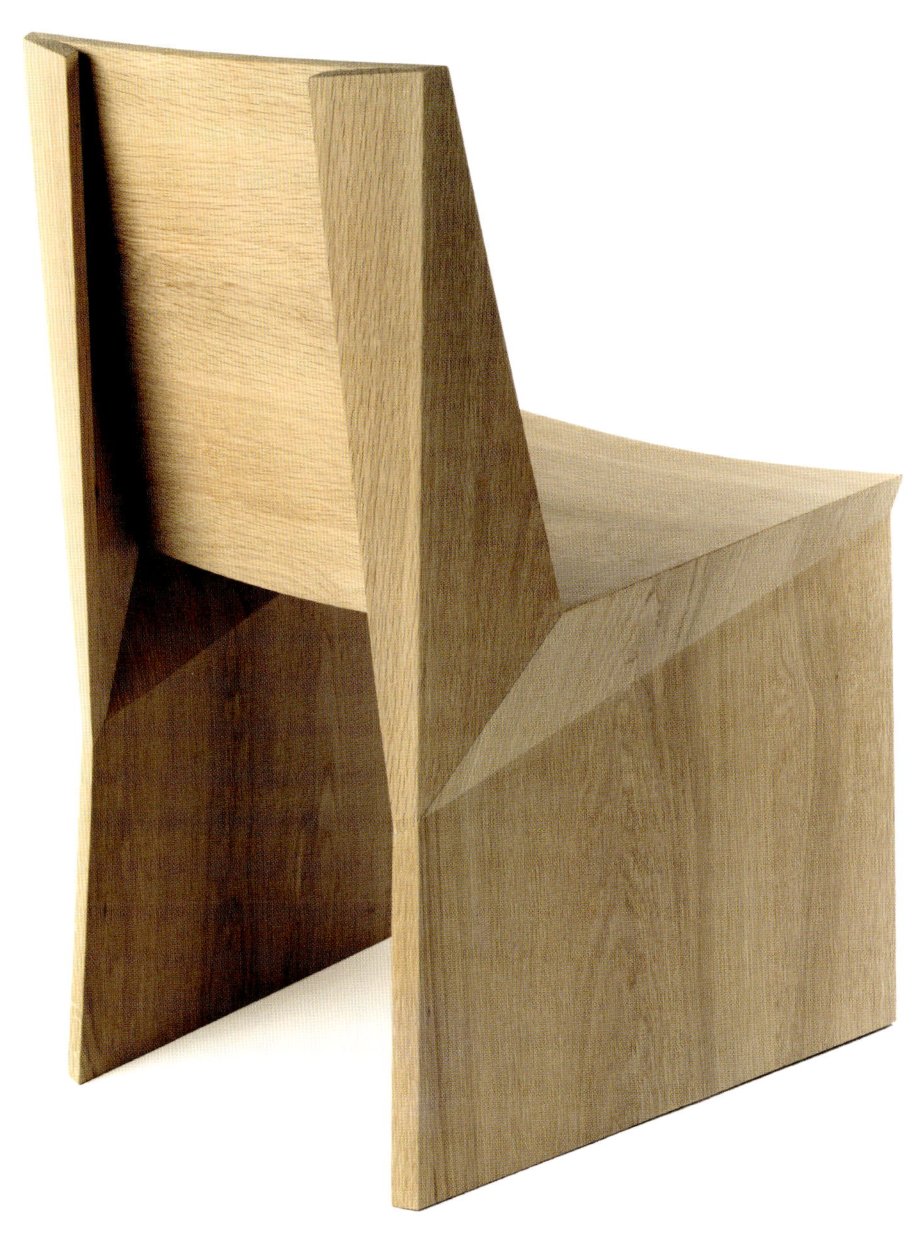

STEPHANIE JAMES-MANTTAN

born 1967, Penrith, NSW
lives in Adelaide, SA

After completing a Bachelor of Arts at Adelaide College of the Arts, Stephanie James-Manttan joined the team in JamFactory's Ceramics Studio in 2007:

Coming to the end of doing my degree at Adelaide College of the Arts in 2006, I had the daunting task of trying to establish my arts practice. Ceramics requires a lot of discipline, practice, a good educated eye and expensive equipment. I felt I still had a lot to learn and being isolated in my backyard shed wasn't going to help. Having done my bachelor degree internship in the Ceramics Studio, I understood how I could benefit from being at JamFactory. I would have all the equipment I needed at my fingertips, I would be exposed to industry leaders both nationally and internationally, and I'd seen how those who had done the Associate program excelled in their chosen field.

James-Manttan fondly remembers the skill, focus and ingenuity of Phil Hart, the studio's Creative Director during her first year as an Associate. She reflects:

When I started at JamFactory, I wasn't a wheel thrower, I would sit there and watch Phil throw these huge platters and pull handles on mugs effortlessly, which, believe me, takes many years of practice. He is an amazing drawer, which can be seen in the inlay and slip trailing on his sophisticated shaped bowls and teapots. Phil was very honest and educated us on form and practice, practice and more practice.

During James-Manttan's second year at JamFactory, Robin Best was appointed Creative Director of the Ceramics Studio. Best, who had previously been instrumental in the establishment of the ceramics studio at Ernabella Arts, experimented with a pilot program in the ceramics studio of Central Craft, Alice Springs, to engage A<u>n</u>angu Pitjantjatjara artists who had relocated to Alice Springs for health reasons. With seed funding from a community development grant from Alice Springs City Council, Best, James-Manttan and studio tenant Sarah O'Sullivan travelled to Alice Springs to present a series of workshops. The resultant works by Nyukana (Daisy) Baker and Jillian Davey were presented as part of JamFactory's groundbreaking exhibition, *From the Earth: Contemporary Indigenous Ceramics.*

The interaction with the Indigenous artists has a lasting effect on James-Manttan. She recalls that while in Alice Springs she had the opportunity to sit in on an Indigenous women's basket-weaving workshop, during which she became transfixed by how the baskets seemingly grew from nothing and she found comfort in the measure of the repetitive weave. Returning to Adelaide, James-Manttan started to manipulate the unforgiving medium, porcelain, which Best had introduced her to earlier in the year.

Starting with a wheel-thrown form, James-Manttan allows her form to partially dry before she steadily manipulates its supple surface with wooden tools to create indentations. These indentations are rhythmically applied to create an organic weave in clay. Capitalising on the strength and translucency of porcelain, she pushes the material to its extremes to create objects of individual beauty.

Margaret Hancock Davis

left
Indent Vessel, *2012*
wheel thrown, altered porcelain
270 x 230mm dia.

Indent Shallow Form, *2012*
wheel thrown, altered porcelain
141 x 310mm dia.

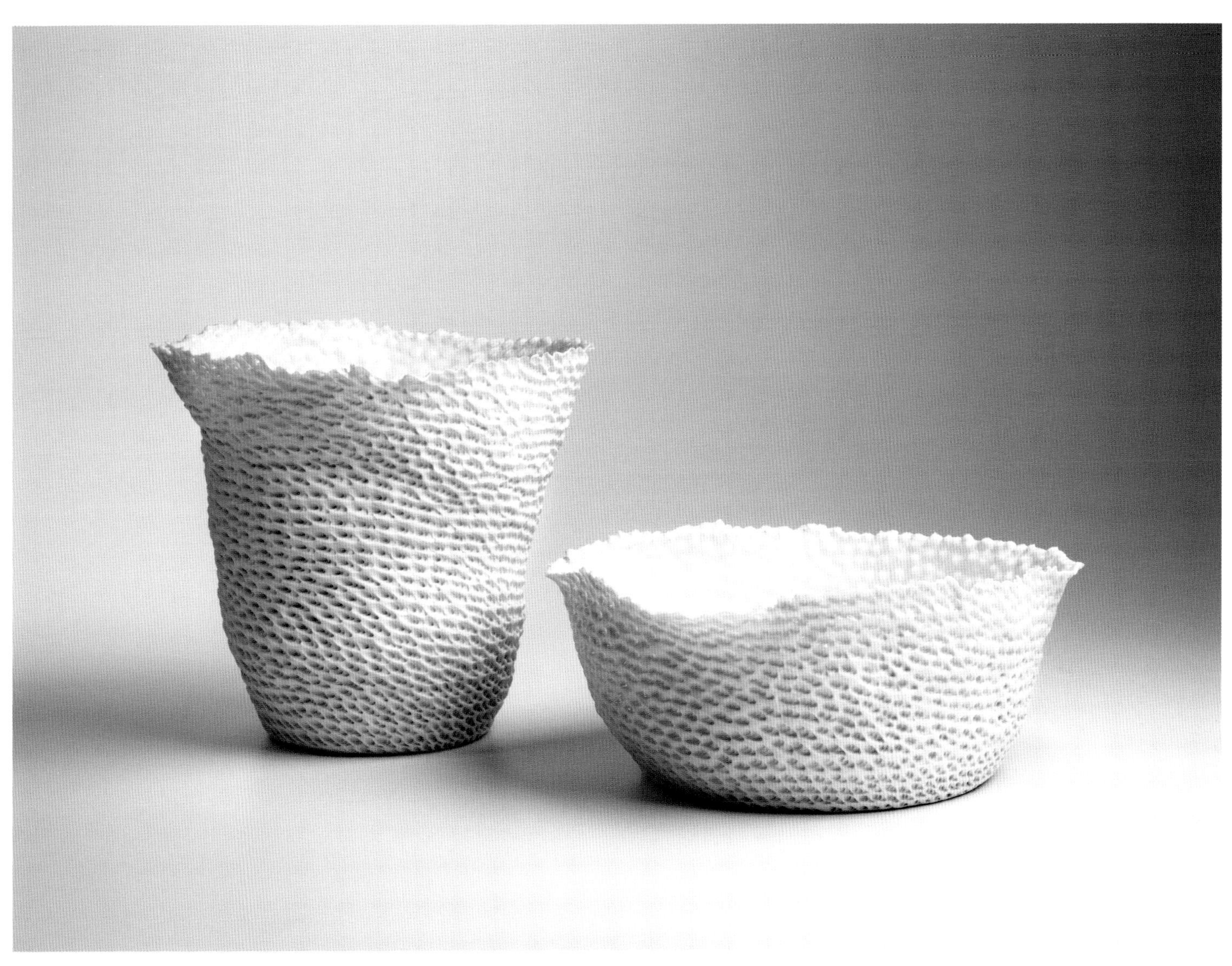

DEB JONES

born 1963, Parkes, NSW
lives in Adelaide, SA

Deb Jones started at JamFactory in 1993 as an Associate in the Glass Studio. Prior to this she had completed a Bachelor of Arts and Graduate Diploma in the Glass Workshop at Canberra School of Art. She has been involved with JamFactory ever since in a variety of roles, including hiring the facilities as an independent practitioner, exhibiting regularly, and being on staff as Production Manager, Commissions Manager, Studio Designer and acting Creative Director. Jones states:

I came to the Jam to spend two years working with glass—day in, day out. It was a good decision. Even though I don't blow a lot these days, working with hot glass helped me understand the material. It also gave me the opportunity to design functional objects, which I love doing ... One of my lucky breaks was when Nick Mount took over the Glass Studio in my second year, 1994. He was a force to be reckoned with, and I was right in there with him. His skills were amazing, his work ethic was profound and if you were prepared to work hard he'd give you the world ... The strength of the Glass Studio program is the opportunity to work factory-style in a repetitive production team. Making wine bottles was always my favourite because I was making something that had a functional practical use, and it allowed us to work very close to tradition ... I started to work part time in the Glass Studio in 2002 and in 2008 I was one of the team who ran the studio for four years. I am now a hirer again. My notion of Adelaide is synonymous with JamFactory.

In 1997 Jones was one of the co-founders of Adelaide's Blue Pony glass studio, where she was based for eight years, while continuing to blow glass at JamFactory. In 2006 she established Gate 8 workshop in Adelaide, with fellow glass artist Jessica Loughlin. She has worked increasingly on public art, architecture and design commissions, including, most recently, glass installations and a water feature sculpture for the Glenside Hospital redevelopment. Other commissions included glass installations for Adelaide City Council, the Adelaide Bus Depot, Appellation at The Louise, Barossa Valley and a joint project with Furniture Studio alumnus, Nico Kelly, for Lyell McEwin Hospital.

Jones's cast glass sculpture, *Support*, 2012 is an exemplar of her minimalist reductionist aesthetic and her ethic of truth to materials. For Jones it is all about minimising her intervention, to let the glass speak and reveal both its inherent properties and the making process. She comments:

I love the relationship between thickness of glass and colour density. I am interested in the inaccessible depth of cast glass. This work, Support, *is another of some maquettes I have been working on, where the glass and structure are intrinsically joined.*

Her major recent exhibitions include *Mind and Matter* (2010, JamFactory and Object, Sydney), and the national touring exhibition *Tour de Force: in case of emergency break glass* (2010–12). Jones's glass is represented in the collections of the Tasmanian Museum and Art Gallery, the National Gallery of Victoria, Artbank and the Parliamentary Library, Parliament House, Canberra.

Margot Osborne

Support, *2012*
cast glass, wood
510 x 265 x 120mm

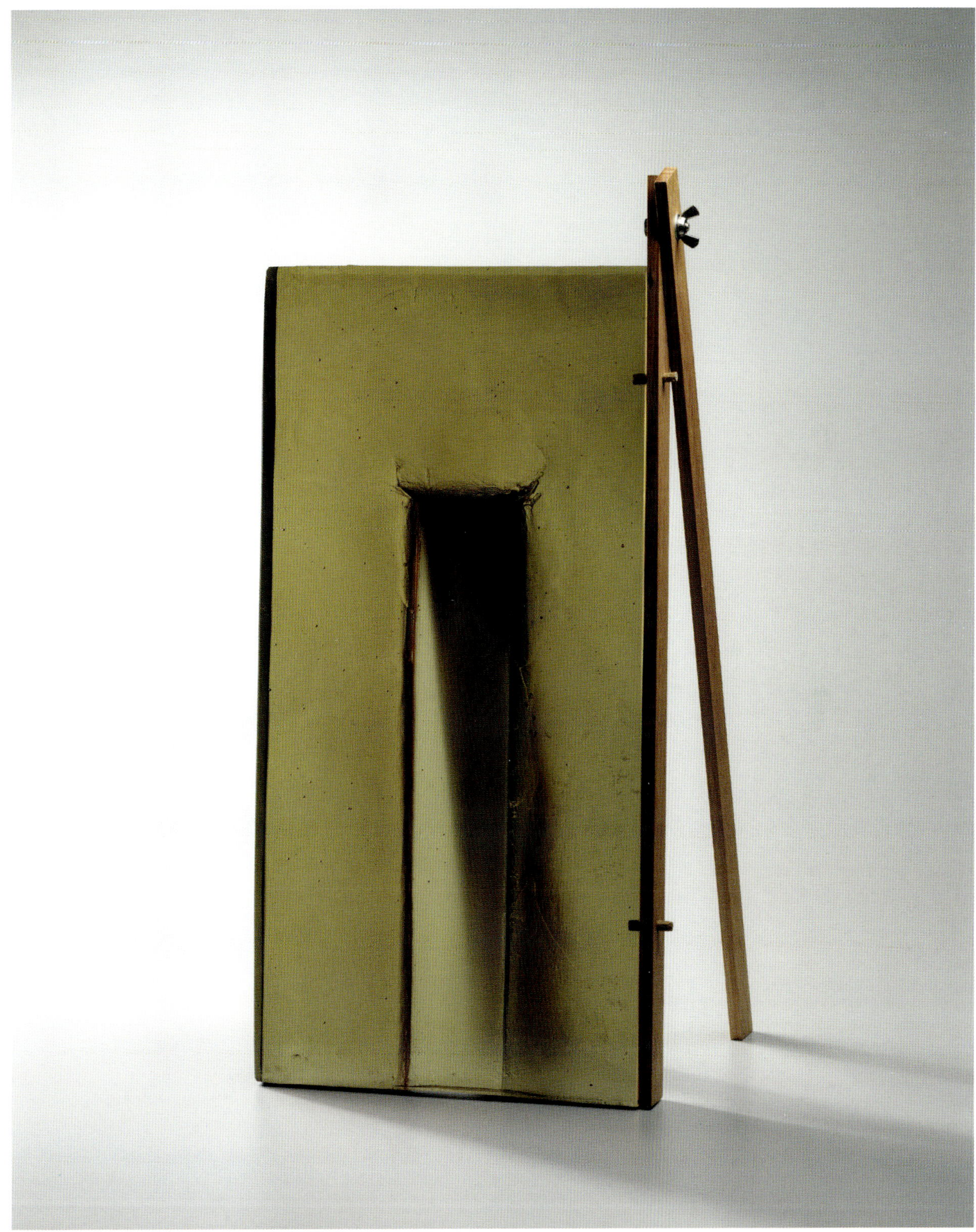

ELIZABETH KELLY

born 1960, Adelaide, SA
lives in Canberra, ACT

Elizabeth Kelly was a trainee in the Jam Factory's Glass Workshop for two years, from 1985 to 1987. After a decade extending her qualifications, first with a Bachelor degree at Canberra School of Art, and then obtaining her Masters degree in Visual Art from Sydney University, she returned to JamFactory as Creative Director of the Glass Studio from September 1997 to December 2000. She recalls:

I had come from an education background, and design theory and art practice were foremost in my recent experience, thus I sought to impart the importance of rigorous design practice into the training program ... The Australia Council funded Press Project was a highlight of my time as Studio Head. I focused on 3D CAD (Solid Works) as a design tool, working collaboratively with tool-makers and other artists. The facility enabled me to investigate industrial design, such as pressing and centrifuge processes, applied to studio glass. I continued the research into colour chemistry that I had undertaken as a Masters candidate at Sydney College of the Arts, and collaborated with other studios in generating a range of different works based on my knowledge of engineering coloured cast glass objects with specific design outcomes.

Close working relationships within a dynamic environment provided conditions to generally raise the bar of standards in the work and outlook of the studio. At times the atmosphere was palpably electric. Training was a key part of the studio operations and I think the most impressive working example was when a large team was operating with professionals alongside trainees, and where interdependence was keenly measured and differences put aside in order to achieve a common commercial goal.

Kelly has paid tribute to the contribution of longstanding Studio Technician Tom Persson, who, over many years, provided invaluable assistance in running the Glass Studio.

She moved to Canberra in 2003 and established her business, Studio Tangerine, to work on commissions with architects and designers in conjunction with her studio practice. Her workshop equipment was purpose-designed for low environmental impact through combustion efficiency and use of recycled materials and industrial waste. She has received a number of significant awards, including a fellowship to the Creative Glass Centre of America, an artist residency in Seto, Japan, a Capital Arts Patrons Organisation Fellowship and, most recently, a Churchill Fellowship. These last two fellowships enabled her to explore the use of cast glass modules to create tower structures.

For this exhibition, Kelly has created an ambitious new sculptural glass tower, *Perilous*, 2012 standing over 2.5 metres tall. This dazzling sculpture extends her recent body of work focusing on glass towers. A major tower sculpture was commissioned for Parliament House, Canberra. *Perilous* is made from a signature shade of purple glass, based on a Studio Tangerine recipe, and includes 50 per cent recycled glass. Kelly engineered the glass components using AutoCAD to model the moulds. She based the patterning on the helical and icosahedral structures of viruses. The modular glass bricks of which the tower is composed are her response to the 20th century hollow bricks that she studied while on her Churchill Fellowship in Europe in 2011.

Kelly's glass is held by major public collections, including the National Gallery of Australia, Parliament House, Canberra, Artbank, Seto Museum, Japan and the Museum of American Glass, New Jersey, USA.

Margot Osborne

Perilous, *2012*
pressed glass
2,700 x 500mm dia.

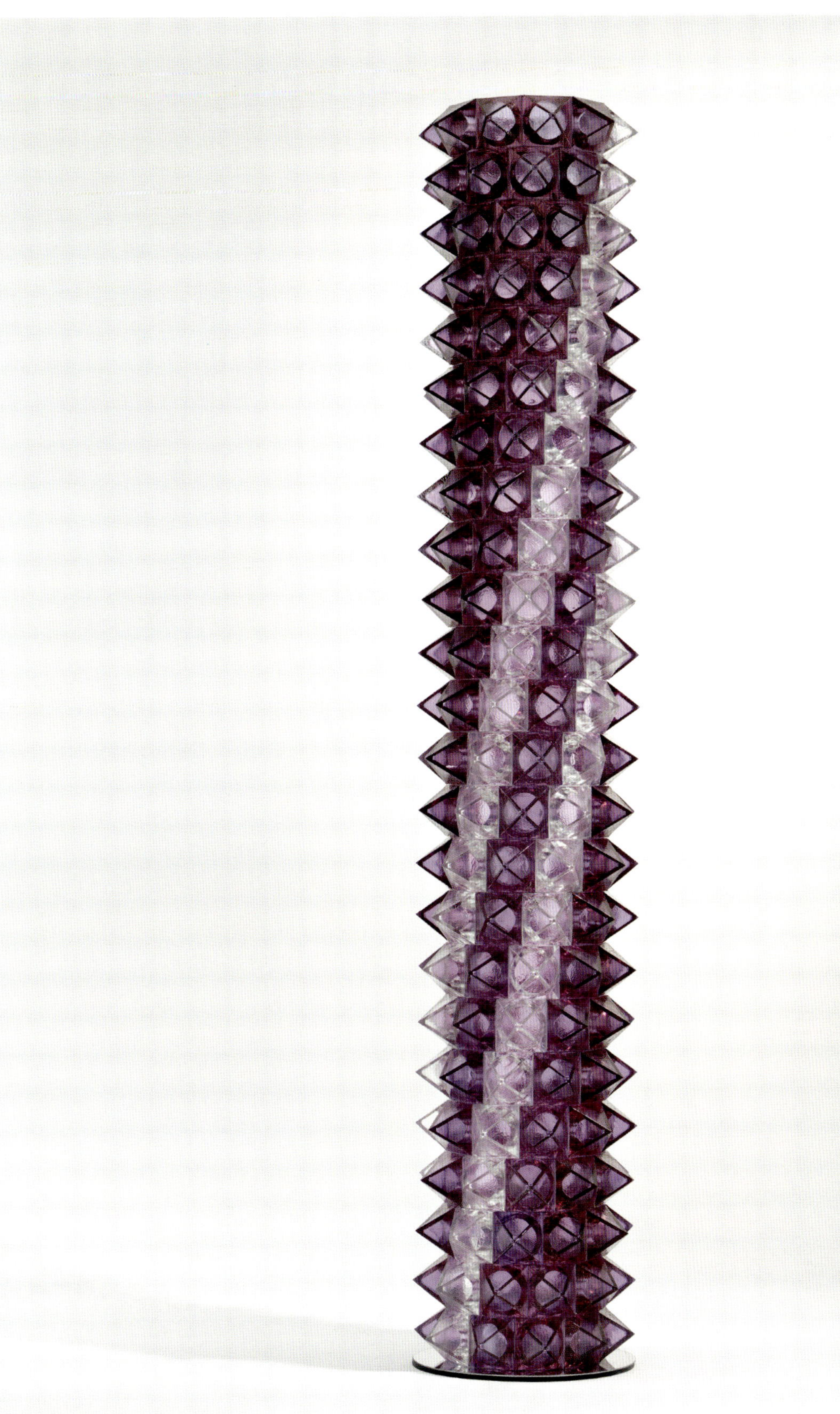

BRONWYN KEMP

born 1952, Broken Hill, NSW
lives in Sydney, NSW

Bronwyn Kemp, alongside Christopher Headley and Peter Andersson, were the inaugural Associates of the Jam Factory's Ceramic Studio in 1979. Under Workshop Head Jeff Mincham, the studio worked steadily to produce one of the Jam Factory's key aims, locally-produced tableware. For Kemp, the Ceramics Workshop was 'definitely a group effort, and a lot of creative energy was generated by the diversity of art making that was happening separately to the production'.

As can occur with any new venture, its participants' expectations may differ and, after several months of focused production work, Kemp left the studio before returning to the Jam Factory in 1980 to take up a rental studio with leading ceramic artists Bruce Nuske and Mark Thompson.

From the late 1970s and early 1980s, Kemp continued to produce her own functional ware and started to make wheel and slab-built sculptural forms decorated with coloured clay as inlays and slips. She experimented with her own clay bodies, and tried new commercial porcelain bodies when they became available.

In 1983 she took over from Jeff Mincham as Head of the Ceramics Workshop and held this position until 1988. During her tenure, Kemp was committed to the training aspect of the JamFactory, regardless of how hard it was to maintain. She remembers vigorous discussions about how training could be retained in a real world/studio model.

During this period the Studio worked very hard on studio production ranges until around 4 or 5pm each day and then, with any energy left, Kemp encouraged her team to work on the development of their own art practice. This sometimes took the form of a separate production line, but most often resulted in individual pieces for exhibition, sculptural works, installations and drawings.

As Phil Hart, one of Kemp's Associates and later a Creative Director of the Studio, reflects:

I was taken on by Bronwyn Kemp as a trainee for 12 months at the old Payneham Road Jam Factory in 1987. A gruelling year of production work lay ahead, along with lots of soul searching and some strange analytical probing. The workshop gang had lots of fun introducing a naive 20-something male to the wider concerns of contemporary art practice, aesthetics and broader social issues of the day. It was really quite a different experience to that which is offered these days. I see myself as fortunate to have experienced this training regime and to have been a part of what nostalgically seems like the halcyon days, sharing the experience with great people: Jo Crawford, Gerry Wedd, John Ullinger, Mellie Stock, Lincoln Kirby Bell and others, Anne Parsons, Freya Povey, Stephanie Livesey, Gary Roberts and of course Bronwyn.

The importance of practitioners continuing their individual practice was clearly confirmed when the then Jam Factory Director Winnie Pelz made the courageous decision to add two local artists—Kemp and textile artist Annabelle Collett—to the British Arts Council touring exhibition *Four rooms* as part of the 1986 Adelaide Festival of the Arts, where it was called *Four Rooms (+ two)*. Devised by Howard Hodgkin, Marc Camille Chaimowicz, Richard Hamilton and Anthony Caro, the exhibition required each artist to design and produce a room, and had premiered in 1984 at Liberty, London, before touring. Kemp relished this opportunity to extend her practice, and produced a highly accomplished, terracotta chicken shed, complete with chickens, chook run and corrugated iron fence covered with inlaid decoration. Politically charged, this work was a response to the exploitation of Asian immigrants and the poor accommodation provided—the shed included a stove, sink and bed.

Inlaid decoration continues to be a feature of Kemp's work today. *Softly Slowly,* 2009 combines her luscious glaze treatment with inlaid decoration to create a work that reflects upon the effects of light and distance in the sprawling Australian landscape.

Bronwyn Kemp's work is held in major collections around Australian and internationally, including the National Gallery of Australia, the Art Gallery of South Australia, Art Gallery of Western Australia, Queensland Art Gallery and the National Gallery of Victoria.

Margaret Hancock Davis

Softly Slowly, *2009*
hand built porcelain, inlaid black slip, glaze
150 x 460 x 130mm

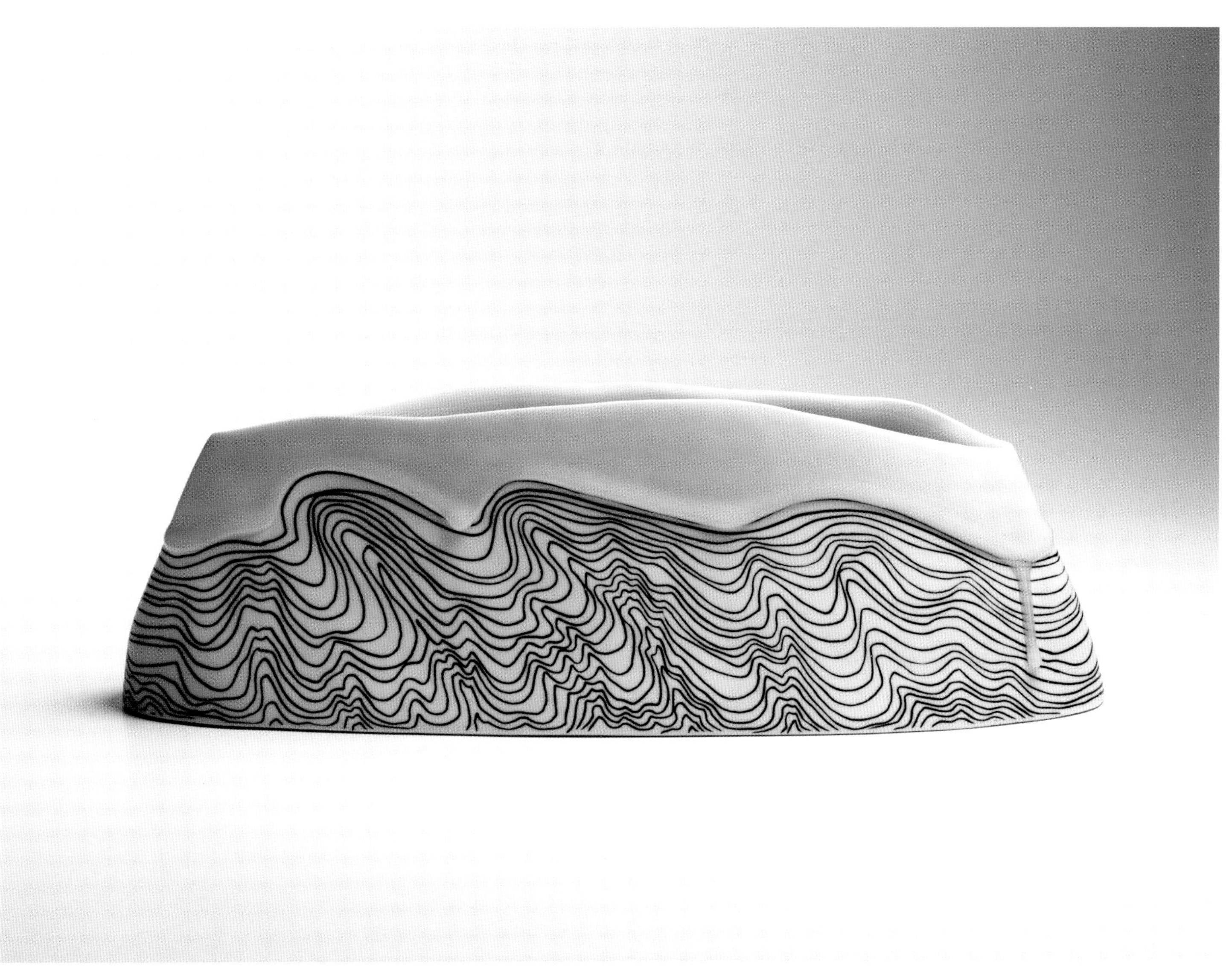

ERIN KEYS

born 1979, Gosford, NSW
Lives in Sydney, NSW

Erin Keys spent two years at JamFactory in 2008–09 as an Associate in the Metal Design Studio. She came to Adelaide after living in Bosnia for a year, and before that graduated in jewellery design from Design Centre Enmore in Sydney, while working as a jeweller's assistant. She regards her time as an Associate as a vital period:

It allowed me the time and space to really hone my skills and create a direction for my arts practice. While I was there I was encouraged to enter many exhibitions and apply for residencies and funding. This built my confidence, my skills and my profile. I made new work for 24 exhibitions during this time, and was handmaking my production line. That resulted in me burning out ... but, the flipside of this was that I was challenged into creating new directions for my work and new ways of making it. I also developed confidence from exhibiting so often, as well as humility when the work wasn't necessarily up to scratch! The social element was fantastic, accessing other creative people and exchanging skills. During this time I was accepted into Talente, *Munich and* Preziosa Young, *Florence as well as developing my own production practice.*

I feel that one's time at JamFactory is more about self-direction and self-motivation than anything else. No-one will ever tell you what to do. I felt challenged and questioned, many times, by what it was that I was doing, but I always felt encouraged to keep going ... Without the space and my own expectations of a result, I would not have my own jewellery design practice today. I probably would have given up!

It was while she was at JamFactory that Keys first evolved her own distinctive style in laser-cut neckpieces, armbands and earrings. Her designs start as intuitive, meandering linear drawings. There is a gestural energy in her drawings, which are imbued with suggestions of a private calligraphy. She scans the drawings and sends the files to be laser-cut in mild steel in Adelaide. A sandblasted and powdercoated finish is then applied. Initially Keys hand-cut her own work, but a minor accident led her to outsource to a laser-cutting company in Adelaide. She realised that the laser was doing a higher quality, more time and cost-efficient job, and since then she has continued to work with the same Adelaide company for the past four years.

Keys now has her own jewellery and design practice at Square Peg Studios in Sydney, selling her work through jewellery design outlets including Zu Design, Adelaide and Studio 20/17 at Danks Street, Sydney.

Margot Osborne

Untitled Necklace #2, *2012*
powdercoated mild steel
1.2 x 200 x 300mm

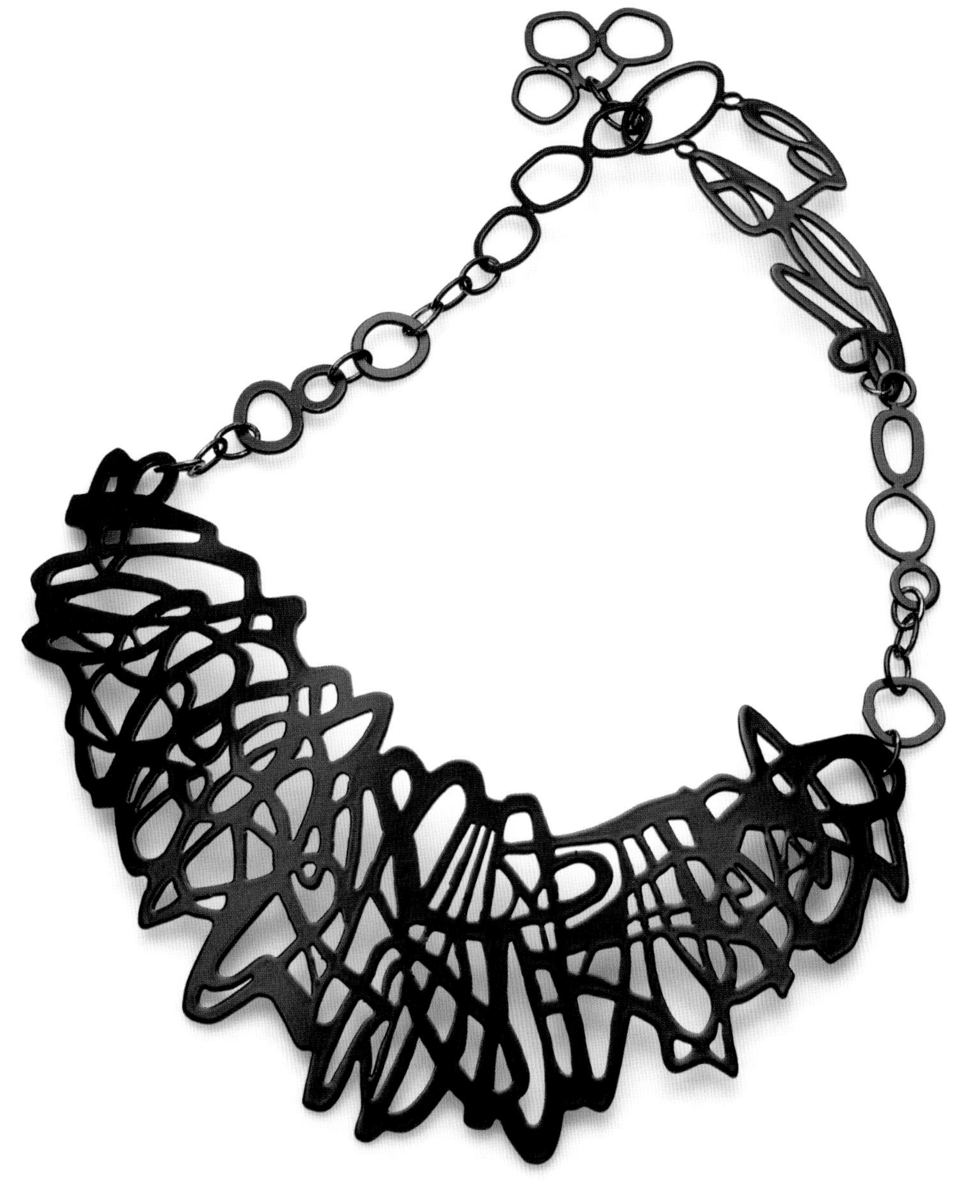

PETA KRUGER

born 1980, Adelaide, SA
lives in Adelaide, SA

After completing a Bachelor of Visual Communication with Honours at the University of South Australia in 2003, Peta Kruger worked as a graphic designer and illustrator. Travelling to London, she worked as an assistant jeweller to Scott Wilson and Jane Adam of Cockpit Arts. The resultant designs by Scott Wilson, which Kruger worked on, were exhibited at the Design Museum, London, as well as being presented at New York, Paris and London Fashion Weeks. Returning home to Adelaide, in 2008 Kruger completed a Bachelor of Visual Arts at Adelaide College of the Arts majoring in jewellery, and joined the team in JamFactory's Metal Design Studio the following year.

Christian Hall was the Creative Director of the studio at that time, and Kruger reflects, 'his advice as a mentor has given me the inspiration and environment to develop a more clever and thoughtful approach to design'.

Under Hall's stewardship, the Metal Design Studio has markedly increased its ability to provide education outcomes for both primary and secondary school students and the general public, through a broad range of workshops and residencies. Teaching workshops and undertaking school residencies enables Associates to further consolidate their skills, and provides important income opportunities throughout their Associateship and into the future. A leading example of these educational programs was the federally-funded Creative Education Partnerships: Artists in Residency Program (CEP), which links professional arts organisations with schools to build relationships between artists, students and teachers.

In 2010, Christian Hall, Kruger and Hannah Carlyle worked with a core group of students at Gilles Street Primary School on a variety of projects, including a range of brooches designed by the student-artists and manufactured and packaged by the Metal Design Studio, plus a large collaborative sculptural work. A further feature of this residency was that the artists introduced students to the skills, practices and ideas of an artist at work. Kruger reflects:

I was thoroughly inspired by the students at Gilles Street Primary School while I was an artist in residence. One of the many facets of this project was that it facilitated a place for my research. We started with a brief: to design a toy. I created a set of building blocks and the students provided valuable critiques—they were very direct and very honest. It created many insightful moments, focusing my attention on some of the finer details of making jewellery, such as collecting all the scrap dust when I cut out shapes from metal, because it looks glittery and beautiful.

Since completing her Associateship, Kruger has remained at JamFactory as an independent studio hirer. This has proven to be a rewarding and inspiring period in her practice, and she has produced work for two solo exhibitions, *Start from Scratch* for the JamFactory's Gallery Two and *This Fool's Gold* for Pieces of Eight Gallery, Melbourne. In 2010, she was awarded the Australia Council's JUMP - national mentoring program for young and emerging artists and received funding from the Ian Potter Foundation to undertake a mentorship with leading contemporary jeweller Karl Fritsch in Germany and New Zealand.

Kruger's current work is inspired by the unique mix of native plants, introduced species and weeds along Adelaide's nature strips. Transforming the humble materials of brass and paint, Kruger creates beautiful brooches inspired by hardy plants, often overlooked in jewellery design's vernacular.

I take great comfort and pleasure in continuing to work with brass. It allows me to cut, bend and stick parts together in a playful and spontaneous way, slowly discovering a collection of shapes and patterns with which I am happy.

I usually start by directly working in metal without many preliminary sketches. I need to be able to turn the work over, feel its weight, look at it from far away and close up, and try it on before I can decide whether it has potential as a finished piece.

Margaret Hancock Davis

top
Geranium, *2012*
brass, paint
60 x 80 x 110mm

Light Green Leaves, *2012*
brass, paint
30 x 50 x 120mm

bottom
Sour Sob, *2012*
brass, paint
30 x 50 x 40mm

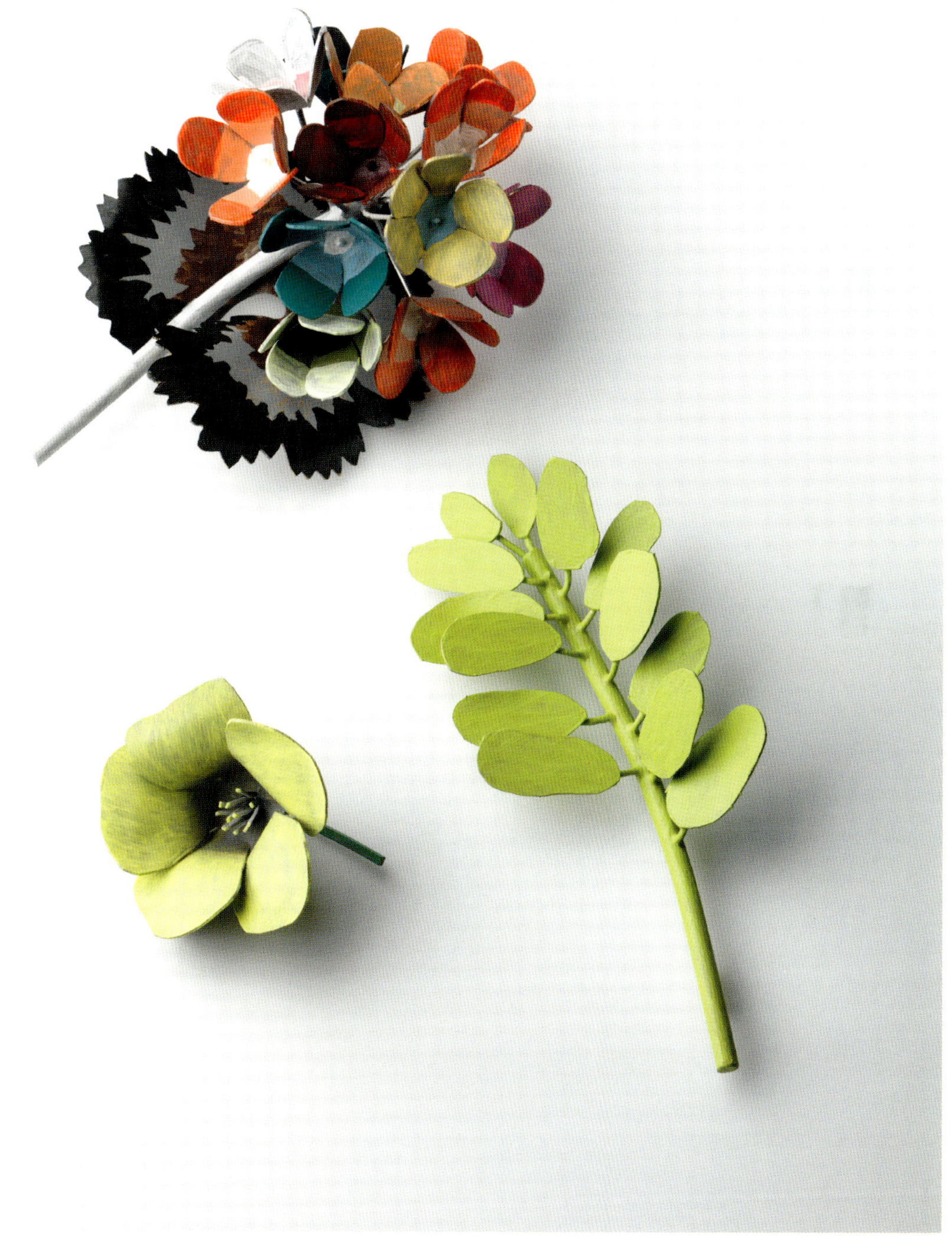

SUE LORRAINE

born 1955, Melbourne, Vic
lives in Adelaide, SA

Sue Lorraine's influence on the careers of emerging jewellers in Australia is not limited by her time as Creative Director of JamFactory's Metal Design Studio. Prior to this, in 1985, Lorraine, Anne Brennan and Catherine Truman established Gray Street Workshop, which has become a model for collectively-run studios both in Adelaide and nationally. To date, more than 90 jewellers from around Australia and overseas have spent time as tenants of the workshop, many of whom were once Associates of JamFactory.

Originally established in Gray Street, Norwood, the workshop has moved several times, and is currently located at Sydney Street, Adelaide. In 1992, the search for new premises saw the then workshop partnership of Lorraine, Truman, Julie Blyfield and Leslie Matthews become tenants in the newly opened purpose-built JamFactory on Morphett Street. Gray Street Workshop remained there until the move to Sydney Place in 1994. Lorraine recalls:

During the time Gray Street Workshop was situated in the JamFactory I concentrated on exhibition work ... making sculptural pieces and objects. I maintained a jewellery production range for local and interstate galleries, and several of these designs are still in production, for instance the Petal brooches *and* Signet rings. *I supplemented my income with a range of part-time jobs, such as setting up exhibitions in GalleryTwo.*

Lorraine became the Creative Director of the Metal Design Studio in 1999. In this role she actively encouraged a dual approach in the studio: firstly as a training facility, providing Associates with the opportunities and support to develop their own studio practice; and secondly as a design and manufacturing unit responding to commissions and retail demand.

She championed the importance of an exhibition practice and provided national and international exhibition opportunities for the Associates and alumni of the Metal Design Studio. Through exhibition work, the Associates were able to explore and consolidate their own distinct styles. The Metal Design Studio exhibited at Fingers Gallery, New Zealand (2005), Velvet da Vinci, USA (2008), Horus and Deloris, Sydney (2005), Studio Ingot, Melbourne (2006), as well as JamFactory's exhibition program.

To provide the Associates with a practical model and to develop their range of skills, Lorraine encouraged the studio to work across scale and media. A portfolio of large-scale architectural commissions and public artworks in Adelaide were developed during Lorraine's tenure as Creative Director: St Mary's College entry gates, the viewing platform balustrades and the undulating playground fence for the Semaphore South Foreshore Redevelopment, *The Wave* fence at the skate park on North Terrace and a series of inlaid artworks for the new Adelaide Tram Stop platforms were all studio projects. Lorraine encouraged a cross-disciplinary approach to commissions and public art outcomes, and the Metal Design Studio regularly worked as a team to produce, for instance, a series of screens and wall relief artworks for the Queen Elizabeth Hospital Development, and the 4.5-metre high forged steel and glass *Dandelion Garden* sculptures at the Lyell McEwin Hospital.

In 2009 Lorraine returned to Gray Street Workshop as a partner. In her recent work she investigates natural history collections, the impulse for collecting and her interest in the theories of natural selection. She has created several ranges of jewellery and objects based on insects: cockroaches made from record vinyl, moths made out of slide transparencies, stick insects fashioned from Cuisenaire rods, and now butterflies cut from iPhone 3 cases, in which Lorraine explores the inbuilt redundancy of consumer goods as a new form of Darwinism.

A little while ago I inherited an iPhone 3 ... for me this was a new and wonderful piece of technology ... but I soon found out that for most people it was old technology and on top of that all the iPhone 3 accessories had disappeared from the shelves ... the iPhone 3 has been superseded, and through the consumer selection process ... gone the way of other species ... perhaps it was just too pretty for its own good.

Margaret Hancock Davis

Too Pretty for Their Own Good, *2012*
heat coloured mild stee, iPhone 3 hard shell covers
100 x 90 x 25mm each

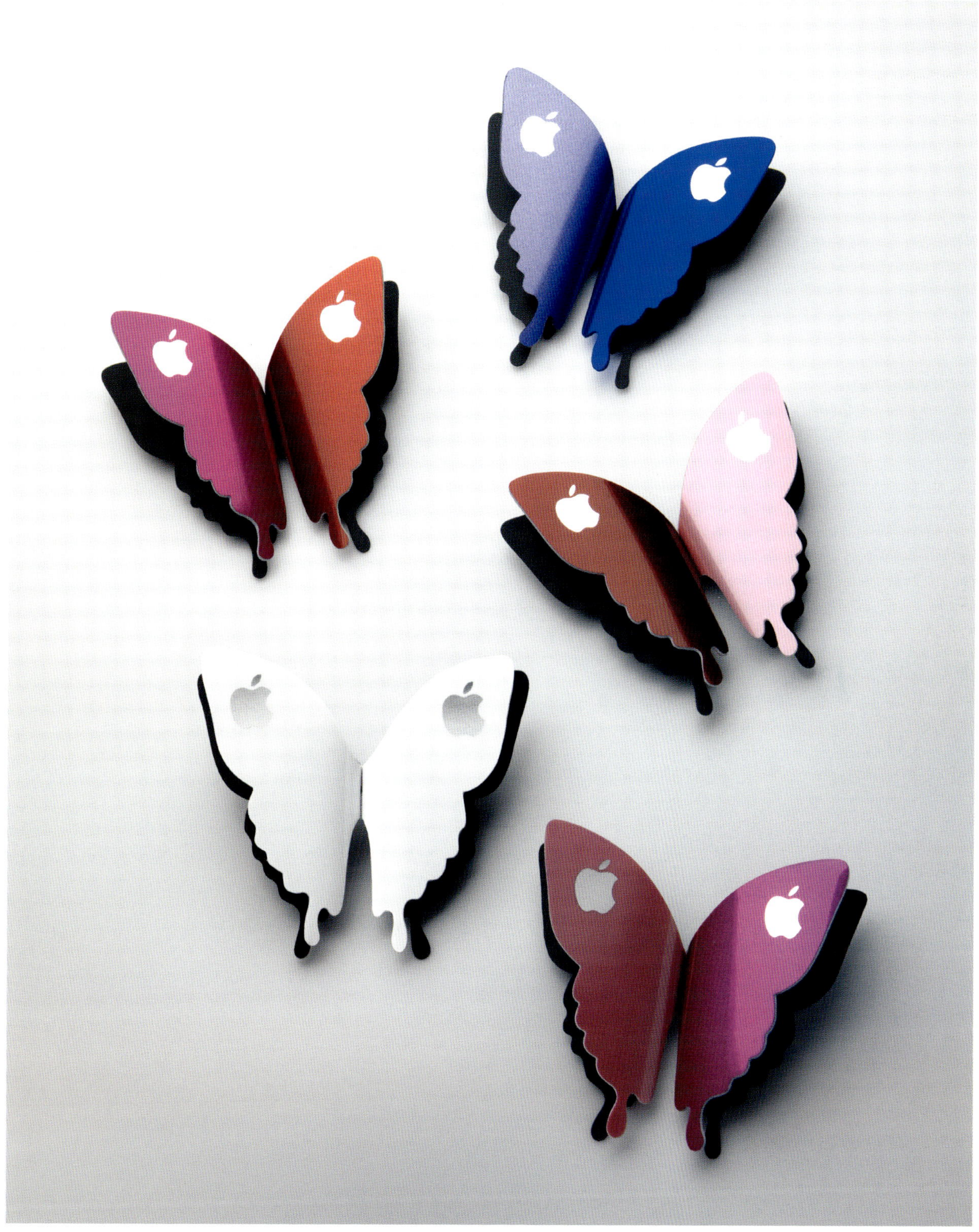

LESLIE MATTHEWS

born 1964, Puerto Rico, USA
lives in Adelaide, SA

With over 25 years' experience, Leslie Matthews is one of Australia's leading contemporary jewellers. Her first association with JamFactory began while she was a member of Gray Street Workshop, which was temporarily housed in JamFactory from 1992 to 1994. Matthews joined Gray Street Workshop upon graduating from the University of South Australia in 1986, initially as an access tenant, though soon becoming one of its partners.

Matthews recalls the achievements from this early time at JamFactory:

While I was there I had my first solo exhibition, Inner Vane *in 1992. I received an Australia Council grant to produce the work—having this opportunity was an important milestone in my career and a positive experience.*

Matthews has held further solo exhibitions at JamFactory, including the 1999 Gallery Two exhibition *An omen in the bone*, and *Chiaro Oscura* held in CollectorSpace in 2012.

Returning to the University of South Australia to undertake a Masters of Visual Arts (Research), which she completed in 2006, she subsequently became the Studio Head of Jewellery and Metal in the School of Art, Architecture and Design, from 2007 to 2010.

In 2010, after many positive years at Gray Street Workshop, Matthews felt it was time to produce work in different surroundings. Deciding on a return to JamFactory to set up an independent studio, Matthews has taken this opportunity to consolidate her practice by experimenting with new materials and processes for a range of exhibitions locally and internationally, while continuing to develop and extend her production pieces.

As an established jeweller, Matthews provides invaluable peer-to-peer support to the emerging jewellers at JamFactory, in particular Peta Kruger, with whom she has shared the studio since 2011. As Kruger states:

As a JamFactory studio tenant, I share my studio with jeweller Leslie Matthews. I admire the way she approaches her work, with careful, cool and thoughtful observations. I hope a little of her influence has filtered into my work over the years.

Throughout her career, the predominant focus of Matthews' practice has been on creating exhibition work. Her most recent group exhibitions include *Schoonhoven Silver Award 2012*, at the Nederlands Zilvermuseum, Schoonhoven, the Netherlands; *The European Fine Art Fair 2012*, in Maastricht, the Netherlands, and *Masterpiece 2011 London art and design fair* (both with London dealer, Adrian Sassoon). In 2010 her work was selected to be in *Abstract Nature*, a major group exhibition held at the Samstag Museum of Art, University of South Australia, and *By Example: Australian Contemporary Jewellery*, at the Museum of Arts and Crafts, Itami, Japan.

Matthews has undertaken several overseas residencies, most recently a studio residency at The British School in Rome (through the Australia Council in 2007) and as an artist/scholar in residence at the Otago Polytechnic, School of Art, Dunedin, New Zealand in 2005.

As part of her independent practice, Matthews has produced public artworks around the city of Adelaide. These include the *Tree of Hope* wall sculpture, Julian Burton Burns Trust, at the Royal Adelaide Hospital (2003); *Drawn Place, Drawn Space*, entrance sculpture at Mawson Lakes Primary School (2004); and *Yungondi: To Give, Impart, Educate, Communicate*, the Yungondi Building Foyer entrance, University of South Australia (1998).

Incorporating highly skilled and subtle lost-wax casting of animal and bird bones, Matthews creates works of a fragile, beautiful nature. Reflecting on the making of her jewellery, Matthews comments:

I focus on creating work that embodies an emotional response, a trace of the body. Bones are often explored, contrasting and merging forms are created, metaphors suggested. These objects are the result of the tactile knowledge held in my hands, touching the forms, being touched and remembering.

Margaret Hancock Davis

Midnight and Midday and Midnight neckpiece, *2012*
sterling silver, antique glass beads
10 x 300 x 200mm

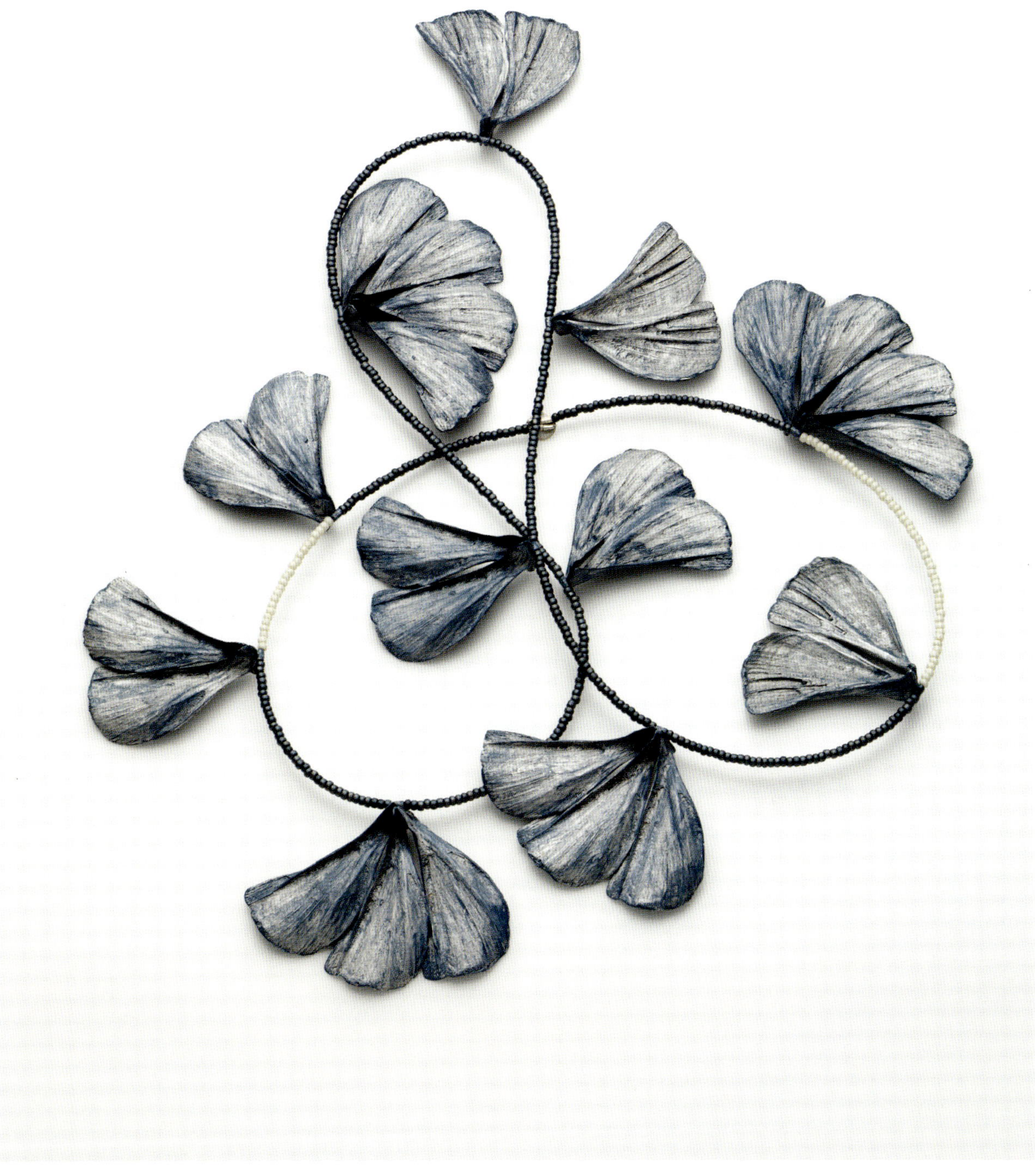

JEFF MINCHAM

born 1950, Milang, SA
lives in Cherryville, SA

Jeff Mincham AM is a towering figure in Australian craft. His lifetime achievement in ceramics and his contribution to Australia's cultural life were recognised in 2011 when he was awarded a Medal of the Order of Australia. In 2009 he was honoured as a Living Treasure, Master of Australian Craft by Object: Australian Centre for Craft and Design. This resulted in a monograph on his ceramics career and a major exhibition, which toured Australia to great acclaim. A selected body of work from this exhibition has been donated by Mincham to the National Gallery of Australia. He is represented in major state and regional galleries in Australia, and in public and private collections throughout the world.

Mincham's career started at the original Jam Factory in its early days at St Peters, when he worked there, first as a tenant in 1976, returning from 1979 to 1983 as the inaugural Head of the Ceramics Workshop. He recalls:

Creating a fully functioning Ceramics Workshop out of the wreckage of previous attempts was not easy. However, not only did we manage it, but a whole range of talented people were given a unique opportunity in the establishment of their careers. I consciously took on a very diverse group of people with widely varying positions on clay, and it all worked out very well with very interesting outcomes—mind you, the institution itself never really understood what we were about and often seemed to have another agenda entirely.

Above all else, the Jam Factory exposed me to the range of possibilities in ceramics, some of which I rejected and others that I embraced. It also enabled me to see the bigger picture of craft practice as it was then, and connected me to a bigger world. Eventually, however, the contradictions that this experience laid before me had to be confronted, and I made a firm decision to work as an individual ceramic artist (the phrase of the time was 'artist potter'). Notions of being a production potter in some imaginary craft industry looked less and less plausible (as it turned out to be); the pathways of art, however, looked challenging and engaging and this they have certainly proved to be.

Mincham had his first exhibition at the St Peters Jam Factory in 1976, but did not have another solo exhibition there until 1990. There was a further gap of 14 years until his retrospective in 2004, *A Potter's Landscape*. Understandably, he has mixed feelings about the organisation. He states:

The Jam Factory was very important to me at the beginning of my career and for a time influenced me greatly ... The downside of the Jam Factory has consistently been to empower and advantage a small group, to the disadvantage of those perceived as outsiders. I have always seen this institution as one for all South Australians and one that needs to be conscious of and proactive in support of the whole crafts community ... My ongoing relationship with the JamFactory is twofold. It will remain an important option for me to show aspects of my work, particularly as there are so few options in South Australia. It will also continue to be a place through which I can make contact with my professional colleagues and fellow practitioners. This does not mean however that I will not take a critical stand on matters of concern from time to time. Indeed, if the JamFactory is to continue to survive as the important South Australian institution that it is, it must always be able to respond to a discourse on its performance. After all, its relationship with its audience is at the very core of its meaning to our community.

Mincham's work for the exhibition is an interpretation of his deeply embedded sense of connection to the South Australian landscape. While the form has been simplified, his surfaces are rich in textural and tonal variation. He has developed a body of glazes in subtle nuances of creams and ochres, which evoke ephemeral changes of light and a bleak, desolate beauty of vanishing salt lakes.

Margot Osborne

Last of the Water (Coorong Series), *2012*
handbuilt, mutiglaze, midfire clay
200 x 380mm dia.

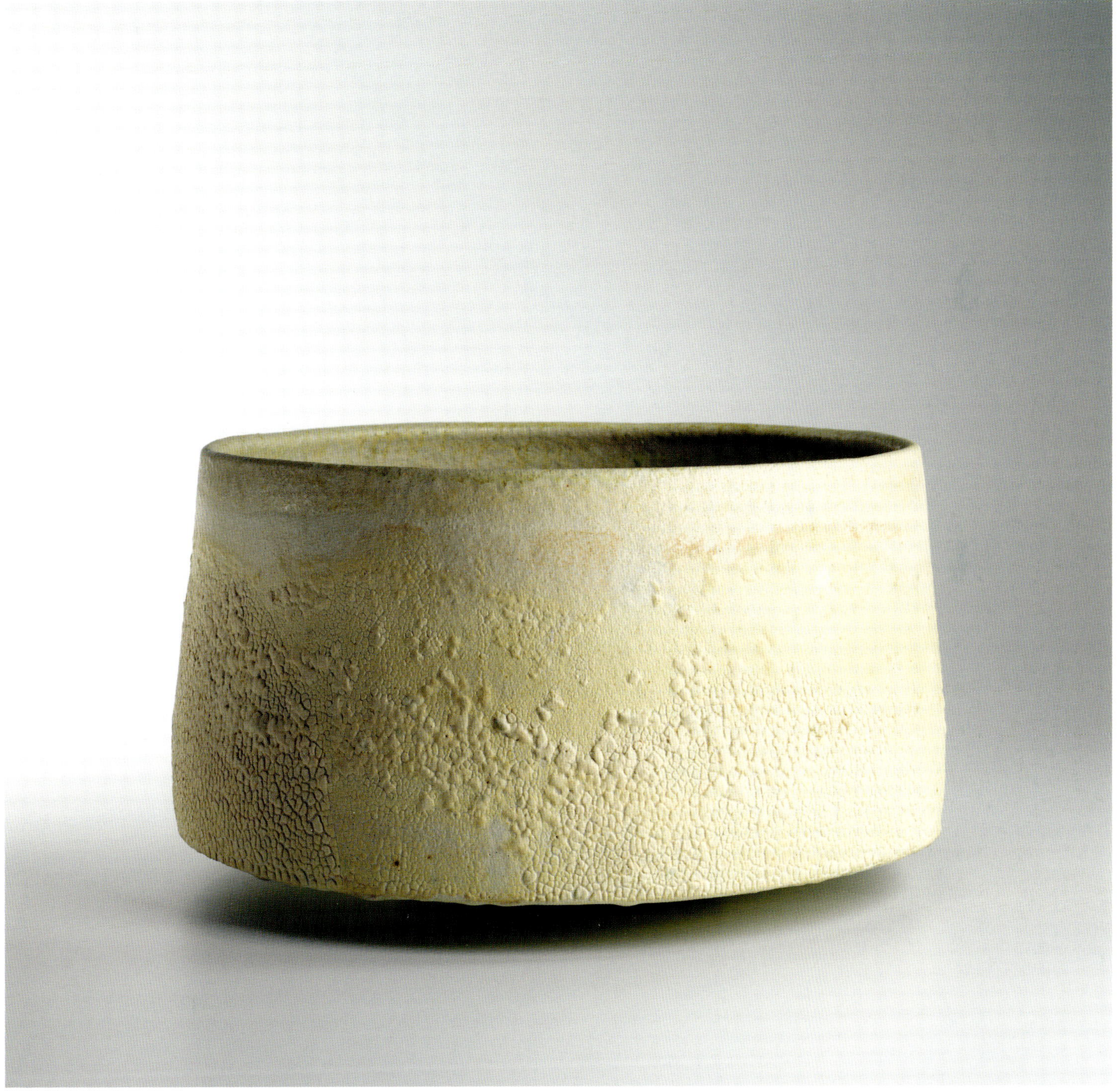

TOM MIRAMS

born1972, Bega, NSW
lives in Adelaide, SA

Tom Mirams is Creative Director of JamFactory's Furniture Studio, and has been in the role since 2006. He studied furniture design at the Tasmanian School of Art in Hobart and on completing his degree was accepted into JamFactory's Associate training program in 1997. Following his two years as an Associate in the Furniture Studio, he maintained a successful independent practice for eight years—focusing primarily on commissioned work—from the George Street Studios in the Adelaide suburb of Thebarton. His major projects during this time included bespoke fit-outs for the Adelaide offices of Microsoft (2005), Adelaide Fringe (2004) and Transport SA (2001).

Mirams was committed to a career in furniture design and making from a young. He saw both the Furniture course in Hobart and the JamFactory program in Adelaide as prominent and effective stepping stones along his chosen path (he had also previously completed an Advanced Certificate in Craft and Design at Mornington College of TAFE in Victoria). His experience as an Associate was during a highly productive period for the Furniture Studio, under the guidance of Studio Head Peter Walker (also a graduate of the Tasmanian School of Art). Mirams was involved in running several large commissioned jobs both within the studio and independently, thus establishing a mode of practice that would sustain him for almost a decade.

In over seven years as Creative Director of JamFactory's Furniture Studio, Mirams' achievements are widespread and varied, yet he is still most inspired by 'seeing the light go on' for an Associate when they make a breakthrough on a design project. He has mentored some outstanding Associates and developed a strong team culture within the studio, harnessing the diverse skills-base that results from attracting graduates from both industrial design and traditional woodworking courses. When asked about personal highlights from the studio's activities in recent years, he says:

There are two projects that really stand out for me ...

Firstly, the opportunity to co-curate an exhibition in JamFactory's main gallery; Resource—Re-Source *(2009), which was a survey of Furniture Studio Associates and staff, who were each asked to create a work based on their particular connection to materials.*

The second relates to the many major commissions the studio has successfully undertaken. The one that stands out most significantly for me is the fit-out for the Mount Gambier Public Library. Our section of this was a $250,000 project run entirely from the Furniture Studio, involving the design and production of some 25 furniture items. The project put me on a huge learning curve and tempered the way I have managed people and projects ever since.

Mirams has continuously produced one-off works for exhibition, and for this show he has created the *Quarter Cut Screen*, 2012, which continues his exploration into structure and pattern. This three-panelled screen is made from recycled Douglas fir. The faces of the screen are embossed with a machined honeycomb pattern, which is then sandblasted through the quarter cut surface, revealing the varied seasonal growth densities. He states: 'I am trying to set a dichotomy between the rugged roughness of the recycled material and the fineness and vulnerability of its treatment.'

Brian Parkes

Quarter Cut Screen, *2012*
recycled Douglas fir
1850 x 1650 x 170mm

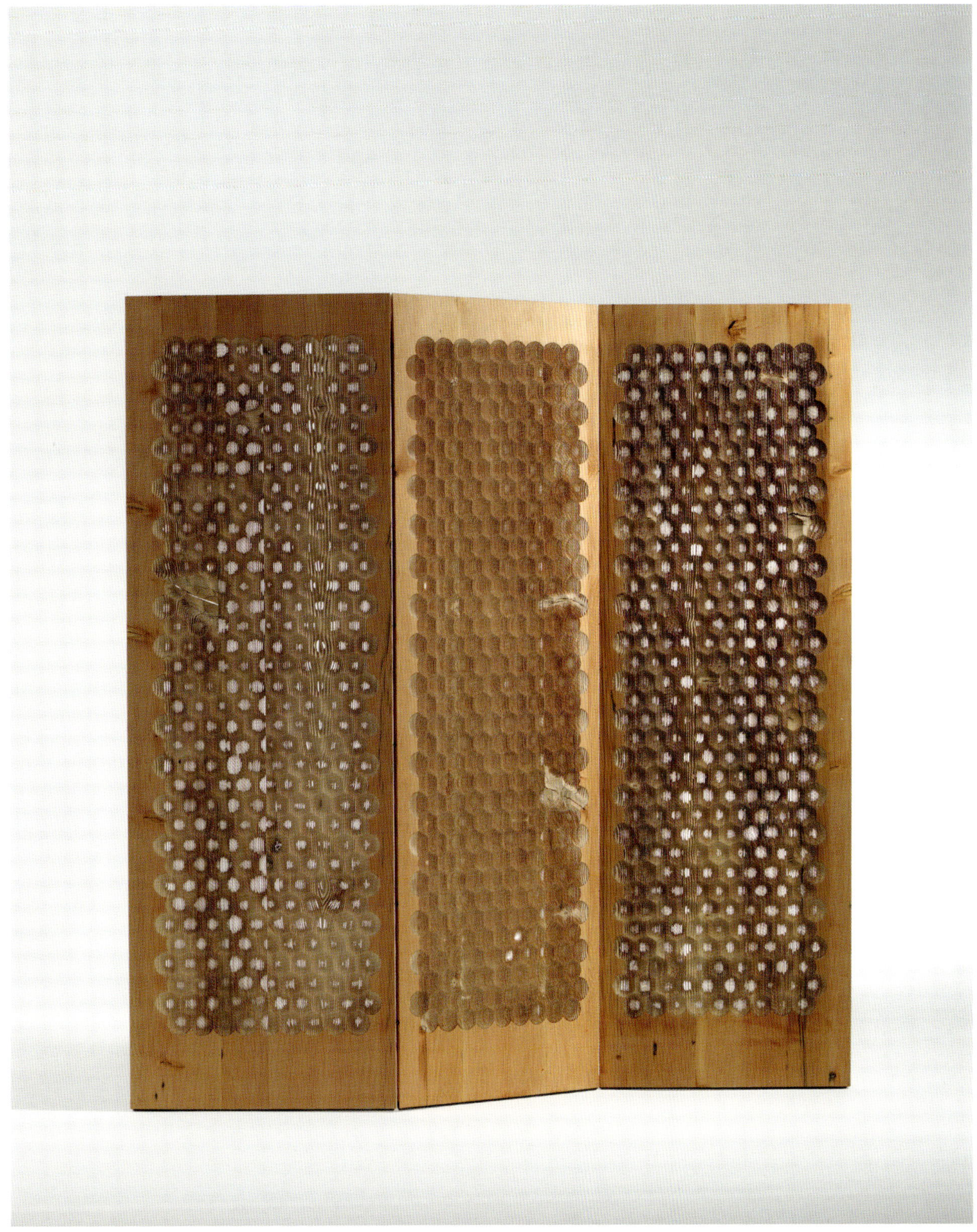

MONO

John Quan born 1977, Saigon, Vietnam
Kumiko Nakajima born 1980, Kitakyushu, Fukuoka, Japan
both live in Adelaide, SA

Former JamFactory Associates, John Quan and Kumiko Nakajima, are the husband and wife designer–makers behind MONO, which derives its name from the Japanese word for 'object', and the English prefix for 'one'. Bringing together their different skills, backgrounds and talents, MONO is the result of two designers working together to create a single design outcome.

Quan completed both a Bachelor of Design (Industrial Design) at the University of South Australia and a Certificate III in Fashion at TAFE SA before joining the Furniture Design Studio in 2007. He takes a very experimental approach to his designs, challenging materials and stretching their capacities to produce clean-lined and fresh products that are often imbued with a sense of fun and play. His designs are driven by the desire to create objects that arouse a sense of surprise in the user.

He has received industry recognition for his designs, such as the *Knife Block,* 2007 and *Woven Form,* 2008. He was a finalist in the Bombay Sapphire Design Discovery Award in both 2008 and 2010, while in 2007 he won the Living Edge Launch Pad award, Best concept award at VIVID, and the JamFactory Italian Centre Design Award. This ABAF (Australian Business Arts Foundation)-recognised award ran from 2006 to 2008, and called for JamFactory Associates to produce objects reflecting Italy's wine and food culture. The winning Associate received funding for travel to Italy, and Quan took this as an opportunity to visit the *Salone Internazionale del Mobile di Milano*. Since undertaking the Associate training program, he has been a studio tenant at JamFactory. His work has been presented in leading exhibitions, including *Prototyping: Making Ideas* (2011) and *WOOD: art design architecture* (2013).

Kumiko Nakajima studied arts curating at Osaka University of Arts, Japan, before undertaking a glass-blowing course at Ezra Glass Studio in Fukui, Japan, with Hiroshi Yamano. A leading Japanese artist, Yamano was well versed in the American glass movement, teaching his students many US-based techniques. In 2005, on a working holiday in Australia, Nakajima visited JamFactory. She was so inspired by the glass scene she found here that she returned to undertake the two-year Associate training program in 2007.

Nakajima's works are inspired by an interest in form, colour and line. She creates works of a subtle refined minimalism which have gained her recognition nationally. She has been a finalist in the prestigious Waterhouse Natural History Art Prize in 2008 and the Ranamok Glass Prize in 2009.

Working from a studio with fellow alumnus Janice Vitkovsky, Nakajima continues to blow glass and assist fellow glass artists at JamFactory. Her work has been exhibited nationally and internationally, including JamFactory's 2012 exhibition *Transparency.*

The cleverly produced MONO product range brings the contrasting qualities of each designer's chosen medium into a unified form. The tactility of each object is of utmost importance, and the challenge of finding the delicate balance between the warmth of wood and cool of glass has allowed MONO to create a sophisticated pared-back aesthetic.

Margaret Hancock Davis

Shiny Box, *2012*
blown and coldwork glass, American walnut
150 x 120 x 130mm

Drop Bottle, *2012*
blown and coldwork glass, Rock maple
145 x 60mm dia

Line Paperweights, *2012*
blown and coldwork glass, American walnut and American cherry
largest 45 x 40 x 40mm

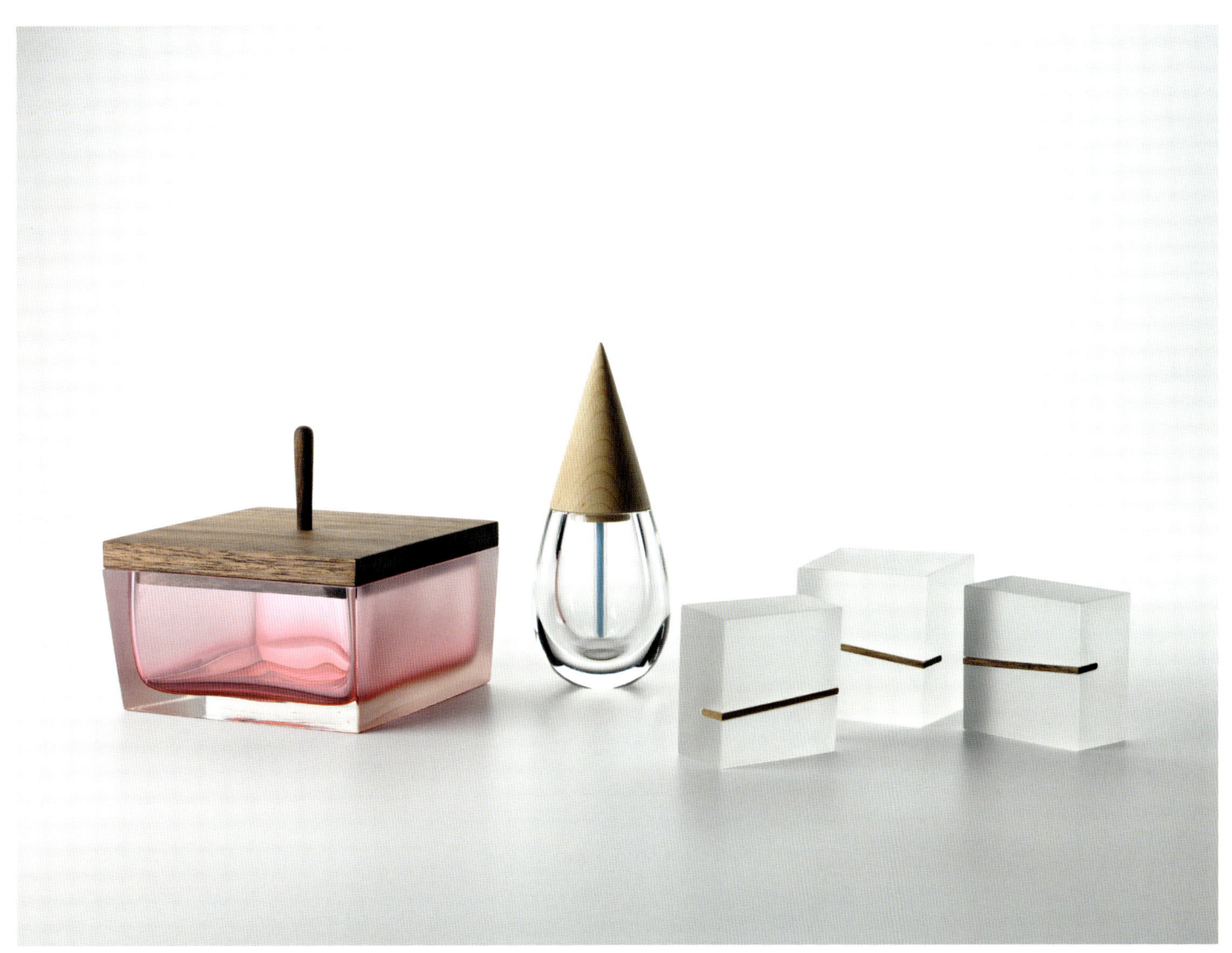

TOM MOORE

born 1971, Canberra, ACT
lives in Adelaide, SA

After completing an undergraduate degree in Glass at Canberra School of Art, Tom Moore moved to Adelaide in 1995 to become an Associate in JamFactory's Glass Studio, which was run at that time by Nick Mount. In 1999 he was appointed as the Glass Studio's Production Manager and has been closely associated with JamFactory ever since. Moore states:

I wanted to blow glass every day and to concentrate on gaining skills through precise repetition. I think it was a very fortuitous time to be at 'The Jam'. Nick was developing a strong client base for commission work, making good changes to the equipment and fostering a healthy hiring community. All of this was contributing to a vibrant training program. Some of the jobs that made the best impression on me involved the whole team each doing their own small part of the process, again and again and again to produce hundreds of bottles. I was aware that we were using the same processes that had been used to make the same forms for thousands of years. For the first time I felt I was connected to the history of the material. My employment at JamFactory continues to provide me with a solid foundation in the repetitive manufacture of functional glassware but also offers the variety of one-off sculptural work. My long association with JamFactory has been pivotal in enabling me to develop my own elaborate and idiosyncratic glass works.

In his studio practice as a professional glass artist Moore has adapted traditional Venetian blowing and hot-forming techniques as a means to create an ever-evolving imaginative universe of hybrid sculptural figures, part animal/part vegetable/part humanoid. Often he displays groups of figures in installations and narrative scenarios against painted or photographic dioramas, and occasionally has expanded these narratives into digital animations.

Moore has exhibited prolifically throughout Australia and internationally, and has been represented in the major touring exhibitions, *Tour de Force* (2010–11) and *White Hot* (Asialink and Craft ACT tour of Asia, 2009). His distinctive glass works have been acclaimed not only within the world of studio glass but also in the wider contemporary art context. He exhibited in *Optimism* (Gallery of Modern Art, Brisbane, 2008) and in *Making it new: focus on contemporary Australian art* (Museum of Contemporary Art, Sydney, 2009). ABC Television made a 26-minute documentary, *Glassorama*, on his work in 2009.

For this exhibition he has created a surreal tableau, a mirror-world above and below ground, in which the principal character is *Ancient Malcontent*, a fish with a mouth where his gills should be, and with plant leaves in place of fins and a tail. According to Moore, 'He has been cantankerous for a long time. His pond is getting hotter, saltier, and he's not meeting any friends.' Then there is *Oily Invertebrate*, a car-creature which is 'quite alien and sinister-looking, but ultimately harmless, going about its own business'. Moore comments:

The bird character with the kinky boots and face-body is my longstanding accomplice called 'Prank'. I always feel things are OK when Prank is in the house. There is a flying potato car floating above all of this. A true ambassador for hybrid vigour, it has human eyes and tentacle/tendrils, the floaty frills of a jellyfish, a somewhat goofy grin. It is an organism that has evolved to simulate some outward aspects of modern automobiles. Nailing raindrops to the wall is a satisfying impossibility that is optically compelling and another symbol of hope, renewal, life.

Margot Osborne

Oily Invertebrate with heaps-good Shrubby Mounds, etc. *2012*
blown and solid glass, silver leaf, fake moss, laminated plywood, dirt, heavy card, paint, particle board
1600 x 1200 x 240mm

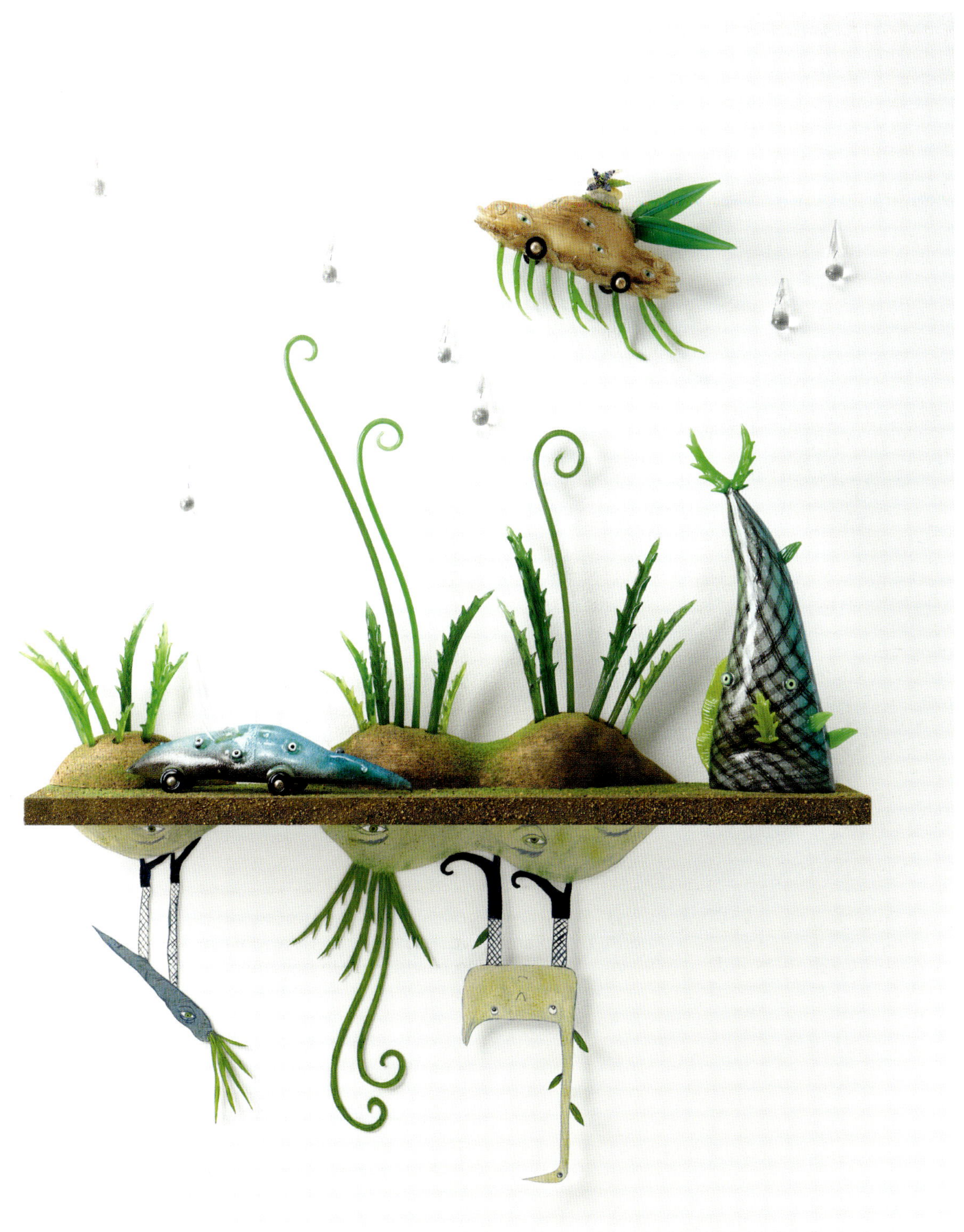

NICK MOUNT

born 1952, Adelaide, SA
lives in Adelaide, SA

Nick Mount has played an influential role in developing JamFactory's Glass Studio into an internationally recognised incubator for emerging glass artists. Initially as Studio Head from 1994 to 1997, and subsequently through his expert advice and mentoring and as a regular presence blowing glass in the hot shop, Mount has helped shape glass practice in Adelaide. Other glass artists in this exhibition, including Clare Belfrage, Tom Moore and Deb Jones, have acknowledged his mentoring role in their creative development.

He comments that when he was Studio Head he set out to foster 'a sense of community'. Focusing on commission work rather than on production ware, he emphasised teamwork and building skills through repetitive work. This not only proved a successful financial strategy, but also engendered a strong spirit of community amongst the trainees. He encouraged casual access to the Glass Studio's hot-glass facilities by the wider community of professional glass artists. This drew practitioners not only from Adelaide but from across Australia. Since Mount's time, JamFactory Glass Studio has been one of the most active and creative hot-glass facilities in Australia.

Mount has always had two aspects to his glass practice, as an artist and as a teacher–demonstrator. In both spheres he has long operated in the international arena, where he has achieved a high standing. He travels overseas regularly for exhibitions and teaching commitments. Mount has demonstrated frequently at Pilchuck Glass School, The Studio, Corning Museum of Glass, and most recently with esteemed US glass artist Dick Marquis at the 2012 Glass Art Society Conference in Toledo, Ohio. The conference celebrated 50 years of studio glass in America.

Mount's lifelong achievements as a glass artist were recognised in 2012 when he was honoured by Object: Australian Centre for Craft and Design with a national touring exhibition and monograph in the *Living Treasures: Masters of Australian Craft* series. That year he celebrated his 60th birthday with an exhibition, *nickmount@60*, at BMGART, and received a ten-year survey exhibition at the Pittsburgh Glass Center, USA, which traced the evolution of his *Scent bottles* and *Plumb bobs*. He is represented in major public collections nationally, including the National Gallery of Australia and most state galleries, and internationally, in collections including the Museum of Contemporary Glass Art, Toyama City, Japan and the Glasmuseum Ebeltoft, Denmark.

Mount's still-life composition for this exhibition is representative of the new direction in his current body of work. To complement his continuing series of *Scent bottles*, which draw on the history of blown glass for inspiration, he has taken a step sideways to draw on the history of still-life painting, introducing a series of blown forms suggestive of vegetables. Each sensuously rounded closed form is exquisitely finished with a range of cold-working techniques and topped with a hand-turned timber 'stalk'. These timber stalks are a natural stylistic progression from the glass flourishes atop his scent bottles, as we see in the current composition. Mount carefully selects the appropriate timber, with Huon pine and local olive wood being particular favourites. The final stage is the arrangement of the forms in meticulously balanced still-life compositions, which are positioned on a finely crafted timber base. Historically, still-life painting was concerned with the imminent decay of the lush fruit and vegetables portrayed, with artists often introducing worms and other symbolic indicators of mortality into the composition. In contrast, Mount's still-life arrangements are redolent with a sense of fullness and ripeness, a moment of fruitfulness immortalised in glass.

Margot Osborne

Still Life with Bosc and Strange Fruit #0806112 (557), *2012*
blown glass, granula murrini, carved, polished , assembled, olive wood, American oak
470 x 890 x 180mm

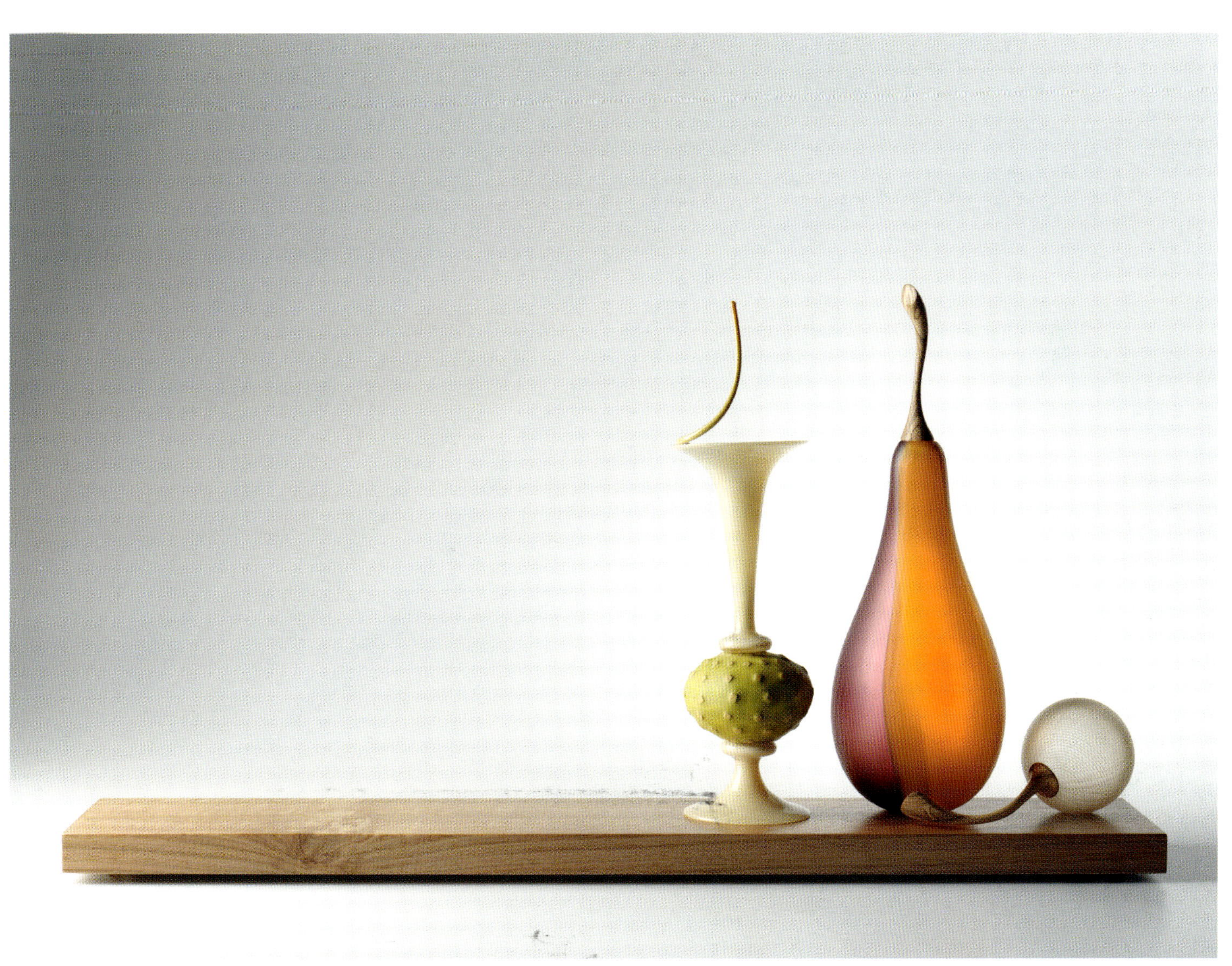

BELINDA NEWICK

born 1975, Perth, WA
lives in Melbourne, Vic

After graduating with a Bachelor of Arts (Visual Arts) from Curtin University in 1995, Belinda Newick spent time expanding her skills and industry knowledge by working with an artisan blacksmith and as a gallery/retail assistant at CraftWest and Gunyulgup Galleries, Yallingup, WA before moving to Adelaide to take up an Associateship in the Metal Design Studio in 1998. The Associateship program was vitally important to Newick as she negotiated the path from undergraduate studies to a career as a designer-maker.

JamFactory is a fine example of an active functioning supportive community that provides space for all people to grow and prosper. It certainly provided me with space, encouragement and guidance to trust myself, to gain confidence to make mistakes and have failures but to also rise to the challenges that stretched my skills and allowed growth and the resultant new pieces.

There is strength in the friendships and relationships formed because everyone is coming from different states and that constant flow of national and international artists/ designers makes everyone participate and connect. Being able to access the other studios, seeing potential in ideas in making collaborative work, really allowed the development of a broad design practice, which is so relevant in the current design climate of multi-disciplinary design practice.

During her Associateship, Newick worked under two Creative Directors, Rik Barnsley and Sue Lorraine.

Rik was so supportive and welcoming when I began at the Jam.
Our studio was a strong team and I was able to benefit enormously from Rik's very strong technical skills. I worked closely with him on the fabrication and installation of the Le Zinc *wine bar, which was a great job to start with. He led a very cohesive group and really supported each individual's growth and development.*

Sue started at the beginning of 1999 Although initially it was a little disruptive to have a change of Studio Head mid Associateship, Sue had a wonderful vision and set the studio on a clear path. We had many fantastic opportunities and great commissions come through the studio with her direction. I gained experience in both the studio jobs and also my production jewellery. Sue's ongoing guidance, support and encouragement of my development in my creative career have continued to offer many opportunities.

On completion of her Associateship, Newick joined the team at Gray Street Workshop and then Zu design—jewellery + objects retail before she made the move to Victoria in 2004. That year she was part of the inaugural representation of Australian Contemporary at *SOFA* Chicago.

For this exhibition Newick has produced a body of work, *De Qi* ('to find the Qi'), 2012. Inspired by her studies in Shiatsu therapies and Oriental medicine, the kidney medulla form has been translated in jade, Huon pine, 9ct gold, copper and fine silver to reflect the Chinese five element theory of wood, fire, earth, metal and water. Each piece is finely engraved with anatomical drawings of the extensive network of nerve endings and touch receptors in the skin, known as the soma sensory system.

Margaret Hancock Davis

Clockwise from left:
De Qi - Wood, Fire, Earth, Metal, Water, *2012*
Huon pine, yellow gold and sterling silver, copper, fine silver, jade
largest (Water)
57 x 48 x 18mm

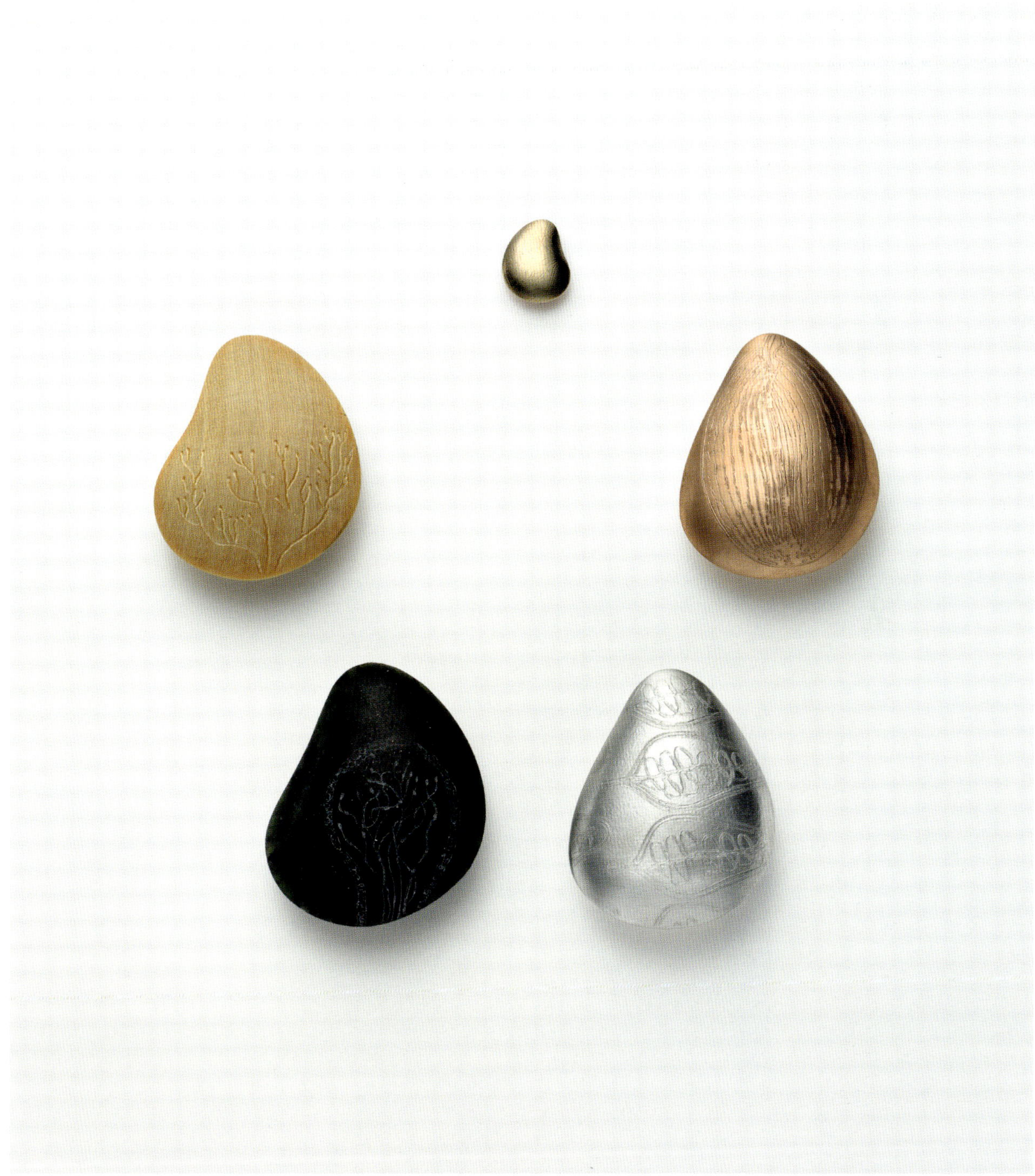

JULIE PIEDA

born 1969, Canberra, ACT
lives in Adelaide, SA

With teaching qualifications from the University of South Australia, Julie Pieda taught art and design at Renmark High School for four years, where she set up a Design Faculty as part of the Art Faculty, before becoming an Associate in JamFactory's Furniture Studio in 1996.

Pieda is Director of Koush Design, a successful design consultancy she established in Adelaide in 1999. Engaging in projects that vary in scale from a custom sofa for a private residence, to detailed interior fit-outs for multi-level commercial spaces, Koush Design creates furniture and interiors with a high level of attention to detail and a quirky edge. Pieda works with local manufacturers and craftspeople—including cabinet-makers, upholsterers and welders—to produce work tailored to each job. Each project requires collaboration between client, designer and manufacturer, with Pieda encouraging clients to express their individual or corporate personality through the creation of bespoke design solutions.

For several years Pieda supplemented her business income with a series of influential part-time roles at TAFE, the University of South Australia and at JamFactory (as Production Manager in the Furniture Studio in 2001) but has, since 2007, focused solely on managing and designing for Koush.

Pieda acknowledges her years as an Associate at JamFactory were pivotal in the development of her career. She believes she learned a great deal from the Heads of the various studios, and adds:

I also learned so much from the other Associates, both in Furniture and the other studios. Experience and skills were so willingly shared ... we gave each other unquestionable support during our time there.

JamFactory's program of visiting artists and designers was, for Pieda—as it is for Associates today—another great source of information and inspiration.

A few weeks after I started my Associateship, designer, furniture maker and bridge maker Richard La Trobe Bateman come out from England. He has an amazing knowledge of traditional techniques and a sense of how the craft of woodwork has evolved over time. I was concerned about my lack of a making background and that I didn't have the construction skills of the other Associates. He told me to look at this as a positive, that I was not burdened by how things 'should be done' and that my design background gave me an opportunity to come at making from a different perspective. This coloured my whole experience at the Jam and, along with the collaboration between studios, taught me to leave room in project teams for everyone's expertise—shared knowledge from varied perspectives can lead to great solutions.

The works included in this exhibition are drawn from the Koush collection of products, which includes pieces that have been produced regularly for over a decade.

Cranberry sofa, 2012 was designed to be a classic item with elegant proportions. It is extremely comfortable and has a solid timber frame. Pieda says, 'The length is critical, as being able to lie down for a nap is the sign of a good sofa!' She adds 'The cranberry colour works with numerous other colours and behaves like a neutral, but with much more personality'. The sofa was manufactured by Design Furniture who Pieda began working with as an Associate. The *Glimpse light,* 2012 is a more experimental response to its ecoboard material, in which Pieda has explored the properties of the material and her own obsession with texture.

Brian Parkes

Cranberry sofa,
2012
timber frame, commercial foam, wool upholstery
850 x 2000 x 775mm

Glimpse lights,
2012
ecoboard, parchment paper, led lights
140 dia. x 50mm

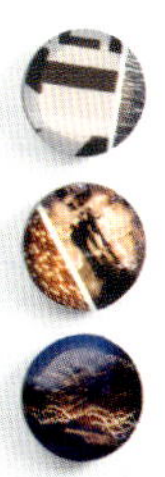

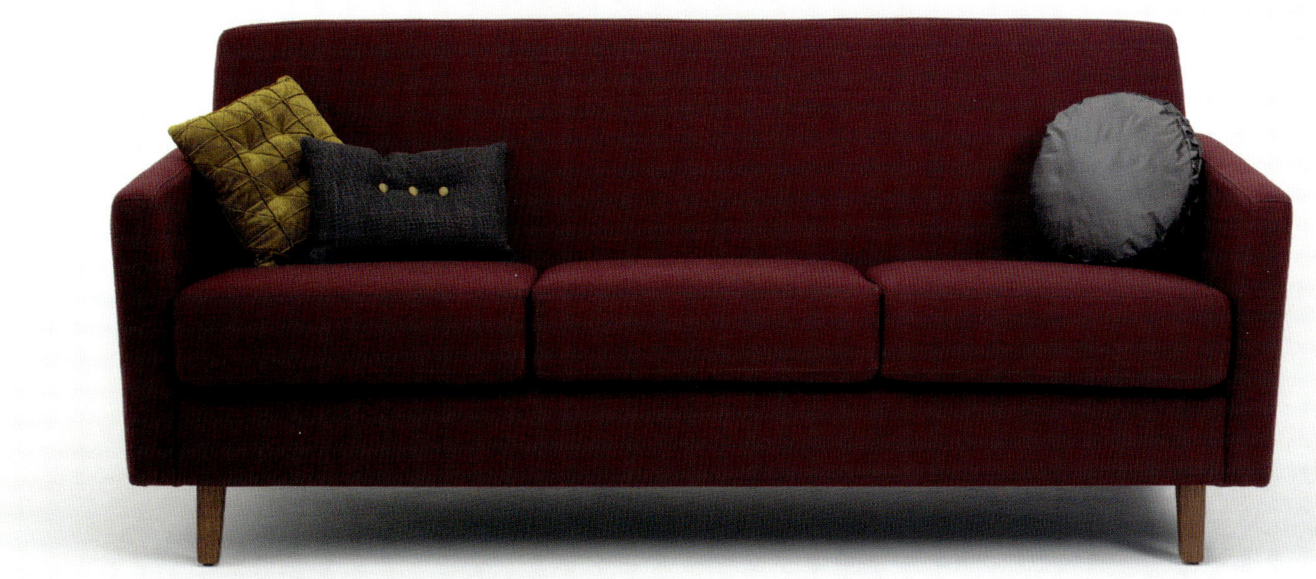

LAUREN SIMEONI

born 1974, Bowral, NSW
lives in Adelaide, SA

Lauren Simeoni is a jeweller, object maker and designer working from Gate 8 workshop in Adelaide. She came to JamFactory as an Associate in the Metal Design Studio from 1997 to 1999, after gaining a Bachelor of Arts degree in gold and silversmithing from Canberra School of Art, where she learnt from luminaries Ragnar Hansen and Johannes Kuhnen. After completing her training at JamFactory she undertook a one-year mentorship at Adelaide's Gray Street Workshop, and then worked for an additional year at Gray Street. From 2002 to 2004 she returned to JamFactory as a studio tenant.

For several years Simeoni worked with collages of images applied to plastics and aluminium, as a basis for brooches, earrings and necklaces. She applied this approach also to larger-scale designs in the public sphere, undertaking commissions for the Anglican Archbishop of Adelaide in 2003 (collaboration with Jan Lackmann), and for Wakefield House, Adelaide in 2004. In 2003 Simeoni held a solo exhibition of this body of work, *Sublimation*, in Gallery Two at JamFactory.

In 2010 she commenced what has become a continuing collaboration with Sydney jeweller Melinda Young to create a new body of work, *Unnatural naturally*. Simeoni and Young send each other packages containing colour-coded 'collections' of random found plastic, mainly representations of nature. Each jeweller then uses these to assemble neckpieces and other jewellery. The resulting jewellery has an esoteric, self-consciously kitsch beauty, which can be attributed as much to Simeoni's keen eye for assemblage of incongruous elements as to the mixed messages of such artificial, plastic 'nature'. *Unnatural naturally* toured to Auckland in 2010, and in 2011 Simeoni and Young jointly curated an exhibition, *Unnatural acts*, featuring eight Australian jewellers, which was shown at Velvet da Vinci Gallery in San Francisco. A further iteration of *Unnatural naturally* was exhibited at JamFactory's Gallery Two in 2011. In October 2012 Simeoni and Young exhibited their latest collaborative jewellery at Craft, Melbourne (formerly Craft Victoria).

For this exhibition Simeoni has created a group of three necklaces based on this approach, fabricating an assemblage composed of 'repurposed' elements: bits and pieces of 'found' plastic representations of nature, sent to her by Young. Using a palette of sludgy 'natural' greens, muddy browns and black she has juxtaposed textures, tones and branchy organic forms to create compelling and very wearable works that have a bizarre, unbeautiful beauty.

Margot Osborne

Wreath, *2012*
artificial foliage, brass, amazonite
30 x 210 x 290mm

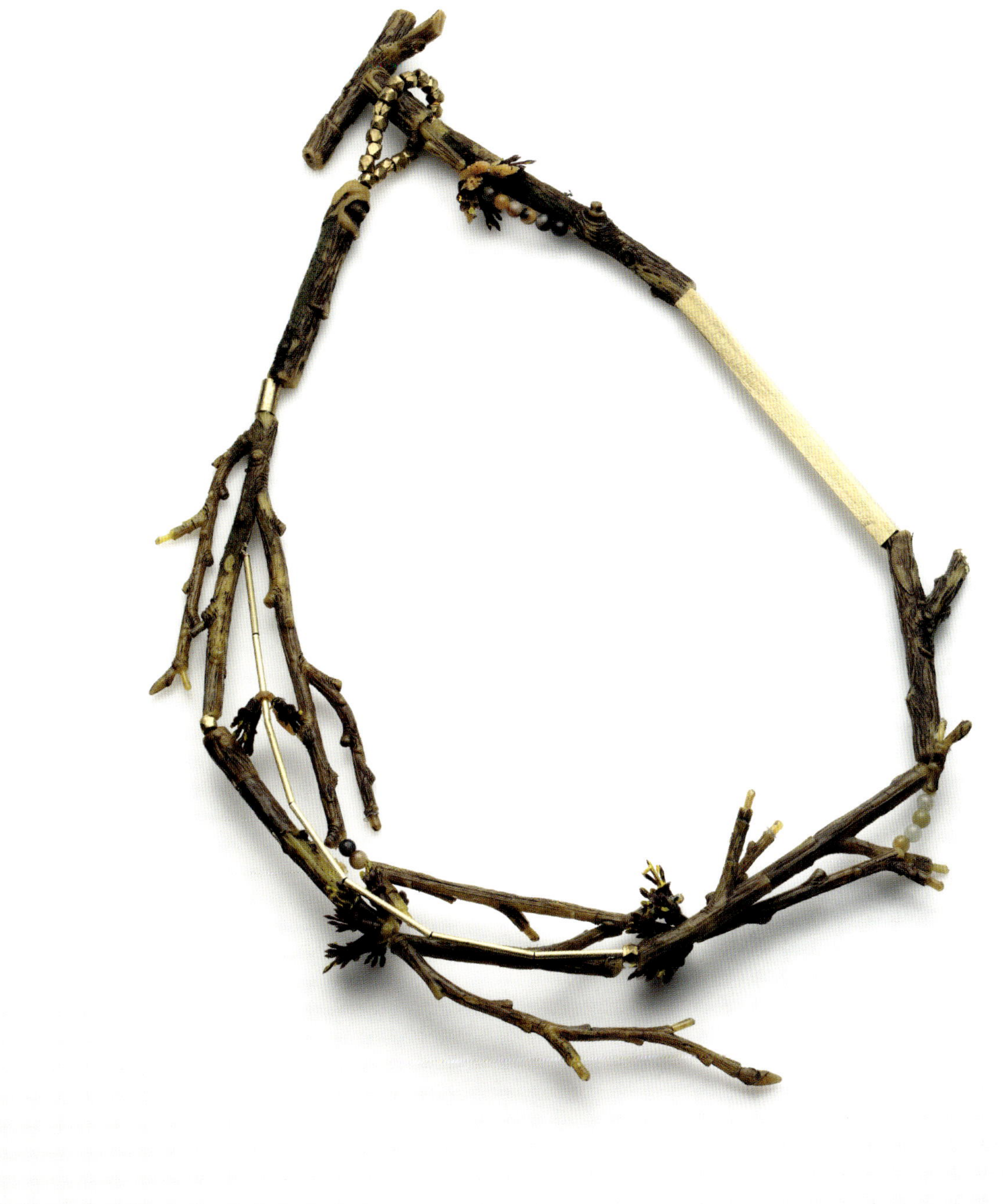

VIPOO SRIVILASA

born 1969, Bangkok, Thailand
lives in Melbourne, VIC

Vipoo Srivilasa received a Bachelor of Arts in Ceramics at Rangsit University in Bangkok before moving to Australia in 1999. After his arrival he obtained a Graduate Diploma of Arts from Monash University, Melbourne in 1997, followed by a Master of Fine Art and Design (Ceramics) from the University of Tasmania in 1998, before heading to JamFactory in 1999 to be a studio access tenant.

Interestingly, Srivilasa and fellow ceramicist Kirsten Coelho both applied for the Associate program for 1999, but due to the planned changes in Creative Directors at the time, there was no intake of first-year Associates that year, and both became studio access tenants instead. Being a studio tenant rather than an Associate did not affect the levels of exchange and support between the studio's Creative Director, Stephen Bowers, and Srivilasa. He describes Bowers as 'kind, fun to be around, full of knowledge and ready to help at any time'.

Srivilasa's work draws directly on his personal experiences and delves into the rich history of ceramics, in particular 18th-century English porcelain figurines, to make wry social commentary. While at JamFactory, he developed one of his favourite series, the subversive, kitsch and humorous *S&M Mermaids,* (2009). In this series he cast himself as a submissive under the control of a fin-tailed dominatrix. The series reflected his bi-cultural experiences, bondage references, and the less than tolerant attitudes towards homosexuality in Thailand compared to the broader acceptance of gay culture he experienced in Australia.

For Srivilasa, some of the best things about JamFactory are the ongoing networks and opportunities it has given him throughout his career. He has recently undertaken residencies at the Pottery Workshop at Jingdezhen, China, where he produced his most recent body of work, *Patience Flower,* 2012. While in Jingdezhen, Srivilasa spent time with Robin Best, who introduced his work to UK-based dealer Adrian Sassoon (who represents a number of Australian practitioners since he travelled to JamFactory supported by funds from the Australia Council).

Patience Flower, so titled due to the time it takes to make, is inspired by the 18th-century Meissen *Teapot with snowball blossoms* by Johann Joachim Kaendler. Impressed by the amount of concentration required to produce a teapot decorated with hundreds of hand-painted three-dimensional blossoms, Srivilasa was keen to create a new body of work that evoked this skill. When he tried to focus his attention on such a labour-intensive task, Srivilasa became aware of the effects social media—in particular Facebook and its constant stream of updates—had on his attention span. It was in Jingdezhen, away from social media's noise, that he was able to obtain the level of focus required to produce such work.

Margaret Hancock Davis

left
Patience Flower 002, *2012*
hand built and cast porcelain
240 x 160 x 150mm

Patience Flower 001, *2012*
hand built and cast porcelain
210 x 170 x 130mm

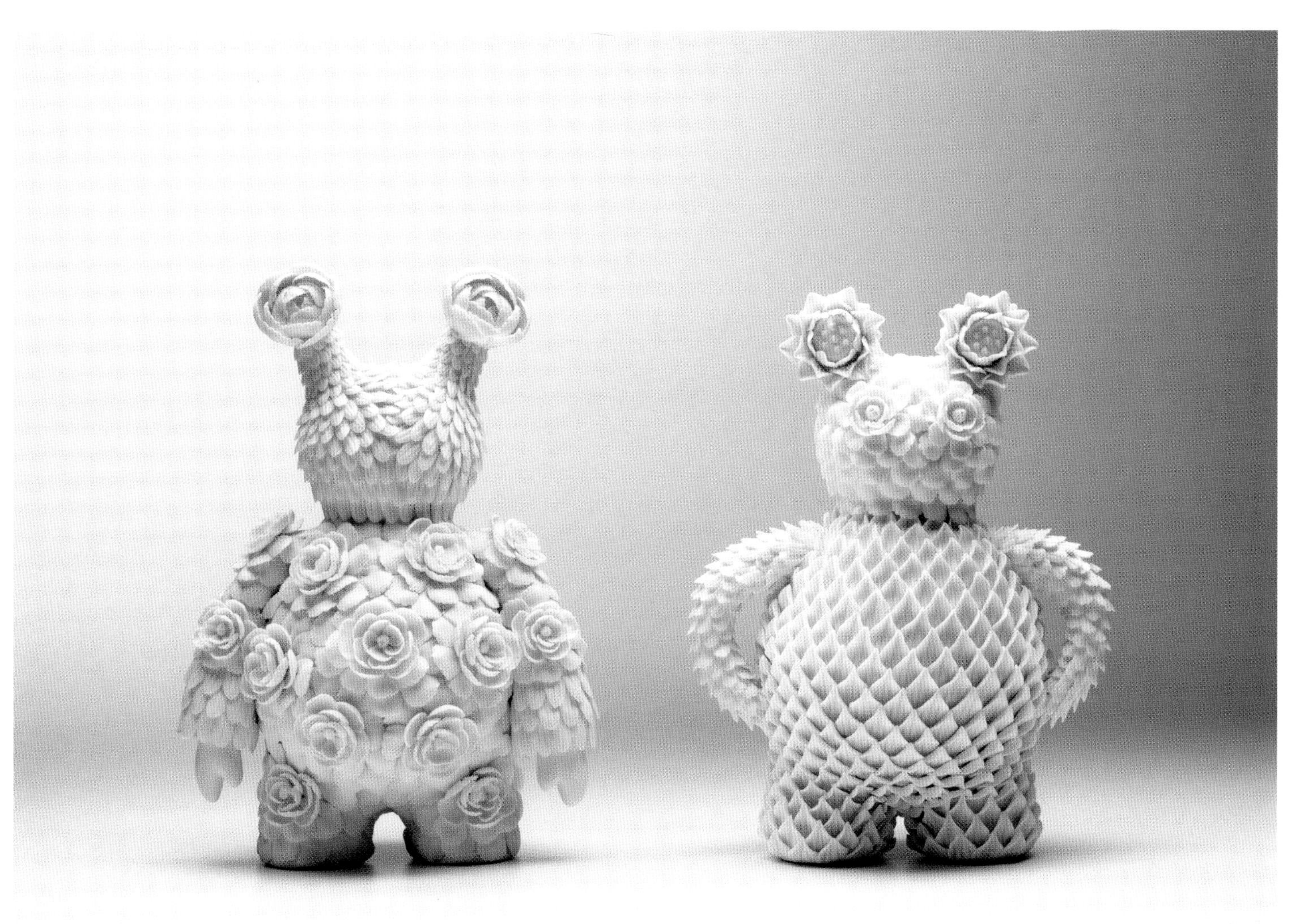

MICHELLE TAYLOR

born 1982, Melbourne, Vic
lives in Melbourne, Vic

Michelle Taylor studied graphic design before undertaking a Bachelor of Arts (with Distinction) (Fine Art) at RMIT University, Melbourne in 2006. She joined JamFactory's Metal Design Studio in 2007, under Creative Director Sue Lorraine.

Rather than develop a production range during her time at JamFactory, Taylor focused her attention on developing one-off pieces for exhibition, and her present practice continues in this vein. In 2007 her work was selected for exhibition, as part of the emerging designers' showcase, at *Talente*, Munich. From this exposure, Taylor was offered representation with Alternatives Gallery in Italy, which has showcased her work at *Collect*, London annually since 2008. This has led to her work being acquired by international collections, including the Alice and Louis Koch Collection of rings, Switzerland, and the Schmuckmuseum, Pforzheim, Germany.

Taylor credits the unique and supportive environment created by JamFactory's team of creative, curatorial and administration personnel for building her confidence and providing opportunities for her to expand her exhibition profile. She adds:

The unlimited access to the mix of studios—equipped with a range of machinery not readily available in independent jewellery, such as sand blasters, spot welders and band saws - provided me a level of experimentation in process and material that I may not have otherwise undertaken.

Taylor is an intuitive maker who works almost exclusively with recovered wood to create organic brooches, necklaces and rings. During her time at JamFactory she often sourced offcuts from the Furniture Studio, but more recently she has found a woodworker close to her house in the Dandenong Ranges, who leaves a box of offcuts out on the nature strip for people to take. She muses that the woodworker possibly expects these offcuts to end up as firewood, not contemporary jewellery.

Taylor's work grows naturally, starting with a carved wood base. She then thoughtfully combines components to add textures and colour, editing and adjusting as the piece develops. Keeping all her offcuts, Taylor rummages through her pile like a child looking for a Lego piece until she finds just the right one, which she then intricately joins with a sturdy mix of pins.

The beauty of the offcut in Taylor's work is that each component is marked by its own history. Enhancing the worn, scuffed, patterned and internal structures with rubbed-back paint, Taylor makes jewellery that becomes a metaphor for man's incursions into, and adaptation of, the landscape.

Margaret Hancock Davis

top
The beanstalk, *2012,*
Bamboo plywood, English limewood, Rimu, walnut, mild steel, paint, timber stain, stainless steel, polyurethane varnish
35 x 90 x 85mm

As green as grass, *2012,*
Bamboo plywood, pine plywood, English limewood, Rimu, walnut, mild steel, paint, timber stain, stainless steel, polyurethane varnish
20 x 100 x 78mm

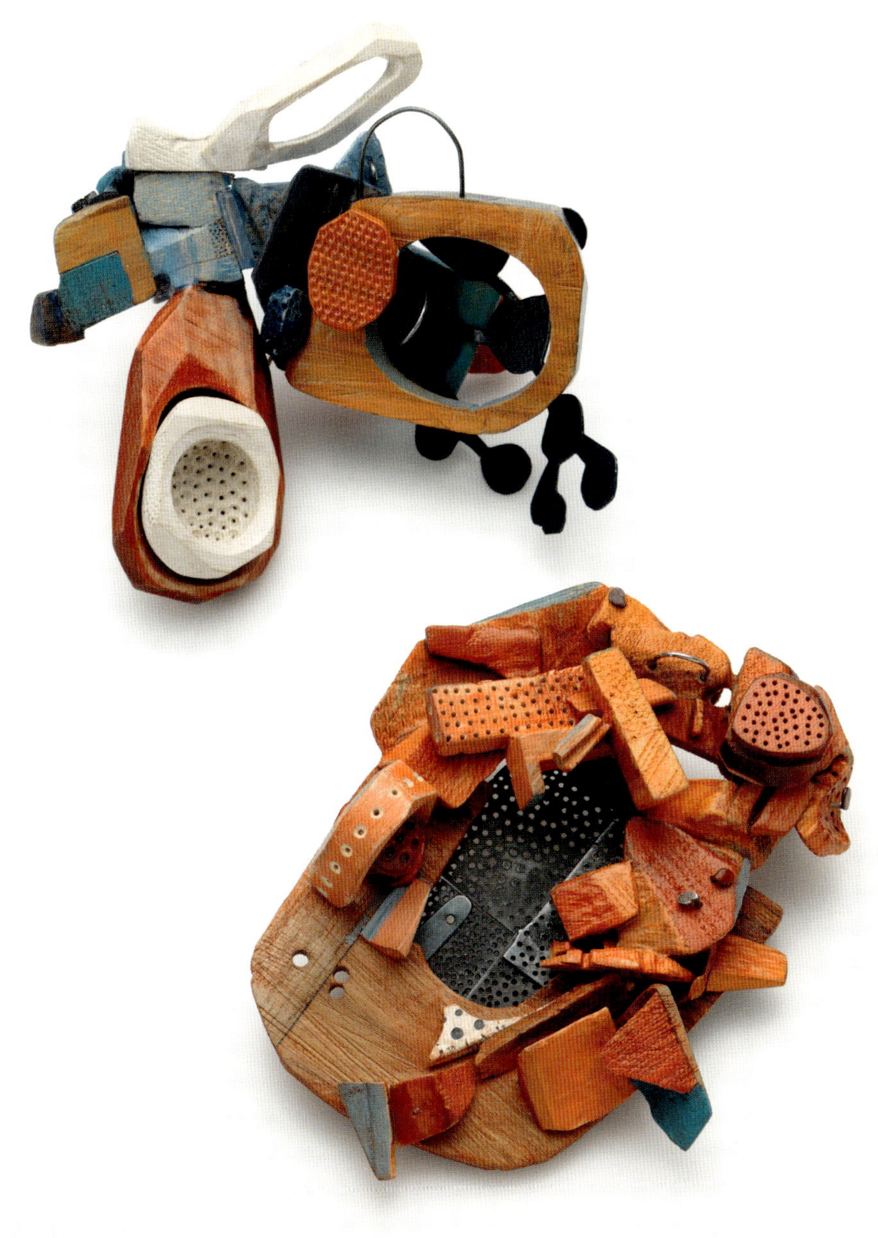

CHRISTOPHER THOMAS

born 1973, Adelaide, SA
lives in Florvåg, Norway

With a passion for the arts from childhood, Christopher Thomas was thinking of becoming an architect when he finished school. After viewing an exhibition by Tasmanian artist-furniture maker Patrick Hall at JamFactory in 1991, Thomas's preconceived notions about objects and their role in our lives were challenged, and this ultimately led him on his journey to become a furniture designer.

He completed a Bachelor of Arts majoring in Furniture Design at the University of Tasmania, before returning to Adelaide to open Christopher Thomas Art & Design in 1997. This was a privately-owned, independent gallery and furniture store, containing specially designed and produced furniture and objects from a broad range of Australian designers, which ran until 2002.

Thomas joined the JamFactory's Furniture Studio under Creative Director Peter Walker in 1998. Thomas says:

I knew Peter from my days at the University of Tasmania—I witnessed with Peter the realities of trying to be a designer-maker, the balancing act of juggling creativity, responsibility, opportunities, financial realities, family and career. You risk a lot being creative and I think Peter's experience as a father made him a good confidante and a memorable studio leader. His style was very casual, loose and free, yet rooted in technical knowledge and the ability to understand people and what they needed. He was also lucky, a trait he said designers need in abundance. He encouraged collaboration, communication, exploration and, in the design world, you don't see that very often.

After completing his Associateship at JamFactory, Thomas lectured at the University of South Australia, the Noarlunga Institute of TAFE and the Douglas Mawson Institute of TAFE, before travelling and working as a designer-maker for Nævdal Snekkeri in Norway, and lecturing at the Royal College of Art, London, and at KHiO, the Oslo National Academy of the Arts. These experiences have enabled him the distance to reflect on JamFactory:

JamFactory is an amazing place and its community truly world class. In my travels I have never come across anything quite like it—it is constantly striving to sustain a venue and give a voice to a new generation of designers and craftspeople, so they can contribute to our cultural environment. I now live on the other side of the world in Scandinavia and directly as a result of my time at the Jam I own and run a successful design and manufacturing company, I exhibit regularly, teach in some of the world's best design schools and support my family. I couldn't be happier with my experiences and the life tools that I picked up at the Jam.

Thomas's practice includes bespoke, and limited-run production furniture, objects and interiors, which blend a range of handmade and computer-aided processes. Produced exclusively for this exhibition, *RoundSquare*, 2012 table has the potential to become a small-run production item for Thomas's design company, Thomas Design. He states:

In this piece I am very much interested in the simplicity of the repeated geometric patterns and their ability to make the viewer become calm and lost in moments of abstract contemplation. The pattern in the top and the relationship of the different elements are very much a merging of the circle and the square, two basic pure shapes ...I enjoy travelling in Morocco, experiencing the craftsmanship, and I see this piece emerging from the tea experiences and highly ornate silver trays and tea tables. I have morphed these experiences into a 'quietly funky' yet functional shape that suits our modern lifestyles.

Margaret Hancock Davis

RoundSquare table,
2012
powdercoated aluminium, highmacs solid surfacing material
450 x 1200 x 690mm

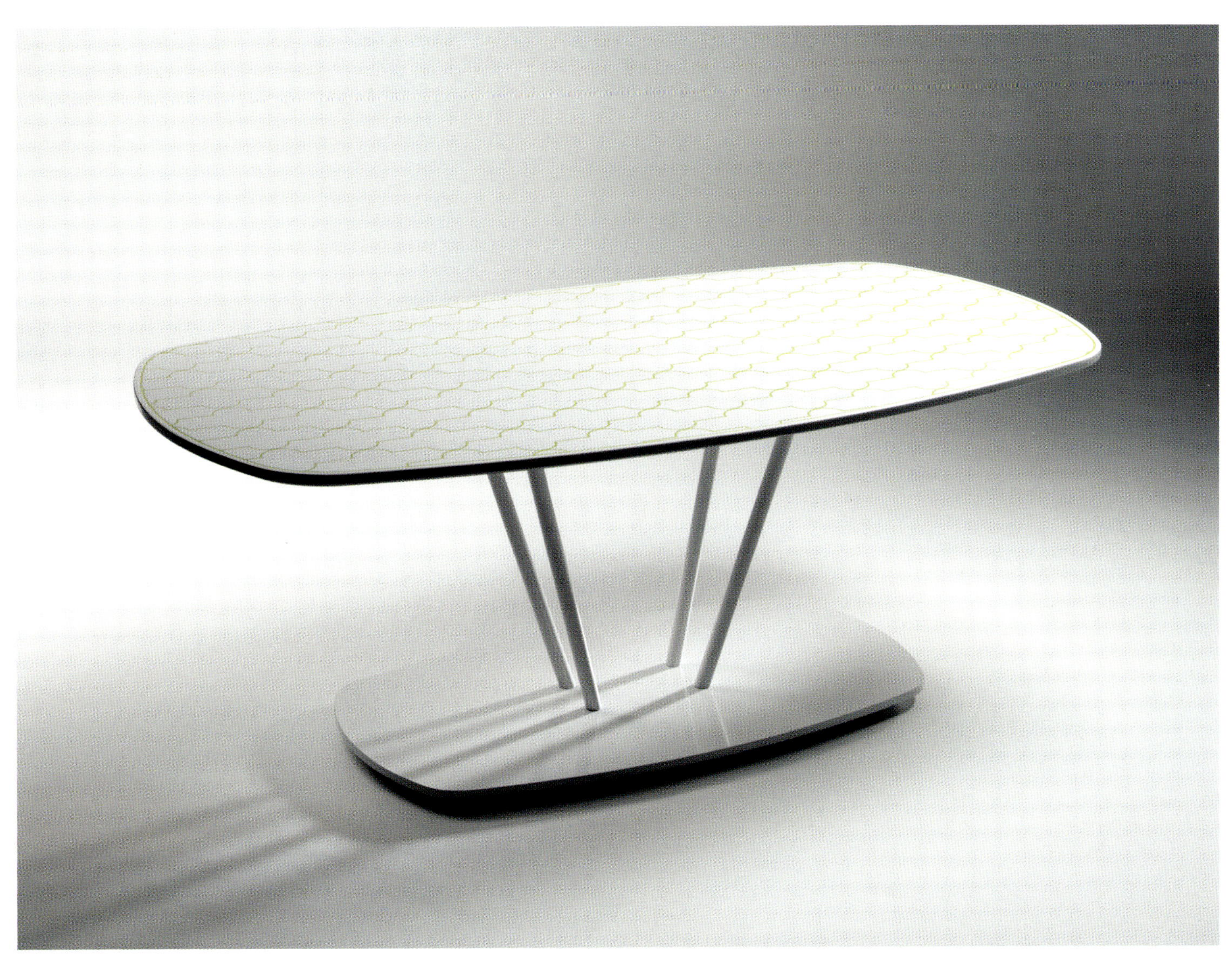

PRUE VENABLES

born 1954, Newcastle Upon Tyne, UK
lives in Melbourne, Vic

After more than 30 years as a studio potter, Prue Venables is widely regarded as one of the most prominent contemporary ceramic artists in Australia. From 2010 to 2012 she was Creative Director of the JamFactory Ceramics Studio.

Venables studied zoology at Melbourne University in the early 1970s, and soon after completing her degree moved to the UK to follow musical interests. Her formal training in ceramics began in 1981 in the Studio Pottery course at Harrow College of Art, London. This rigorous program, taught by influential lecturers such as Walter Keeler and Richard Slee, instilled in Venables a disciplined work ethic and a strong philosophy of making, which she has since sought to convey to students and emerging artists in her various teaching and mentoring roles in Australia, and through guest lecturing in Sweden, Denmark, the UK, New Zealand, Pakistan, South Korea and Taiwan.

It was not until Venables returned to Australia from the UK in 1989 that she began to work with Limoges porcelain—the luminous and refined material that is now synonymous with her work.

There is a deceptive simplicity in her minimalist works, which explore utilitarian forms. What appears light and delicately effortless actually requires great skill and precision in manipulating thrown forms, and in propping and cradling these forms during the firing to prevent warping and collapse. Of her work in this exhibition, she says:

The search for an apparent simplicity, quietness, and an essential stillness motivates my work and yet there are contradictions hidden here. The finished objects stand innocently, as if oblivious to the complexities of their history of skilful and rigorous making and firing processes, while still containing covert references to the sprung tensions of their thrown and altered origins. These objects are made to be used and handled, but also embody sculptural and spatial interactions that reflect both musical and gestural references.

Venables' first formal engagement with JamFactory was in 1993, when she exhibited in the main gallery with acclaimed Japanese ceramic artist Takeshi Yasuda. Interaction through other exhibitions and invitations to conduct workshops ultimately led to Venables applying for the Creative Director's role in 2010.

One of the Ceramics Studio's most significant achievements under Venables' leadership was the completion of a commission for 1,000 hand-thrown bowls—at relatively short notice—for a major event on the beach at Port Willunga coordinated by renowned chef Gay Bilson for the Adelaide Film Festival in February 2011. This project was valuable in bringing a strong sense of community back to the Studio, with many potters contracted to assist in production. This reconnection with local ceramic artists was maintained throughout the lead-up to the 2012 Australian Ceramics Triennale, and Venables championed comprehensive involvement by JamFactory in this important event.

Brian Parkes

Trio, *2012*
wheel thrown, altered and pierced Limoges porcelain
bottle 255 x 120 x 85mm
pierced spoon
85 x 330 x 65mm
oval bowl
135 x 320 x 270mm

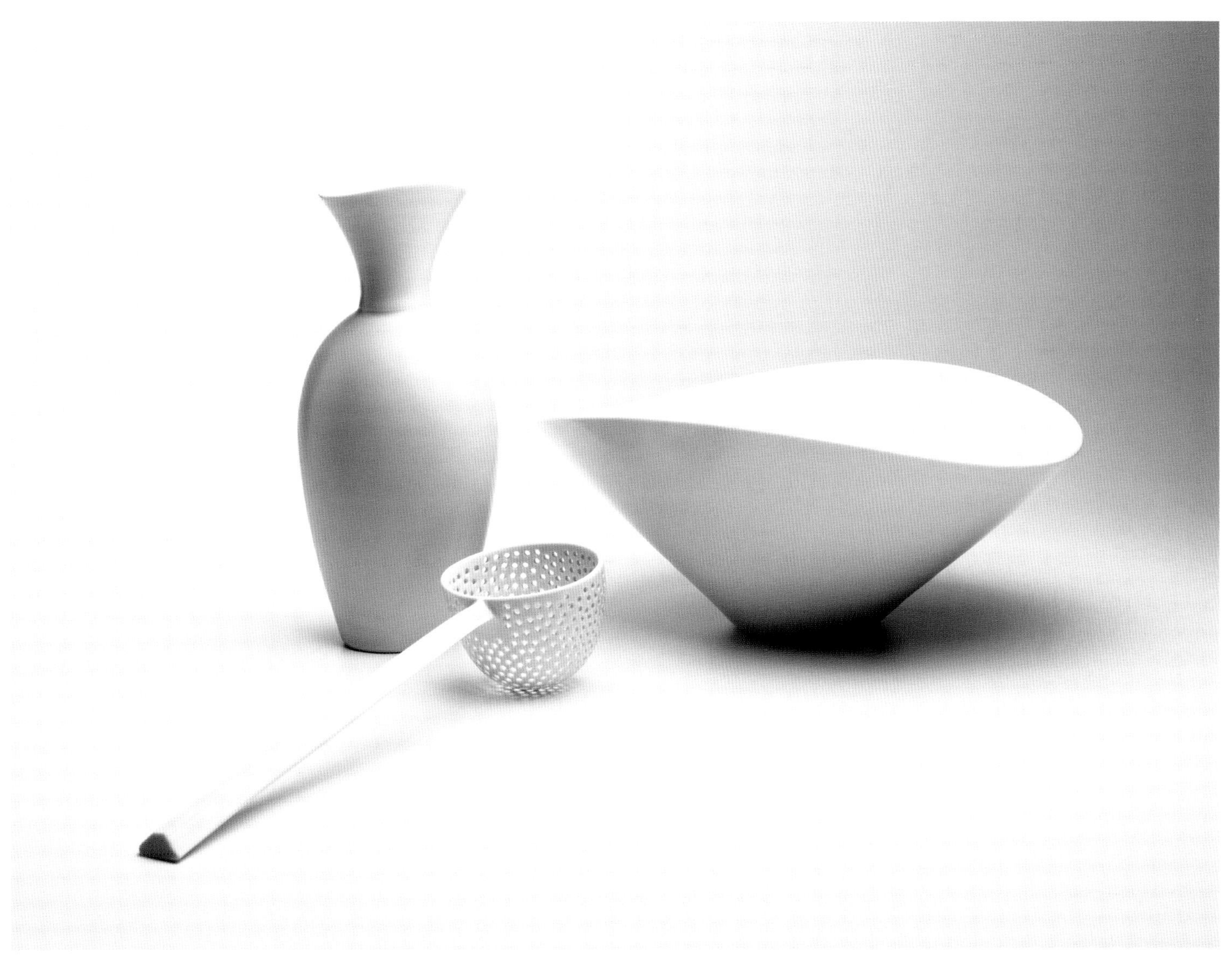

JANICE VITKOVSKY

born 1977, Adelaide, SA
lives in Adelaide, SA

Janice Vitkovsky was an Associate in the Glass Studio from 2000 to 2001. During that time she was awarded the inaugural JamFactory scholarship to attend Pilchuck Glass School, USA, where she had the opportunity to experience glass in the international arena. She regards her experience at Pilchuck and at JamFactory as pivotal points in building her skill. She states that, for her, 'the intensive training was fundamental to understanding glass as a material and its technical capacities'. In 2002, Vitkovsky was selected to exhibit at *Talente*, Munich.

At this time she was working primarily in blown glass and making production lines for JamFactory's retail operations. However, she had become drawn to the fused *murrine* glass made by glass artist Giles Bettison, and asked if she could learn from him. Assisted by a grant from the Australia Council, she undertook a mentorship program with Bettison in his New York studio, assisting him at master classes in New York and France. She then went to Canberra School of Art to complete an honours year, and followed this with a further year as artist in residence. It was there that Vitkovsky refined some of the technical issues underlying her approach to *murrine* glass. She won the *Object (New Design) National Graduate Award* and a scholarship to attend North Lands Creative Glass in Scotland.

Vitkovsky has evolved a distinctive interpretation of *murrine*, creating intricate monochromatic patterns that sometimes seem to flicker in response to the moving gaze of the viewer. She is interested in resonances between tonal diffusions of colour and shifting emotional frequencies.

Since she returned to Adelaide in 2007, Vitkovsky has established a studio-based practice, creating *murrine* wall panels and freestanding forms for exhibitions in Sydney, where she is represented by Sabbia Gallery, and in the USA, where she is represented by Bullseye Gallery, Portland, Oregon. She participated in the international Asialink touring exhibition, *White Hot* (2008) and the JamFactory exhibition *Mind and Matter* (2010).

Her work in this exhibition, *View*, 2012 represents an extension of her approach to *murrine*. She states:

My work is centred around notions of perspective, and how our experiences colour and shape our perspective on things. By working with intricate patterns that depict fluidity and motion, I am interested in exposing the immersive nature of our experiences and in creating an impression of impermanence. By employing a historic Venetian murrine technique I am able to create lines that travel through the glass, where a moiré effect is created. This effect plays with the viewer's interaction with the work, changing as you move around it.

Margot Osborne

View, *2012*
murrine technique, fused, cast and hand finished glass
590 x 590 x 20mm

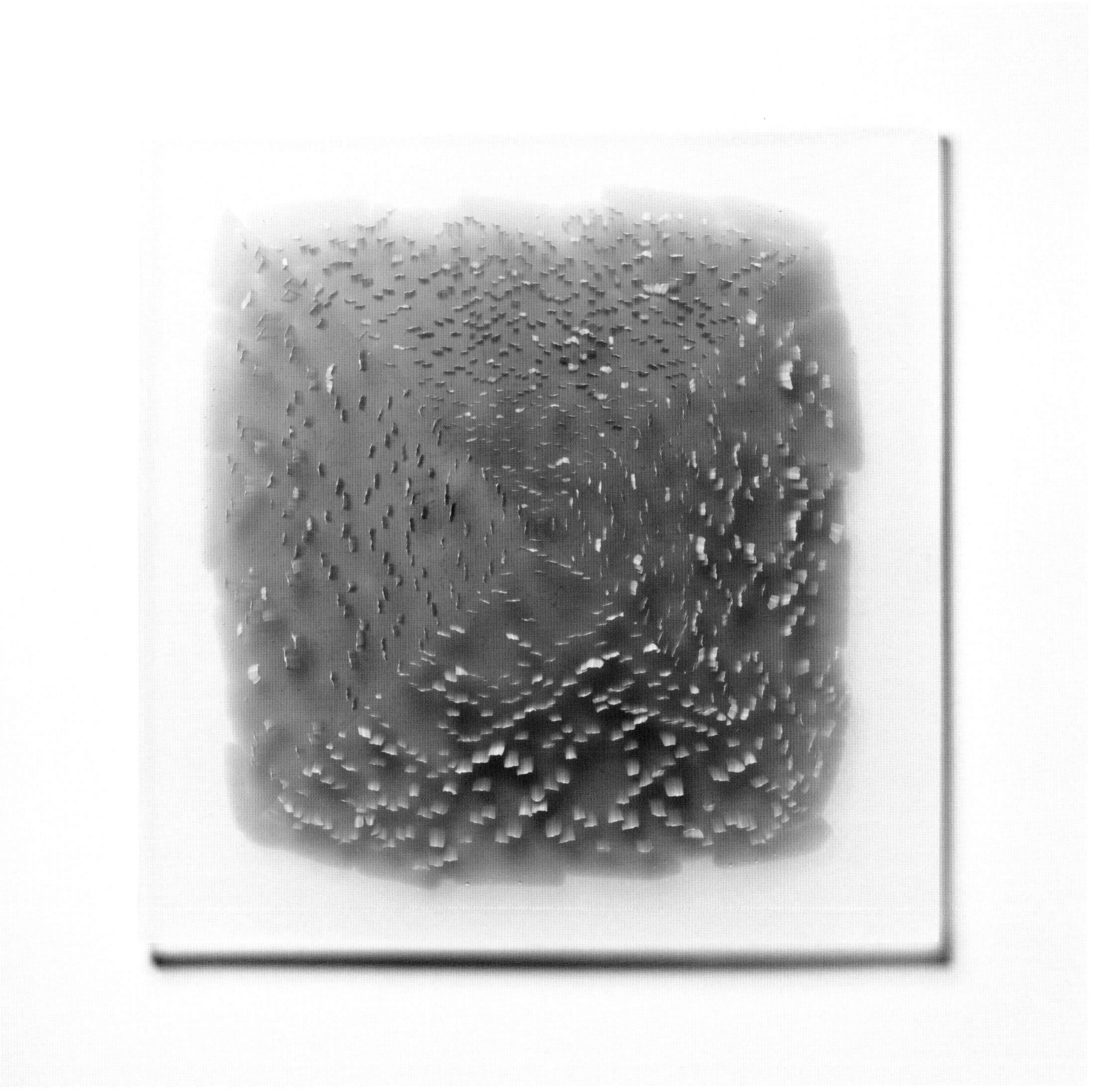

PETER WALKER

born 1961, Sydney, NSW
lives in Adelaide, SA

Peter Walker was an early graduate from the groundbreaking Design in Wood program at the University of Tasmania in Hobart in the mid 1980s. Having established a successful practice as a designer–maker, combining sculptural work and functional design, he moved to Adelaide in 1997 to take up the role of Head of Furniture Design. He says:

I came to the JamFactory attracted by the prospect of melding my professional practice experience with the opportunity to train others. JamFactory provides a unique contribution in developing craft and design professionals. It is not possible for universities and art schools to teach the realities of making a living as a professional designer/craftsperson, nor is it their role, as they concentrate on historical and aesthetic foundations for a career in the creative arts. The JamFactory picks up the process and provides this essential component.

During Walker's three-and-a-half years in the role, the Furniture Studio thrived, undertaking important commissions, developing Associates' design skills and exhibiting work as a studio. One of the many notable activities of this time was a major project with visiting Sydney-based designer Caroline Casey, in which former Associate, Adrian Potter, was employed by the studio to work with Casey to develop prototypes for a series of tables and stools to be produced at JamFactory and marketed and sold through Anibou. Major commissions included suites of furniture for the Abache hair salons in Burnside and Glenelg—a collaboration with the Metal Design Studio that picked up a Design Institute of Australia Gold Medal—and the seating for a new chapel at Pedare Christian College.

Working with Philips/Pilkington Architects, we designed seating for 900. Brought on to design at the early stages of the process, before the building was built, we produced prototypes and oversaw the sub-contracted process and carried out the critical installation. This was an enormous space, where the furniture became an integral architectural element.

Walker's success in his role at JamFactory and within his own practice resulted in an appointment as Honorary Research Fellow at the University of Wisconsin and later to the Rhode Island School of Design. During ten years at RISD as Associate Professor, he served in the roles of Graduate Research Director and Department Head of Furniture Design. Walker attributes his international career and outlook to his time at JamFactory.

Probably the most significant change for me as an artist was to have the potential of a global career become part of my thinking. Watching the glass artists' phenomenal success in marketing themselves internationally inspired me to think about my own work in an international context. I actively started looking outward and took my work and the JamFactory story to the United States through presentations at the Furniture Society Conference in San Francisco and at Anderson Ranch, Colorado in the late 1990s.

Walker maintained strong links with Australia through this time and helped create opportunities for artists and designers on both sides of the Pacific. He returned to Australia in 2012, and is currently Program Director for the Masters of Sustainable Design and Senior Lecturer in Interior Architecture at the University of South Australia.

Walker's sculptural work in this exhibition, *The Moon*, 2012 is a geodesic sphere made from organic wooden elements and has been created in reference to geodesy—the science of measuring the size and shape of the earth. He notes that 'whether the moon is crescent, full, waning or waxing, it remains constant across the hemispheres'.

Brian Parkes

The Moon, *2012*
eucalyptus, aluminium
900mm dia.

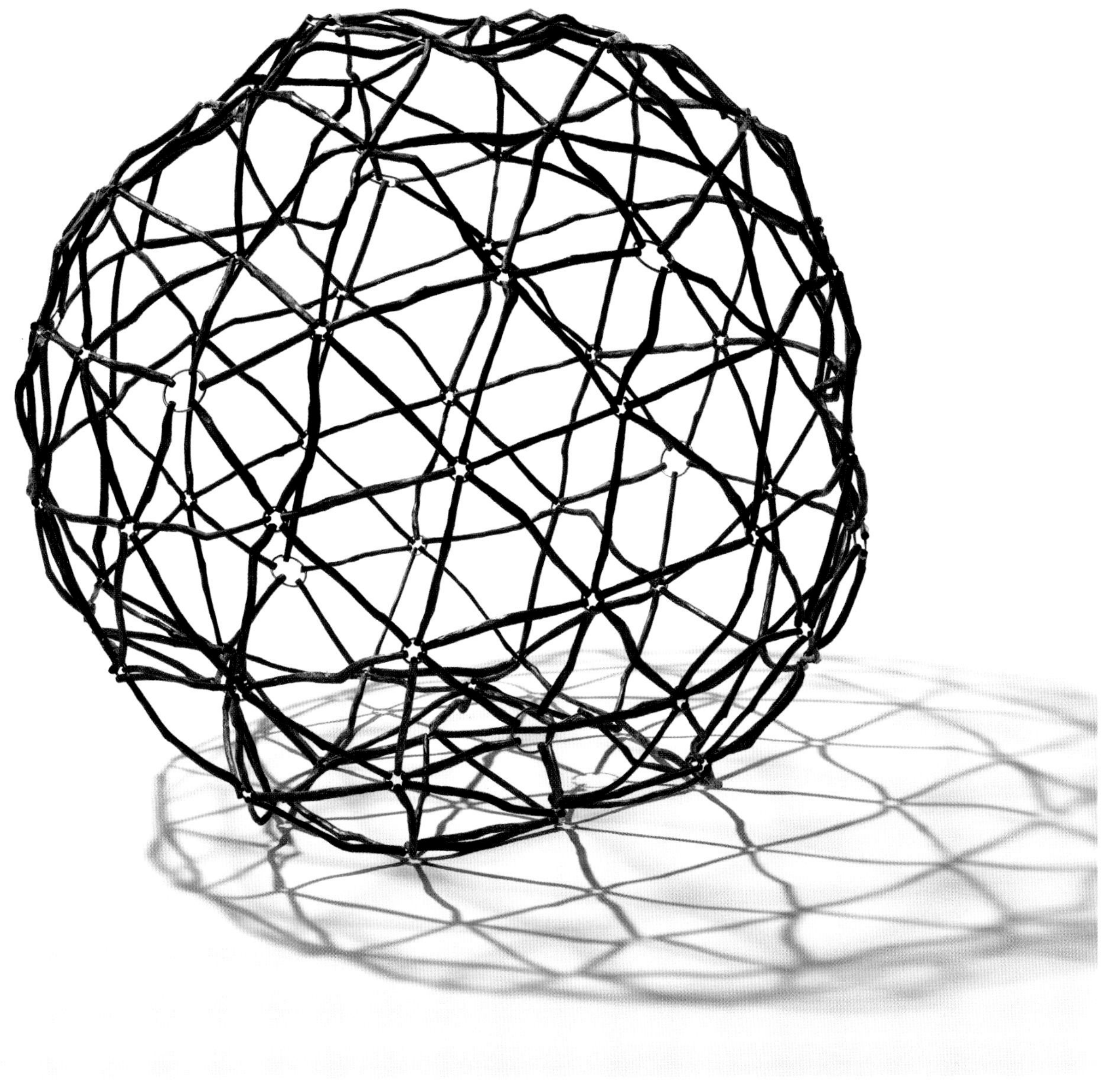

GERRY WEDD

born 1957, McLaren Vale, SA
lives at Port Elliot, SA

Gerry Wedd's time at the Jam Factory as a studio tenant from 1985 to 1986 was relatively brief, but it has remained a key moment in his career as a ceramicist. He states:

Every aspect of what I do has been influenced by my time at the Jam—technically, aesthetically and professionally. It was a ceramics melting pot and meeting place, a natural networking hot-house situation. It was also a focal point for visitors, curators and the like ... For me it was all positive, I came and went as I liked and was able to glean things from the various Heads and tenants. Good socially as well. The Bull Ring gallery was also really significant in exposing craft practitioners to the visual arts and vice versa. There was always the issue with the role of the Jam—that has been there from the beginning. The training system had terrific results when Bronwyn (Kemp) was running ceramics. Most educators contributing now are ex-trainees or tenants from that period.

Wedd has a diverse creative career. He is highly regarded in Australia not only as a ceramicist, but also as a jeweller, and as a designer for surfwear company Mambo. He has exhibited frequently at JamFactory in solo exhibitions—*Thong Cycle* (2008), *Willow* (2005–06), *Material Narratives* (2001) and *Scratch: an exhibition of applied art and crafts* (1993)—and in major group exhibitions including, most recently, *A Secret History of Blue and White* (touring 2006–09) and *Porcelain* (2009). He has achieved an international presence in exhibitions in Germany (2011) and as part of the *10th Biennial of Havana*, Cuba (2009), and has won the major national awards, the Hobart Art Prize (2010) and the Sidney Myer Fund International Ceramics Award (1998).

Wedd has a strong profile as a public artist, with some of his major commissions in Adelaide including *Brain*, a play-sculpture for Glover Playground (2010), sculptures for Hindmarsh Square (2009), *Under the arches*, Torrens River bank (2007) and *Drift* sculptures for the Glenelg foreshore (2006). He has worked regularly for South Australia's artist-in-schools program (2001–11) and is a lecturer in ceramics at the University of South Australia, where he obtained his Masters in Visual Arts degree in 2009. He was the recipient of the SALA (South Australian Living Artists) monograph in 2008, with a book, *Gerry Wedd: thong cycle*, written by Mark Thomson and published by Wakefield Press.

For this exhibition he has created a large coil-built ceramic urn with cobalt slip decoration, *Towards a Standard*, 2012. The surface of the urn is covered with Wedd's drawn and painted vignettes and cameo portraits of the people who have figured in the history of JamFactory's Ceramics Studio over the years. He states: 'The urn is a tribute to my time at the JamFactory and the people I came across while I was working there'.

Margot Osborne

Towards a Standard, *2012*
coil-built ceramic, cobalt slip decoration
560 x 400mm dia.

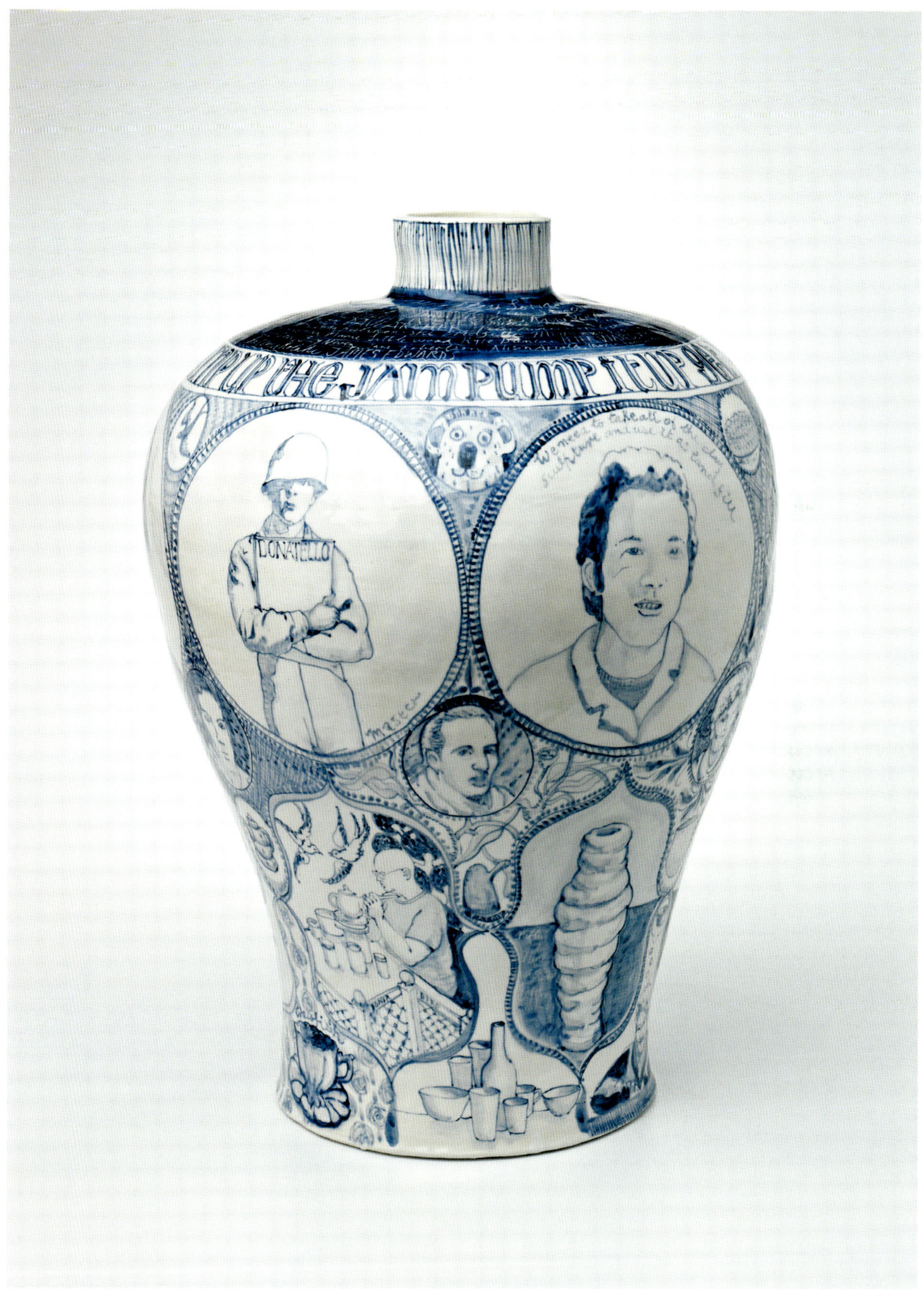
UP THE JAM PUMP IT UP
DONATELLO

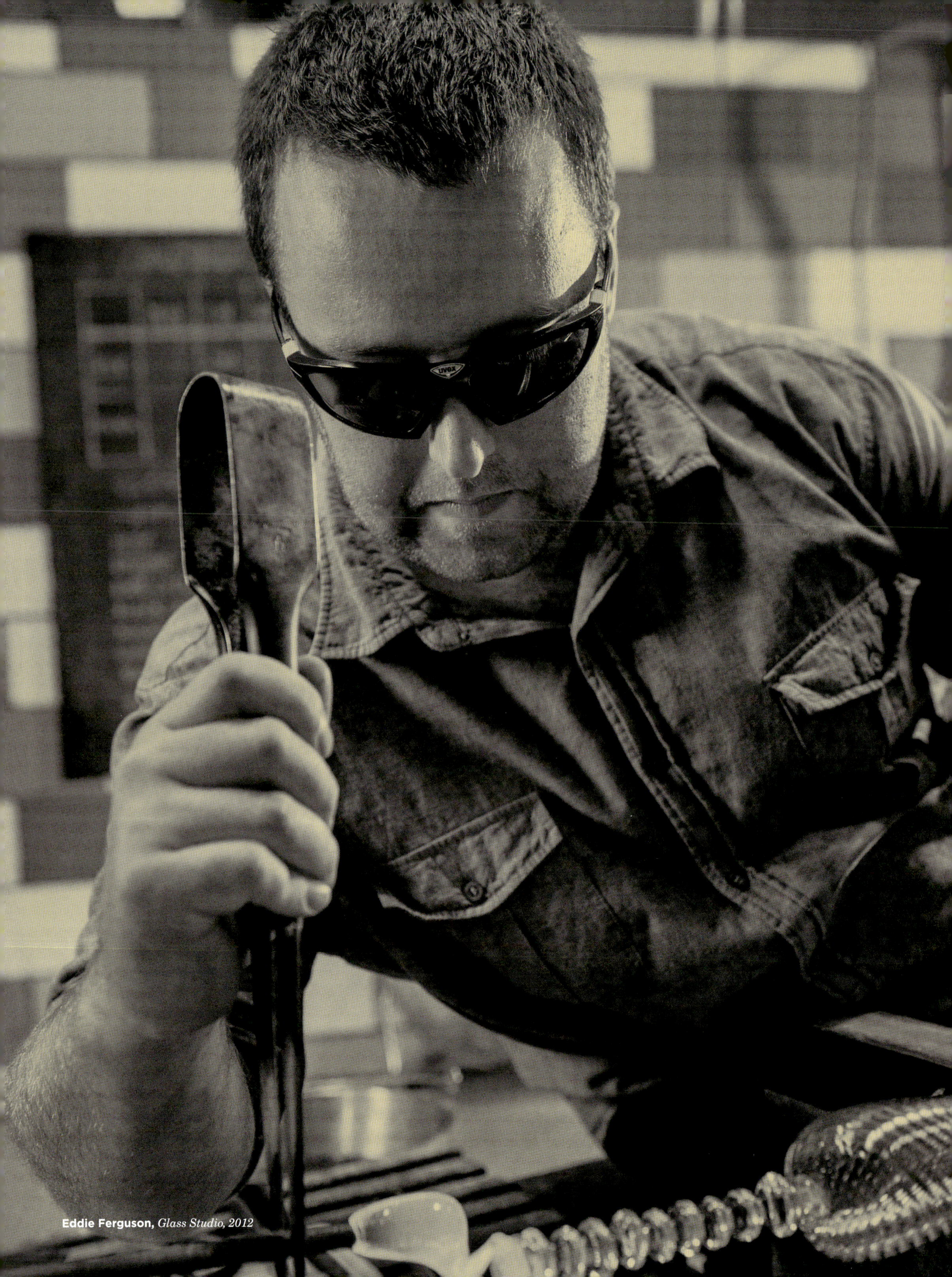

Eddie Ferguson, *Glass Studio, 2012*

CREATIVE DIRECTORS, ASSOCIATES AND TENANTS 1973 - 2013

CERAMICS STUDIO

Past Creative Directors
2010 - 2012
Prue Venables

2008 - 2010
Robin Best

2006 – 2007
Philip Hart

1999 - 2003
Neville Assad Salha

1990 - 1999
Stephen Bowers

1989 - 1990
Peter Andersson

1983 – 1988
Bronwyn Kemp

1979 - 1983
Jeff Mincham

From 1976-1977 a pilot workshop was run by Wally Shwab

Current Associate
2012 - 2013
Ulrica Trulsson

Past Associates
2012
Alison Smiles

2011 - 2012
Wayne McAra
Sophia Philips
Hilary Jones

2010 - 2011
Maria Chatzinikolaki
James Edwards

2009 - 2010
Susan Frost

2008 - 2009
Tamara Hahn
Suzanne Gregor

2007 - 2008
Stephanie James-Manttan
Erin Lykos

2006 - 2007
Mercedes Mangnall
Maria Parmenter
John Colman

2004 - 2005
Charmain Hearder
Isabella Niven
Jane Robertson

2003 - 2004
Alison Arnold
Peter Anderson

2002 - 2003
Zoe Warburton
Tracey Rosser
Honor Freeman

2001 - 2002
Jane Burbidge
Peter Ward
Lee Marshall

2000 - 2001
Judy Griffith
Vicki Xiros
Karen Warburton

1999 - 2000
Marie Littlewood
Kylie Duncan

1998 - 1999
Ben Booth

1996 - 1997
Elodie Barker
Jacinta Ivory
Jane Bamford

1995 - 1996
Jutta Kulikowski
Bridgette Minuzzo
Bronwyn Lennox
Denise Angus
Lesa Farrant

1993 - 1994
Naomi Boxall
Nico Petho
Georgia Rydon

1991 – 1992
Richard Doheny
Tim Edwards
Yvonne Nitschke

1989 – 1991
Joanne Fraser

1989 – 1990
Rosalind Hoskin
Christopher Harford

1988 – 1990
Gerard Slade
Peter Andersson

1988 - 1989
David Archer
Moira Corby
Liz Eakins

1987 – 1988
Robyn Herriman

1986 - 1987
Jo Crawford
Phil Hart

1985 – 1986
Merrilyn Stock
Stephanie Livesey

1984 – 1986
Lincoln Kirby Bell
Georgia Hale

1984 – 1985
Kay Pemberton

1983 – 1985
Philipe Lakeman

1983 – 1984
Peter Rose

1982 – 1985
Kate Jenkins

1982 - 1984
Gary Roberts

1982 – 1983
Gail Barwick

1982 – 1983
Anne Parsons

1981 – 1983
Stephen Bowers

1981 – 1982
Janis Heston
Kathy Alty

1980 – 1982
John Odgers

1980 – 1981
Timothy Strachan
Mark Heidenreich
Pamela James-Marti
Lorraine Lee

1979 – 1980
Peter Andersson
Christopher Headley
Bronwyn Kemp

FURNITURE STUDIO

Current Creative Director
2005 - present
Tom Mirams

Past Creative Directors
2002 - 2003
Michael Searle

2000 - 2002
Gregory Gilmour

1997 - 2000
Peter Walker

1994 - 1996
Donald Fortescue

1990 - 1994
David Adderton

Current Associates
Andrew Gregg
Daniel Guest
Liam Mugavin
Matthew Taylor
Stephen Soeffky
Miao Wang

Past Associates
2011 - 2012
Jorge Criollo-Carrillo

2010 - 2011
Samantha Bosward
Adam Cantwell

2009 - 2010
Andrew Bartlett
Michael Garrett
Caren Ellis
Nick Koschade

2008 - 2009
John Hallett

2007 - 2008
Gareth Brown
Norhani Modh Ali
John Quan

2006 - 2007
Alucius Turner
Takeshi Iue
David Potts

2003
Peter Williams
Jim Hannon-Tan

2002 - 2003
Kelly-Anne Capuano
Amanda Twyford
Anne-Claire Petre

2001 - 2002
Toyotake Yamauchi
Michael Hill
Toby Thomas

2000 - 2001
Anne Harry
Craig English
Nico Kelly

1999 - 2000
Guy Parmenter
Penny Gough-Harper
Mac Young
Saul Scanlon

1998 - 1999
Chris Letch
Christopher Thomas
Mark O'Ryan

1997 - 1998
Ian Hope
Anna Brown
Tom Mirams

1996 - 1997
Julie Pieda
Michael Searle

1995 - 1996
Gray Hawk
Adrian Potter

1993 - 1994
Andrew Osbourne
Malcolm Thompson

1992 - 1994
Kestie Lane
Martin Murray

1991 - 1992
Richard Butcher
Michael Kumnick
Ian Lewis
Elena Tay

GLASS STUDIO

Current Creative Director
2012 - present
Karen Cunningham

Past Creative Directors
2007 - 2011
Deb Jones
Christine Cholewa
Tom Moore
Nick Mount
(Management Team)

2000 - 2006
Matthew Larwood

1997 - 2000
Elizabeth Kelly

1994 - 1997
Nick Mount

1985 - 1994
Peter Tysoe

1983 - 1985
Tom Persson

1978 - 1982
Stanislav Melis

1974 – 1977
Sam Herman

Current Associates
George Agius
Llewelyn Ash
Diego Vides
Boreel
Liam Fleming
Marcel
Hoogstad Hay
Katie-Ann
Houghton
Alexander Valero

Past Associates
2011 - 2012
Eddie Ferguson
Emma Klau
Katherine Plunkard

2010 - 2011
Kristel Britcher
Andrea Fiebig
Madeline Prowd

2010
Aogu Takano

2009 - 2010
Jaan Poldaas
Danielle Rickaby

2008 - 2009
Amanda Dziedzic
Clare Wilson
Marielle McKinley

2007 - 2008
Jess Fisher
Kumiko Nakajima

2006 - 2007
David Yule
Vickie Melanson
Mandi King
Karen Cunningham

2005 - 2006
Annette Blair
Brenden Miller

2004 - 2005
Elizabeth Newman
Jacqueline Knight
Christine Cholewa
Yuri Tamura

2003 - 2004
Yvette van Berkel
Laurel Kohut
Dale Roberts

2002 - 2003
Louise FitzGerald
Wendy Meyen
Luke Mount
Shizuko Somadori

2001 - 2002
Bronwyn Black
Andrew Baldwin
Aanya Roenfeldt

2000 - 2001
Janice Vitkovsky
Aaron Robinson

1999 - 2000
Emma Petersen
Mark Thiele

1998 - 1999
Mel Fraser
Troy Tirrell
Brenden Scott
French

1997 - 1998
Tegan Empson
Wendy Hannam

1996 - 1997
Hilary Crawford
Tyrone Renyon

1995 - 1996
Tom Moore
Tim Edwards
Sophia Emmett
Sarah Jane Fieldsend

1994 - 1995
Miles Johnson
David McLeod

1993 - 1994
Joyce Louey
Greg Gepp
Deb Jones

1992 - 1993
Yolanda Blans

1991 - 1992
Irena Kaluza
Clare Belfrage
Gabriella Bisetto

1990 – 1992
Meg Caslake

1989 - 1991
Matthew Larwood

1989 - 1990
Jane Cowie
Louella Giles

1988 - 1990
Mikaela Brown

1987 - 1989
Brian Chaseling
Effie Halkidis
Jonathon Westacott

1986 - 1988
Bettina Visentin
Kate Forest

1985 – 1987
Elizabeth Kelly

1986 - 1987
Alex Wyatt

1985 - 1986
Ross Hall

1984 - 1986
Ian Driver

1984 - 1985
Steve Davies

1983 - 1985
Setsuko Ogishi

1982 - 1985
Scott Chaseling

1981 – 1984
Eileen Gordon

1980 - 1984
Pauline Delaney

1982 – 1984
Christopher Wright

1981 - 1982
James Dodson
Nikki Stern

1979 - 1982
Michael Hook
Akihiro Isogai

1980 – 1981
Graham Crosby
Judith Hancock
Donald Wreford
Ivan Polak
Maria Polette

1979 - 1981
Alex Mitrovic

1979 - 1980
Graham Mcleod

1978 - 1979
Neil Roberts

1977 - 1979
Fred Tessari

1976 - 1977
Peter Goss

1975 – 1977
Rob Knottenbelt
Tom Persson

1974 - 1977
John Walsh

1974
Bruce Nuske
Cedar Prest
Mark Thompson

METAL DESIGN STUDIO

Current Creative Director
2009 - present
Christian Hall

Past Creative Directors
1999 - 2008
Sue Lorraine

1995 - 1998
Rik Barnsley

1991 - 1994
Greg Healey

Current Associates
Tania Black
Courtney Jackson
Nadja Mayer
Kate Sutherland

Past Associates
2011 - 2012
Natalie Gock
Minnette Michael

2010 - 2011
Jessamy Pollock

2010
Jonathon Sinclair

2009 - 2010
Hannah Carlyle
Vanessa Williams
Sorcha Flett
Peta Kruger

2008 - 2009
Leonie Westbrook
Erin Keys

2007 - 2008
Sun-Woong (Chris) Bang
Michelle Taylor
Sarah Rothe

2006 - 2007
Michelle Kelly
Meghann Jones
Meghan O'Rourke

2005 - 2006
Tassia Joannides

2004 - 2005
Shauna Mayben Swanson
David Zitnick
Sally Mahony
Carmen Liang

2003 - 2004
Sim Luttin

2002 - 2003
Katrina Freene
Kath Inglis

2001 - 2002
Marie-Jane Ryan Bennett

2000 - 2001
Petrina Kernchen
Shine Myung-ok shin

1999 - 2000
Brendan Adair Smith

1998 - 1999
Belinda Newick
Jan Lackmann
Anika Williams

1997 - 1998
Bronwen Riddiford
Lauren Simeoni

1996 - 1997
Alisa Dewhurst
Mark Tatarinoff
Melissa Turner
Stephanie Wood

1995 - 1996
Cassandra King
Rodney Mosel
Selina O'Connell

1994 - 1995
Vizma Bruns
Tim Elsom

1993 - 1994
Anna Eoclidi
Khamal Hamdan
Jane Ruljancich

1991 - 1993
Jason Moss
Belinda Powels

JEWELLERY STUDIO

Past Head of Workshop
1973 – 1978
Vahn Hemmingsen

Past Trainees
1977- 1978
Won Ho Chong
Bretton Jones

1976- 1979
Stephen Moore

1976- 1978
Peter Amadio
Christopher Lund

1976- 1977
Peter Cunningham
Barry Edwards
Mark Goldsworthy
John Heller
Christopher Mullins
Andrew Wells

1973- 1974
Diane Boynes
Don Ellis
Mary Michelmore
Chris Neave
Peter Savage
Bev Silver

The following trainees participated in programs of the jewellery studio from 1973 - 1991 but due to incomplete records dates are not available

Jonanna Antonelli
Matthew Arkins
R J Benham
Ian Butterfield
Roy Cooper
Andrew Gasner
Michael Gee
Franco Guidetti
Patricia Hagan
Susan Harle
W L Harman
Lillian Jackson
Roman Kielczweski
Greg King
Robert King
Anthony Levinson
Kevin Mangan
Linda Menzies
Raoul Monot
Andrew Muller
Jeffrey Muller
Greg Nylan
Joseph Orbuso
Colin Osborne
Wayne Pedemonte
Margaret Russell
Susan Smythe
Gerry Staruchowicz
Bep Swinkels
J Tegan
Alan Tilsley
Peter Van Czarnecki
Michael Vivian
Dean Watson
Geraldine Winzar
Grant Wishart
John Wishart
Brian Wood

LEATHER

Past Head of Workshop
1988 – 1990
Steve Bates

1980 – 1988
Ian White

1976 – 1978
Pietro Salemme

Past Trainees
1989 – 1990
Andrew Badinski
Gale Carney

1989
Therese Czislowski
Julia Banvers

1988 – 1990
Stephen Edwards

1987 – 1988
Elizabeth Abbott
Wendy Driver
Ruth Fitzgerald
Hugh Jardine
Louise Pope

1986 – 1987
Tim Morris
Jenni Oldfield

1985 – 1987
Chris Somogyi
John Francis

1985 – 1986
Jessica Ainsworth

1983 – 1985
Pauline Griffin

1983 – 1984
Ian Hicks

1982 – 1985
Jan Simons

1981 – 1984
Robert McRae

1981 – 1982
Steve Bate
Lorraine Gill

1980 – 1981
Margaret Lucy

1980 – 1981
Gordon Halliday
Richard Rowland

1979 – 1982
Dianne McKenzie

1978 – 1979
Penny Amberg

1977 – 1980
Ian White

1976 – 1979
Paolo Cerro

TEXTILE DESIGN

KNITTED
Past Head of Workshop
1982 – 1990
Jennifer Layther

WOVEN
Past Head of Workshop
1975 – 1979
Pru Medlin

KNITTED
Past Trainees
1989 – 1990
Karen Mole

1988 – 1989
Nicole Foster

1988
Elizabeth Queale

1987 – 1988
Lee Oddy
Nicole Thiele

1987
Barbara Davitt

1986 – 1987
Helen Evans
Holly Landgren

1985 – 1986
Jenny Alland
Alison Laycock
Meredith
Middleton

1984 – 1986
Kirstie Stewart

1984 – 1985
Louise White

1983 – 1985
Isobel Kindley

1983 – 1984
Sharon
Kaesehagan
M Sheridan

1981 – 1983
Anne Berry
Gunda Rosskamp

WOVEN
Past Trainees
1977 – 1978
Silvana Angelakis
Annabel Ayers
Lucy MacDonald

1976 – 1977
Yvonne Loosli

1975 – 1977
Jun Tomita
Helen Bennett

JAMFACTORY TENANTS AND STUDIO ACCESS TENANTS

* based on available records

Brendan Adair-Smith
Adelaide Festival Centre
Catherine Aldrete-Morris
Ruth Allen
Kathy Alty
Jane Andrew
Denise Angus
Anima Gallery
David Archer
Dan Armstrong
Alison Arnold
Richard Ayliffe
Nicole Ayliffe
Andrew Baldwin
Elodie Barker
Andrew Bartlett
Frank Bauer
Clare Belfrage
Douglas Bell
Robin Best
Giles Bettison
Gabriella Bisetto
Annette Blair
Sue Bogner
Chris Boha
Robyn Born
Jane Bowden
Lionel Bowen
Noel Bowen
Stephen Bowers
Naomi Boxall
Kristel Britcher
Matt Burgess
Tricia Burrows
Simon Butler
Pablo Byass
Mark Callin
Anni Callinan
Mark Capon
Hannah Carlyle
Peter Carrigy
Kris Carter
Meg Caslake
Cast Lab Project
Suzanne Charbonnet
Scott Chaseling
Maria Chatzinikolaki
Christine Cholewa

Martin Cielens
John Clift
Gus Clutterbuck
Kirsten Coelho
Zara Collins
Alison Cooper
Peta Cowan Goh
Jane Cowie
Crafts Council of Australia
Craftsouth
Sarah Crowest
Hilary Crawford
Jo Crawford
Karen Cunningham
Peter Cunningham
Cindy Czabania
Reene Damiani
Petra de Mooy
Darren De'lacy
Department of Technical and Further Education
Richard Doheny
Margaret Dodd
Mark Douglas
Stephen Dounton
Ian Driver
Chantal Duffy
Danielle Duvoisin
Amanda Dziedzic
Liz Eakins
John Easton
Margaret Edgecombe
Barry Edwards
Tim Edwards
Caren Ellis
Tim Elsom
Tegan Empson
Craig English
Helen Evans
Experimental Art Foundation
Wendy Fairclough
Lesa Farrant
Andrea Fiebig

Stevie Fieldsend
Jess Fisher
Louise Fitzgerald
Bert Flugelman
Nicholas Folland
Jo Fraser
Mel Fraser
Honor Freeman
Katrina Freene
Brendan Scott French
Susan Frost
Greg Fullarton
Helen Fuller
Penny Fuller
Lorraine Gill
Gobelin Tapestry
Agnieszka Golda
Peter Goss
Holly Grace
Susan Graham
Gray Street Workshop
Suzanne Gregor
Pauline Griffin
Klaus Gutowski
Tamara Hahn
Christian Hall
Rita Hall
Ross Hall
Gordon Halliday
Leslie Halliday
David Halsey
Glenistair Hancock
Gwyn Hanssen Pigott
Rosie Hannam
Wendy Hannam
Chris Harford
Peter Harris
Philip Hart
Rebecca Hartman-Kearns
Sophie Hastwell
Gray Hawk
Charmain Hearder
Mark Heidenreich
Robyn Henwood
Robin Herriman
Michael Hill
Jenny Hogben
Rosalind Hoskin

Kath Inglis
Ipsius Design
Takeshi Iue
Jacinta Ivory
Sarah James
Stephanie
James-Manttan
Peter Jeffery
Tassia Joannides
Martin Johnson
Neil Johnson
Peter Johnson
Philippa Jolliffe
Deb Jones
Virginia Kaiser
Michelle Kelly
Nico Kelly
Bronwyn Kemp
Roman
Kielczewksi
Isobel Kindley
Bob King
Gerry King
Mandi King
Lincoln Kirby Bell
Joseph Kivubiro
Emma Klau
Max Klubal
George Koleff
Vanessa Kovarskis
Peta Kruger
Ella Kuhnert
Jutta Kulwikowski
Philipe Lakeman
Matthew Larwood
Ali Lawson
Alex Leckie
Bronwyn Lennox
Ian Lewis
Linda Lin Tai
Marie Littlewood
Stephanie Livesey
Erin Lykos
Dianne MacKenzie
Mercedes Mangnall
Anne Manning
Nora Mantzioris
Leanne Marshall
Leslie Matthews
Shauna Mayben
Swanson
Wayne Mcara
Brenda McKay
Mariella McKinley
Anna Medlin
Vickie Melanson
Minnette Michael
Meredith Middleton
Bridgette Minuzzo
Tom Moore
George Morgan
Rodney Mosel
Nick Mount
Ian Mowbray
Kumiko Nakajima
Sandra Naulty
Juliet Nelson
Elizabeth Newman
Yvonne Nitschke
Bruce Nuske
Mark O'Ryan
Tony Oakey
John Odgers
Tiffany Parbs
Anne Parsons
David Pedler
Jenny Pedlar
Malcolm Pedler
Emma Petersen
Jaan Poldaas
Wayne Pollard
Adrian Potter
David Potts
Freya Povey
Belinda Powles
Cedar Prest
Madeline Prowd
John Quan
Stephanie Radke
Louise Ramsay
Dianne Richards
Danielle Rickaby
Bronwen Riddiford
Guy Ringwood
Gary Roberts
Dale Roberts
Jane Robertson
Sue Rosenthal
Tracey Rosser
Sarah Rothe
Richard Rowland
Jane Ruljancich
Randal Sach
Naomi Schwartz
Regine Schwarzer
Katrina Shaw
Tim Shaw
Lauren Simeoni
Stephen Skillitzi
Jo Spencer
Vipoo Srivilasa
Sylvia Stansfield
Kirstie Stewart
Simon Sturt-Bray
The Gold Fish Studio
Mark Thiele
Toby Thomas
Mark Thompson
Toby Tomas
Pavel Tomecko
Vicki Torr
Anne Trebilcock
Fiona Truman
Yvonne Twining
Jan Twyerould
John Ullinger
Uz Associates
Ruth Venner
Bettina Visentin
Janice Vitkovsky
Peter Walker
Zoe Warburton
Gerry Wedd
Chris Wells
Leonie Westbrook
Carolyn Weston
Liz Williams
Peter Williams
Vanessa Williams
Clare Wilson
Gay Wilson
Patricia Wise
Sun Woong Bang
Ross Wootten
Amy Worth
Susan Worthington
Toyotake Yamauchi

CONTRIBUTORS

Margaret Hancock Davis (co-curator) is Curator and Exhibitions Manager at JamFactory. She joined the team there in 2004 as Project Coordinator of the International Craft Initiative (Australian Contemporary)—which presented exhibitions at *SOFA* Chicago, *Collect*, London and *Talente*, Munich from 2004 to 2008—and as the Gallery Assistant. Since 2007, she has been responsible for JamFactory's exhibitions program, and her curatorial projects have included *From the Earth: Contemporary Indigenous Ceramics* (2008) and *Prototyping: Making Ideas* (2010).

Margot Osborne (co-curator) is an independent curator and arts writer. Over a long career in the visual arts she has held a range of key positions in Adelaide and Sydney. She has been curator of numerous exhibitions for JamFactory, both as Exhibitions Curator (1998-2001) and subsequently as a guest curator, including most notably *The Return of Beauty* (2000) and the national touring exhibition, *Wild Nature* (2002-05). She is the author of three books: monographs on Jeff Mincham and Nick Mount, and the acclaimed survey *Australian Glass Today*. She has written on art and design for artist catalogues, art journals and newspapers, is a former editor of *Broadsheet* and guest editor of two issues of *Artlink.*

Brian Parkes (co-curator) is Chief Executive Officer and Artistic Director at JamFactory. For ten years prior to this, he was Associate Director and Senior Curator at Object Gallery in Sydney and has curated numerous exhibitions, including the landmark survey of contemporary Australian design, *Freestyle: new Australian design for living* (2006–08), and he was co-curator of the acclaimed touring exhibition *Menagerie: contemporary Indigenous sculpture* (2009–12). In 2007 Parkes was one of ten curators invited by Phaidon Press, London to contribute to &Fork, a book profiling 100 emerging product designers from around the world, and in 2008 he was an Adjunct Curator for the Museum of Arts and Design, New York.

Dick Richards (essayist) has almost 50 years' experience as a teacher, writer, curator, researcher and consultant in the visual arts and crafts. He was employed in various roles at the Art Gallery of South Australia from 1965 to 2000, including as Curator of Decorative Arts. From 1990 until his retirement in 2000, he was the Gallery's Curator of Asian Art.

Ian Were (essayist) has written regularly for Australian art and culture journals—beginning, in the late 1970s, with *Preview* and *The Adelaide Review*. From 1996 to 2002 he edited 26 issues of *Object* magazine and, from 2002 to 2009, as Senior Editor at the Queensland Art Gallery/Gallery of Modern Art, he edited or co-edited around 12 exhibition publications and edited 23 issues of *Artlines* magazine. Since 1997 he has edited more than 20 art books and publications, including six recent books as a freelance editor and writer. He writes on contemporary art, design, architecture and associated issues and, more recently, has written short stories. Recent articles appear in *Indesign* and *Eyeline* magazines.

ACKNOWLEDGEMENTS

A project of this scale requires the input and energy of many individuals and organisations and we, would like to thank everyone involved. First, we wish to thank the 40 exhibitors for their enthusiasm for the exhibition and for the information they provided for the development of this publication. Many of these artists are represented by commercial galleries and we gratefully acknowledge the assistance of Adrian Sassoon, BMGArt, Edwina Corlette Gallery, Ferrin Gallery, Gallery Funaki, Galerie Ra, Gray Street Workshop, Helen Gory Galerie, Lauraine Diggins Fine Art, Matin USA, Moss Green, Nellie Caston Gallery, Olsen Irwin, Robin Gibson Gallery and Sabbia Gallery.

We also thank the dedicated JamFactory staff who have been involved in the development, production and promotion of the exhibition, in particular: Andrew Bartlett, Brad Bonar, Peter Carroll, Tom Mirams, and Emily Troon.

We are grateful too, for the support of this important project by JamFactory's current Board of Directors; Peter Vaughan (Chair), Jim Carreker, Tim Horton, Kay Lawrence, Jane Lomax-Smith, John Ranaldo and Libby Raupach.

We would like to thank our exhibition touring partner Country Arts SA, in particular Craig Harrison and Katinka Bracker who have developed an extensive national tour for the exhibition. Thanks too, to the Directors and relevant staff at each of the confirmed tour venues who will be hosting the exhibition as it tours throughout Australia from 2013–2016. Barossa Regional Gallery in Tanunda, Western Plains Cultural Centre in Dubbo, Tweed River Art Gallery in Murwillumbah, Ipswich Art Gallery, Artspace Mackay, Gold Coast City Gallery, Moree Plains Gallery, ANU School of Art Gallery in Canberra, Wagga Wagga Art Gallery, Latrobe Regional Gallery in Morwell, Design Centre Tasmania in Launceston, Riddoch Art Gallery in Mount Gambier, Murray Bridge Regional Gallery, Signal Point Gallery in Goolwa and Port Augusta Cultural Centre - Yarta Purtli - Gallery.

We are proud of this exhibition catalogue and would like to thank essayists Dick Richards and Ian Were for their wonderful contributions as well as former executive officers Winnie Peltz, Lynn Collins, Leone Furler, Mark Ferguson and Stephen Bowers who each provided insightful comments and observations for the research. Thanks also to Serena Wong, Alex Hurford and Stephanie James-Manttan for their assistance in research.

A very special thank you must go to Grant Hancock for the photography of the exhibition works as well as access to his image archive. Dating back to 1976, this archive has been an important source of imagery for the publication. Grant's outstanding photographic skills have played an important role in assisting the success of many art, craft and design practitioners in South Australia.

We are also grateful to printing coordinator Kirsty Wright from Imago and copy editor Theresa Willsteed and our final thanks go to designer Sophie Guiney for her tireless work in making this publication, as well as all of the interpretive and marketing material associated with the exhibition, look so completely wonderful.

Margaret Hancock Davis,
Margot Osborne and Brian Parkes